1992

SPECIAL EDUCATION SERIES
Peter Knoblock, Editor

Achieving the Complete School:
Strategies for Effective Mainstreaming
Douglas Biklen
with Robert Bogdan, Dianne L. Ferguson,
Stanford J. Searl, Jr., and Steven J. Taylor

Classic Readings in Autism
Anne M. Donnellan, Editor

Stress in Childhood:
An Intervention Model for Teachers and Other Professionals
Gaston E. Blom, Bruce D. Cheney,
and James E. Snoddy

Curriculum Decision Making for Students with Severe Handicaps:
Policy and Practice
Dianne L. Ferguson

Community Integration for People with Severe Disabilities
Steven J. Taylor, Douglas Biklen,
and James Knoll, Editors

Helping the Visually Impaired Child with Developmental Problems:
Effective Practice in Home, School, and Community
Sally M. Rogow

Progress Without Punishment:
Effective Approaches for Learners with Behavior Problems
Anne M. Donnellan, Gary W. LaVigna,
Nanette Negri-Shoultz, and Lynette L. Fassbender

Issues and Research in Special Education, Volume 1
Robert Gaylord-Ross, Editor

Cultural Diversity, Families, and the Special Education System:
Communication and Empowerment
Beth Harry

Cultural Diversity, Families, and the Special Education System

Communication and Empowerment

Beth Harry

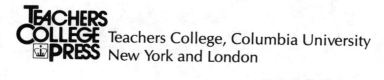

Teachers College, Columbia University
New York and London

Published by Teachers College Press, 1234 Amsterdam Avenue
New York, NY 10027

Library of Congress Cataloging-in-Publication Data
Harry, Beth.
    Cultural diversity, families, and the special education system :
communication and empowerment / Beth Harry.
      p.   cm.
    Includes bibliographical references and index.
    ISBN 0-8077-3120-X (alk. paper). — ISBN 0-8077-3119-6 (pbk. :
alk. paper)
    1. Handicapped students—Education—United States.   2. Minority
students—Education—United States.   3. Puerto Rican children—
Education—United States—Case studies.   I. Title.
    LC4031.H373   1992
    371.9′0973—dc20   91-32033

    ISBN 0-8077-3120-X
    ISBN 0-8077-3119-6

    Printed on acid free paper
    Manufactured in the United States of America

    98   97   96   95   94   93   92   8 7 6 5 4 3 2 1

Contents

Foreword

It is well established that systems, both human and biological, tend to maintain themselves. In the case of human organizations, the mission of the system is usually legitimated with reference to certain "immutable truths" and core values that rapidly attain the status of common sense and consequent immunity from critical scrutiny. As systems expand, so too do the number of people who have a direct stake in maintaining the system because their status, credibility and income are invested therein. It is not surprising, therefore, that it takes a massive amount of evidence of dysfunctionality and internal contradiction to bring about fundamental changes in most human systems.

I believe that we are close to this point of "paradigm shift" within the special education systems that exist in most North American schools and it is a privilege for me to write a foreword to a book that so eloquently documents the need for this shift. Beth Harry's study provides a medium through which the silenced voices of parents can be heard as they and their children travel through what often appears to be a Kafkesque labyrinth of special education "delivery systems."

Central among the "immutable truths" that sustain these delivery systems is the belief that categories such as "learning disability" and "speech impairment" exist in reality, independent of the social construction process that gave rise to them. This process of defining deviance through categorical labeling serves two functions of system maintenance. First, it deflects critical scrutiny of mainstream programs and pedagogy by deporting all students for whom these programs and pedagogy have failed; location of the problem within the student is clearly an essential part of this process. Second, it provides a continuous flow of clients for services that are legally mandated and externally funded and for which a variety of categories of expertise have been defined. The expertise and credibility of professionals who provide services to those labeled "learning disabled" (or some other category) depends directly on the existence of such a category of client.

While few would dispute the genuine commitment of most special educators and assessment specialists, there is an inexorable logic in the system that largely determines the kinds of outcome that can result from the initial referral. For example, if a sufficient number of psychologists were to attribute bilingual children's present level of academic functioning either to inappropriate programs or pedagogy, or to inadequate time to attain grade norms in English (as considerable research indicates they should), they would cause a crisis for both the mainstream and special education systems. Mainstream teachers would be forced to adapt their programs to take account of much greater cultural and linguistic diversity than they have become accustomed to, while special educational professionals would lack the clients required to sustain their jobs as well as their personal sense of expertise and credibility within the system.

The evidence of internal contradictions and system dysfunctionality has accumulated steadily over the past 15 years. For example, close to half of the special education service dollars go to the assessment process in order to determine the appropriate category within which to place a child, raising the issue of whether the interests of children might be better served if at least some of these funds were to go into intervention; in addition, the construct of "learning disability" is so conceptually confused that no battery of tests has shown any degree of validity in identifying children who suffer from such presumed disabilities. As Rita, one of the parents in this book, so aptly notes about her son: "Maybe they decided to call him learning disabled/language because they don't know what else to call him!" Further evidence of the doubtful status of special education categories is the lack of data to support the effectiveness of any specific set of pedagogical procedures for children labeled as "learning disabled" or "speech impaired." Finally, there is little evidence for the overall effectiveness of special education programs in view of the fact that relatively few children return to the mainstream from special education placements.

These problematic issues are compounded when attempts are made to apply special education services in culturally diverse contexts. As this book so clearly shows, the special education system operates as part of the overall education system not only to maintain itself but also to preserve structures of power in the society at large. The virtually exclusive use of English as a language of instruction combined with the monocultural content of the curriculum means, as Beth Harry points out, that the burden of acculturation rests squarely on the shoulders of children and their families. Schools that operate in this manner clearly do not see it as part of their role to challenge the division of status and resources within the wider society. As a consequence, they structure the discourse between teachers and children and between professionals and families in such a way that the students' and families' inferior status is clearly communicated to them.

The irony of this situation is that dysfunctional educational systems are frequently kept from complete collapse (although their internal contradictions have become very evident) through the outstanding dedication of a few committed individuals. For example, Elizabeth, a member of a small group of bilingual personnel in this study, who were attempting to bring about change, described their efforts as "five people trying to do the work of 15." While such efforts can result in system improvement, they also frequently result in the burn-out of key professionals prior to any form of system restructuring.

Clearly, a radical restructuring of the entire special education system is required if the rhetoric underlying P.L. 94-142 is to have any bearing on reality. Minimally, this restructuring will involve abandonment of most categorical labels, provision of culturally-responsive mainstream programs aimed at *preventing* academic difficulties rather than creating them, and involvement of parents in what Beth Harry calls reciprocal rather than one-way discourse—a process that would include parents as equal partners in the entire assessment and placement procedure as well as in advocacy and policy-making roles in the school as a whole.

Continued investment in a special education system as inherently dysfunctional as that portrayed in this important book will serve only to perpetuate the alienation of culturally diverse families from the education system and from society at large. Restructuring the system so that the voices of parents and students can be expressed and amplified within a collaborative rather than an adversarial paradigm will ultimately also serve the interests of education professionals as well as families and students. While the current practice of "blaming the victim" mystifies for both professionals and families the inherent logic of the special education system, there is only so long that we can obscure from our own consciousness that the persistent failure of particular groups of children reflects our own failure and that of the system we uphold.

Jim Cummins
Ontario Institute for Studies in Education

Acknowledgments

I would like to thank my doctoral dissertation committee — Robert Bogdan, Doug Biklen, Ellen Barnes, and Alejandro Garcia, all of Syracuse University — for their encouragement and guidance in the conduct of the research which forms the centerpiece of this book, and for convincing me that it was worth trying to get it published. I thank Peter Knoblock of Syracuse University for recommending the project to Teachers College Press, and Brian Ellerbeck of the Press for the enthusiasm with which he responded to the original manuscript and the keen insights he shared with me regarding the interpretation of the study data. I thank also Carol Collins of Teachers College Press for her meticulous editing, and her patience with my never-ending technical errors. I thank Cynthia Reid, without whose assistance the bibliography for this project might never have been in publishable form, and Nadya Molina and Rita Dealy for their invaluable help with the documentation of the Spanish passages.

I also thank my mother, Grace Harry, my friends Carl and Denise Belcher, Marsha Smith-Lewis, Eileen Ball, and Maya Kalyanpur for their support and encouragement over several years of research and writing. Heartfelt thanks go to my son, Mark Teelucksingh, for his patience with a workaholic mother.

In particular, I thank the twelve Puerto Rican families who shared their views and feelings with me regarding matters that were very sensitive and dear to their hearts. Their openness and hospitality transformed an academic exercise into an opportunity to make new friends and to be introduced to another vibrant Caribbean culture.

I dedicate this effort to these twelve families, in the hope that it will make some small contribution to the futures of their children and others like them.

Dedicatoria

Quiero darle las gracias a mi comité de disertación doctoral, Robert Bogdan, Doug Biklen, Ellen Barnes y Alejandro García, todos de la Universidad de Syracuse, por su estímulo y por haberme guiado por los caminos de la investigación la cual es la pieza fundamental de este libro, y por convencerme de que valía la pena publicarlo. Le doy las gracias a Peter Knoblock de la Universidad de Syracuse por recomendar el proyecto a Teachers College Press, y a Brian Ellerbeck de la editorial por el entusiasmo con el cual respondió al manuscrito original y la perspicacia que compartió conmigo en relación a la interpretación de los datos del estudio. Le doy las gracias también a Carol Collins de Teachers College Press por su meticulosa redacción, y su paciencia con mis interminables errores técnicos. Gracias a Cynthia Reid, sin su ayuda la bibliografía para este proyecto pudo no haber estado en una forma publicable, y a Nadya Molina y Rita Dealy por su ayuda inestimable con la traducción de los pasajes en español.

Le doy las gracias también a mi mamá, Grace Harry, a mis amigos Carl y Denise Belcher, Marsha Smith-Lewis, Eileen Ball y Maya Kalyanpur por su apoyo y estímulo en muchos años de estudio y escritura. Gracias de todo corazón a mi hijo, Mark Teelucksingh, por su paciencia al tener una madre "workahólica".

En particular, le doy las gracias a las doce familias puertorriqueñas quienes compartieron sus puntos de vista y sus pensamientos conmigo en relación a situaciones muy sensitivas y apegadas a sus sentimientos. Su hospitalidad, y su forma de ser tan abierta hacia mi, transformaron un ejercicio académico en una oportunidad para hacer nuevos amigos y para ser integrada en otra vibrante cultura caribeña.

Le dedico este esfuerzo a estas doce familias, con la esperanza de que esto va a hacer una pequeña contribución para el futuro de sus niños y el futuro de otros como ellos.

Introduction

The problem addressed by this book is that parents of poor, minority, handicapped children are at a triple disadvantage in dealing with school systems. It is known that, in the United States, ethnicity and poverty are likely to place children at an educational disadvantage (Heller, Holtzman, & Messick, 1982; Mercer, 1973). It is also known that the diagnosis of a child's disability has a powerful impact on families (see a substantial review by Turnbull & Turnbull, 1986). Herman (1983), in discussing the potential effects of this combination, says:

> When the three status distinctions of poverty, minority and childhood exceptionality intersect, the families involved are uniquely vulnerable to systematic discrimination. (p. 47)

Many minority families face a fourth disadvantage—they do not speak the language of the school.

ETHNIC MINORITIES OF COLOR IN THE UNITED STATES

While the United States is a nation made up of many cultures, the dominant cultural ethic has been one of assimilation into a "melting pot," envisaged as a uniquely "American" yet essentially racially homogenous, neo-European culture. Two facts, however, belie that image. First, the image of the melting pot was never intended to include the descendants of Native Americans or African slaves. Second, the waves of immigration in the latter half of this century have been predominantly non-White, providing a very different picture from that of previous centuries. Indeed, it is predicted that, by the turn of the twenty-first century, one-third of the population of the United States will comprise people of non-White racial origins (Hodgkinson, 1985). The cultures represented by these peoples will be as varied as their physical characteristics.

The challenges facing many of these peoples, particularly when combined with poverty, include some salient differences from those faced by the generations of European immigrants whose cultures were more similar to that of mainstream America. For example, it is known that the linguistic, religious, and cultural incongruities encountered in schools by immigrants in the late nineteenth and early twentieth centuries were more readily resolved by Irish and German than by Italian groups (Kitano, 1969; Sarason & Doris, 1979). The greater difficulties of Italians have been interpreted as reflecting a clash in values related to formal education (Covello, 1967), as well as the prejudicial attitudes of mainstream America towards Southern Europeans (Gould, 1981).

It is evident that cultural incongruities will be even greater for people of non-European heritage, and there is the additional fact that, for non-White minorities, racial difference remains visible in succeeding generations. In a society with a history of intense racial discrimination, this difference is central and stands as the strongest answer to the charge by Caucasian Americans that "my grandmother made it, why can't yours?"

The challenge for schools is immense. It is not that students of non-White races or non-European cultures are harder to educate than those of the mainstream U.S. culture. It is that they may be, in many important ways, different and that the education system simply has not been geared to understand, respect, and address the needs of such tremendous heterogeneity. Indeed, it is well known that many minority students, whether indigenous or immigrant, do not achieve well in U.S. schools and that they are overrepresented in special education programs.

It is crucial to note, however, that it is societal attitudes toward the combination of poverty with cultural, linguistic, and racial difference that adds up to an overwhelming situation for many minority families. It is the children of low-income families who are most devastated by these experiences, partly because of the absence of various material and social supports that may be more available to financially stable families, and partly because acculturation may come more easily to higher social class.

Helpful here is the concept of "ethclass," which relates to individuals' having a strong sense of identity, or "peoplehood," with their ethnic group, while also acquiring behaviors more typical of their social-class peers of a different ethnicity (Gordon, 1978). Thus middle- and upper-class minority peoples may make significant modifications to their behavior that bring them in line with those of Whites of their own class, while still retaining a primary identification with their ethnic group. Many of the generalizations made about ethnic minority students' difficulties in American schools are therefore most relevant to those from poor or working-class backgrounds, those whose sense of identity, as well as behavioral patterns, is tied to a culture that is generally devalued and rejected by schools.

Indeed, poverty has been shown to be correlated with academic failure

(Chan & Rueda, 1979). Thus the children of non-White immigrant groups, many of whom enter the United States at the bottom of the socio-economic ladder, as well as indigenous groups whose histories have been tied to low status and poverty have the triple, in some cases quadruple, disadvantage referred to above.

CULTURALLY DIVERSE PARENTS AND THE SCHOOLS

This book is primarily concerned with the way parents of minority students perceive the special education system, with specific attention to their views of the process by which their children are designated "handicapped." In order to provide a backdrop to this issue, the book will begin by summarizing who these students are. Chapter 1 will use the U.S. Department of Education's (1987) racial classification system as a framework for describing the diversity of students served in schools in the United States. The five categories currently used are: American Indian or Alaskan Native, Asian or Pacific Islander, Hispanic, Black (not of Hispanic origin), and White (not of Hispanic origin). The first four categories of students are subsumed under the classification "minority," while the fifth category is recorded as "White."

Chapter 2 will offer a summary of what is known about the general cultural ethos of these groups and concepts of disability among them. Tremendous caution is advised in making generalizations from this outline because of the heterogeneity both within and among the groups. Thus the emphasis of the chapter will be on common points of difference as compared to mainstream U.S. society.

Chapter 3 will summarize relevant research on the patterns and prevalence of special education placement among these groups. The review will focus on investigations of how schools interact with cultural, linguistic, and socioeconomic factors to result in academic underachievement and consequent special education placement.

Chapter 4 will then outline the literature, both empirical and conceptual, regarding the experiences of minority families as they interact with schools in general and the special education system in particular. This has been examined mainly in terms of cultural differences in child-rearing practices, interpersonal behavior, social roles, family structures, and interpretations of disability. The majority of this literature has been based on Black families (Heath, 1983; Lowry, 1983; Marion, 1979, 1980a; Nebgen, 1979; Sullivan, 1980; Tomlinson, Acker, Canter, & Lindborg, 1977) and Hispanic families (Ada, 1988; Baca & Cervantes, 1984; Bennett, 1988; Bram, 1968; Canino & Canino, 1980; Casuso, 1978; Condon, Peters, &

Sueiro-Ross, 1979; Cordasco, 1968; Curtis, 1988; Delgado, 1980; Delgado-Gaitan, 1990; Diaz, 1981; Sour & Sorell, 1978). A smaller but growing body of literature also gives insight into other minority families' interaction with the schools, such as Asian Indians (Gibson, 1987), Southeast Asians (Blakely, 1982; Chan, 1986; Chan & Kitano, 1986; Leung, 1986; Leung, 1988; Morrow & McBride, 1988; Tran, 1982), and Native Americans (Connery, 1987; Cunningham, Cunningham, & O'Connell, 1986; Johnson, 1987; Sharp, 1983).

In addition, considerable information about home-school interaction can be extrapolated from literature attempting to find culturally appropriate solutions to instructional issues and appropriate home-school transitions for culturally different children such as the Hmong (Trueba, Jacobs, & Kirton, 1990), Native Americans (Deyhle, 1987; Macias, 1987; Philips, 1983; Van Ness, 1981; Walker, 1987), and Hawaiians (Au & Jordan, 1981; Boggs, 1985).

Despite specific differences among cultures, a common theme in this growing body of information on parent-school interaction is a striking pattern of cross-cultural dissonance that results in inadequate understanding by parents of the educational system in the United States and an apparently passive approach to home-school interaction, along with expressions of either extreme cynicism or extreme trust regarding the school system. Chapter 4 examines the way professionals' interpretations of the law contribute to parents' exclusion from genuine communication and decision making.

The chapter points to the fact that the legalistic framing of services to students can serve both to protect and to constrain. The concept of disability on which the law is based is specific to Western culture, as is the framework of services it offers. Yet the legal mandate has the effect of reifying these concepts, so that professionals treat them as objective reality and, in so doing, delegitimate all others. Thus the voices of culturally different parents are excluded from a discourse that defines the categories into which all interpretations may fit and limits the areas to which parents may contribute.

AN ETHNOGRAPHIC STUDY OF
PUERTO RICAN AMERICAN PARENTS' VIEWS

Against the background of the difficulties of many culturally diverse students and their families, Chapters 5 through 9 use the findings of a study of Puerto Rican American parents' views to illustrate the tremendous misunderstanding and inappropriate educational practice that can result when discourse is structured in such a way as to disempower parents. Compliance with the letter of the law is grossly insufficient for the challenge of cross-cultural communication. It will also show, however, the potential for learning and for positive service that can result when professionals engage in culturally responsive practice. The study focuses on the experiences and views of twelve low-income Puerto Rican families whose children have been placed in special education programs in a small, inner-city school district in the Northeast.

This study of the views of parents breaks new ground in three ways. First, it is concerned with meaning as defined by the parents. Thus, proceeding from the observation that the concept of disability and the attitudes surrounding it are social judgments defined by culture, the study begins by asking what the classification "handicapped" means for low-income families from a Puerto Rican background and what impact this event has on them. Further, how do they explain their children's educational difficulties? How do such parents, who, by U.S. standards, have had relatively little formal education, see their role in their children's educational careers? To what extent is their potential and the mandate for their participation realized?

Second, the study is one of only a few in the field of special education that has utilized an ethnographic approach, emphasizing the role of culture and cross-cultural communication in determining the meanings families attach to their children's special education placement. Since most studies have been based on more structured surveys of parents' views and participation, this study presents a somewhat different picture. The study is based on 9 months of in-depth, unstructured interviews, conducted in both Spanish and English, with twelve mothers and four fathers. The interviews are supported by participant observation of community and family events and of meetings between parents and special education personnel. In addition, further information was gleaned from interviews with twelve professionals directly involved with Hispanic families in the school district.

Third, the findings of the study are important in that they reach beyond the surface of passivity, satisfaction, and trust usually described in the literature on Hispanic parents. Numerous probing interviews, and observation of a wide range of situations, reveal that what seems like trust may often be an ingrained, habitual deference to authority. What seems like passivity and satisfaction may be a mask for a sense of alienation, resignation, and powerlessness.

Chapter 10 concludes that the findings of this study corroborate what is known about dissonance between school systems and culturally diverse families of differing racial/ethnic backgrounds. It cannot be argued that this small group of parents is representative of all minority parents in similar situations, but it is clear that the experiences of these parents are real, probable, and explainable in terms of what is known about cross-cultural conflict. Most important, the study provides an analysis of how such misunderstandings may occur and how a willing and concerned school system can begin to bridge the gap between the mainstream and what is increasingly being referred to as "the other America."

Overall, the challenge facing schools is to revise not only assumptions, expectations, and instructional methodologies but also the essential ethos that conveys to students and their families the message that power and right reside only in the culture of mainstream America. Although all the participants in the study emphasize that they are American citizens, they always describe themselves as Puerto Rican–American. The irony of this perception is evident in one mother's summary of her feeling of frustration with the school system:

Es fuerte bregar con estos americanos. Aquí en america, las escuelas son para los americanos!

(It is very hard to deal with these Americans. Here in America, the schools are for Americans!)

Cultural Diversity
and Minority Status

On any street corner on the West Side, within about a 10-block radius of Spruce Street, a greeting of "buenos dias" is likely to receive a response of "bueno dia" with a noticeable omission of the final *s* in both words. "'Tá bién" (it's okay) to speak Spanish here since the area is dominated by an estimated 5,000 Spanish-speaking people, most of whom are from Puerto Rico. It would not do, however, to assume that color of skin or other racial features will give a clue as to whether to use English or Spanish, since Puerto Ricans come in all colors.

The hub of this community is a small, 2-story brown building with the sign "La Asociación Latina Americana." The Latin American Association (LAA) is predominant among several voluntary agencies serving this area, and their presence indicates the widespread dependence of many residents on various kinds of public assistance.

"Mucho Daño a los Niños"
(A lot of Harm to the Children)

On a mild spring morning, an old woman about 4 feet, 10 inches tall, with dark brown skin and a heavily wrinkled forehead barely visible beneath a mop of graying hair, stands at the doorway of the LAA. She could be anybody's grandmother. Actually, she is Gina's, one of the children in this study.

Gina's grandmother, and a few of the other older people in the community, such as the fair-skinned Cuban man from across the street, can find any number of excuses for going to the LAA for assistance, but most often they go just to feel at home and to find out what is happening in the neighborhood. The younger people in the tiny foyer sit or stand with a greater urgency: they have come to seek an interpreter to accompany them to an unexpected appointment or to translate a document, or, perhaps, they are waiting for the daily English class to begin. But today everyone may have a long wait, because a tall, dark young man needs someone to take his wife to the hospital — she has gone into labor prematurely. Gina's grandmother and the Cuban will not leave until they see a solution to this emergency.

Back at Gina's home, I wander between the dining room and kitchen, admiring the island mementos, family photographs, and handmade centerpieces that decorate the shelves and walls of the room. Her mother, Ana, cooks piononos — crisp, round balls of fried plantain stuffed with spicy ground beef — while my tape recorder captures the sizzling of her kitchen. Her high-pitched, rapid "Spanglish" soars above it all and I listen, savouring traditional island hospitality — piping hot delicacies and heavily sweetened Puerto Rican coffee:

Mira! (Look!) Hay muchas personas that try to help Puerto Ricans, pero in a way nos ayudan, and in another way nos desayudan! (There are many people that try to help Puerto Ricans, but in a way they help us and in another way they hinder us!) At first you think you can trust somebody and then behind your back they are talking about you. That's why I tell you I don't trust nobody!

Hay mucho daño down here a los niños. He visto tantas cosas! (There is a lot of harm down here to the children. I have seen many things.) My son say "I want to go outside, pero (but) I don't let him. In Puerto Rico it's different—everybody know you. Pero here it got trouble everywhere. When I moved down here in esto apartamiento (this apartment) I got a lot of trouble with the kids. In the summertime, José me dice (said to me) "Mammy, I want to go in the porch" so I say, "okay, pero stay where I can see you." But his friend got matches and cigarettes! He got only 9 years, and he smoking cigarettes! I say, "What kind of friend is that? You need to have good friends or when you grow up you are no good, you are nothing."

So I put José in the room. I don't want to hit him because when he grow up he is mad with me. I don't like hitting, I see a lot of kids their father hit them and he don't know what's going on with the kids. They don't tell him nada (nothing)! So I tell them, "I am no just your mother, I am your friend too, trust me!" I tell him, "No take off your clothes outside your home, no let anybody see you." I tell him, "Try no go in the bathroom at school." I tell Gina, too.

You see, I love my children more than my life! When they go in the school my heart is broken! What I mean is I try to keep my kids more at home than outside.

Ana speaks for all the mothers in the study of Puerto Rican parents reported in this book. Her words echo familiar themes of cultural alienation, mistrust, and a continuing struggle to draw a protective boundary between home and "outside."

Ana and Her Family

Ana Diaz-Quintero (pseudonym) was born in Puerto Rico and came to live on the U.S. mainland in 1976 at the age of 16, having left high school in the eleventh grade. Her eldest child was born in Puerto Rico, while his younger brother and sister were born on the mainland. At the time of the study, José, age 12, was in the fifth grade; Gina, age 9, was in a special education class for students classified mildly mentally retarded; and Elizabeth, age 4, was attending a neighborhood preschool program.

About five feet tall, plump, with light brown skin, piercing gray eyes, and brown hair pulled back tightly in a bun, Ana has just a trace of Africa in her features. Always dramatic in manner, she is quick to smile, frown, or laugh, and, when speaking of something that makes her angry, there is no concealing the sudden flush of her face or the sharp edge to her voice. She talks a mile a minute as she moves in and out of the kitchen or sits, for a moment, to sew a flowing mantilla onto the dark hair of a doll dressed in flounces of red lace and ribbon. Ana dresses as many as ten of these dolls per week and sells them for $10 or $12 each. This helps, since her family was cut off from welfare when her husband quit the required English class. He became angry because, he says, they expected him to learn English from a blackboard when he told them he cannot read or write in Spanish.

Certain aspects of Ana's family defy easy categorization. On a racial dimension, her husband, Pedro, is the only immediate family member who would readily be classified as Black according to the U.S. system. But Ana would not use this term; she would use, instead, the more descriptive term *piel oscura*, which simply means "dark-skinned." Their son, José, fair-skinned with straight black hair, would probably be seen as White in the United States, while the girls, just a bit darker than their mother, with curly black hair, would be hard to categorize. In terms of nationality, both Ana and Pedro were born U.S. citizens, yet they spent their formative years in a culture very different from that of the U.S. mainland. Ana's words, quoted above, leave no doubt that she considers herself a stranger in a foreign land.

The minute fraction of the U.S. Department of Education's statistics represented by Ana and Pedro's children, however, reflects none of this ambiguity. According to the classification system used by the Department of Education's Office of Civil Rights (OCR), these students would first be classified as Hispanic (regardless of race), which category is then collapsed into an amalgam of all non-White groups, designated "minority." Thus, for the record, José, Gina, and Elizabeth Diaz-Quintero are minority students.

CULTURAL DIVERSITY AND MINORITY STATUS

The family described in the foregoing section belongs to one of four groups classified as "minority" in the United States. While the Diaz-Quintero family falls within one national subgroup of the larger category Hispanic, the attitudes expressed by this mother cannot be assumed to be representative of Puerto Ricans in general. They do, however, seem to be fairly typical of many Puerto Ricans of a similar educational and socio-economic background who are only minimally acculturated to life on the U.S. mainland. They also bear a strong resemblance to the attitudes of some other Hispanic families of similar background. These distinctions, among many others that will be discussed in this book, are important influences on the way we think about groups of people, because without attention to such detail, we too readily fall into the trap of developing stereotypical images and expectations.

This book is concerned with the way families from culturally different backgrounds view the special education system and with the quality of their interaction with professionals in that system. This topic is of great concern to educators today for two reasons. First, the children of such families are disproportionately classified as handicapped and placed in special education programs. Second, the input of parents is not only mandated by law (P.L. 94-142 and, more recently, P.L. 99-457) but is increasingly being seen as a crucial element in the adaptation and success of students from culturally different backgrounds.

This chapter will present an overview of the surface characteristics of the four groups referred to as "minority" in the United States and will discuss their status in the society. I will begin with a discussion of the U.S. perspective on race and then attend to factual information on the social, economic, and educational status of the different groups.

In a nation as heterogeneous as the United States, it is inevitable that attempts at classification by race will be fraught with ambiguity. The goal of the following discussion is to sharpen readers' awareness of the complexities of such classification and of the impossibility of stereotyping large groups of people along discrete and static racial or cultural dimensions.

Minority as a Racial Concept

Not all students in the United States whose families could lay claim to a nonmainstream culture are necessarily minority. For example, students from distinctly non-Anglo-Saxon cultural backgrounds, such as Southern or Eastern Europe, including people from Spain and Portugal, would not, despite their cultural differences, be designated minority. These people are considered White, as is specified by the following quote from the U.S. Congress Subcommittee on Census and Population (1987): "For civil rights and affirmative action purposes," a person from Spain falls within the European category, since "persons from Spain are not part of Hispanic as an ethnicity, nor are Portuguese" (p. 104). This distinction points to the political aspects of racial classification, a feature that has been particularly influential in the conceptualization of the category Hispanic. This aspect will be discussed in more detail in the discussion of the notion of a Hispanic identity contained in Chapter 2.

In the United States, the use of the term *minority* essentially represents an attempt to categorize by race, not by culture. Yet the specifics of race are only important on one dimension: whether one is White or not. This is evident in the OCR's annual survey of elementary and secondary schools (U.S. Department of Education, 1987). The survey first distinguishes between five possible classifications, based on geographic and/or racial features, and then, for the purpose of summary tables, condenses the original five categories into two—White and minority. The racial category White comprises the majority group, and to be other than White is to be a member of the minority group.

The OCR classification system reads as follows:

AMERICAN INDIAN OR ALASKAN NATIVE. A person having origins in any of the original peoples of North America and who maintains cultural identification through tribal affiliation or community recognition.

ASIAN OR PACIFIC ISLANDER. A person having origins in any of the original peoples of the Far East, Southeast Asia, the Pacific Islands, or the Indian subcontinent. This area includes, for example, China, India, Japan, Korea, the Philippine Islands and Samoa.

HISPANIC. A person of Mexican, Puerto Rican, Cuban, Central or South American, or other Spanish culture or origin—regardless of race.

BLACK (NOT OF HISPANIC ORIGIN). A person having origins in any of the Black racial groups of Africa.

WHITE (NOT OF HISPANIC ORIGIN). A person having origins in any of the original peoples of Europe, North Africa, or the Middle East. (U.S. Department of Education, 1987, Form ED102, Appendix A)

The OCR classifications do not address the common fact of mixed racial origins. What this means is that a person of mixed origin may not choose White, since one cannot be mixed and still be White. One can, however, be mixed and still be Black or Asian or Native American. This suggests that a notion of racial purity is attached to being White but not to being of any other race. For many people, however, the choice of Black, for example, is no more meaningful than the choice of White would be. This is particularly true for Hispanics, since many people from the Spanish-speaking Americas reflect mixtures that may include African, European, and native Central and South American races. Of course, this is also true for many Native and African Americans, among whom mixtures with other races are very common. Within this White/non-White framework, however, the racial heterogeneity of Hispanics presents a unique anomaly, because they are the only ethnic group who are likely to include many Whites along with a host of mixed races. Of course these people could choose the category White, but to do so would mean not choosing Hispanic.

The corollary "regardless of race" attached to the definition of Hispanic reflects the anomalous character of this group. The category Asian or Pacific Islander, for example, clearly includes a mixture of racial groups, yet the classification system does not specify "regardless of race" for this group, presumably because Whites are not likely to be among them; this group is already clearly non-White and therefore minority. It is not required, then, to distinguish between the dramatically different racial characteristics of people from India and China, or between people from Japan and Samoa or the Philippines. To be consistent, logic would have required the category Asian or Pacific Islander also to carry the corollary "regardless of race." Nor does the category Black (not of Hispanic origin) reflect any more logic, since many Hispanics from Caribbean and Central American territories have origins in the Black racial groups of Africa.

This approach to classification of students is, of course, not peculiar to education but is deeply ingrained in the U.S. way of thinking about race — that the important thing is whether or not one is White. Regarding Hispanics, this is part of an ongoing controversy over classification for national census taking, the current outcome being that the 1990 census continues to present Hispanic as a separate category with no dominant racial distinction. Indeed, Hispanics have actively resisted being forced to choose along racial lines, but nonetheless they are classified as minorities in schools, regardless of race. The census is more discriminating than the OCR classifications, with the 1990 questionnaire separating American Indian from Eskimo and Aleut, while also leaving room for designation of particular American Indian tribes. Similarly, while Asian or Pacific Islander is retained as a "race" (U.S. Bureau of the Census, Form D-61, 1990, Item 4, p.

2), space is also allotted for specification of national groups, such as Chinese, Guamanian, and so on. Nevertheless, "race" is a misnomer as an umbrella term for these racially heterogeneous peoples.

These classification systems reflect the unremitting commitment of American society to the goal of classifying people according to a presumed race. A look at current demographic projections, however, suggests that the minority/majority perspective will be required to undergo an essential revision in the coming century.

The Year 2000: Minority or Majority?

Minority groups currently comprise about a third of the U.S. population and are increasing in numbers more rapidly than the White majority. Minority students are projected to account for over 50 percent of the school-aged population by the turn of the century (Hodgkinson, 1985). Indeed, the use of the term *minority* is already meaningless in many large urban school districts, such as Baltimore, where 80 percent of the student body is Black (Maryland State Department of Education, 1988), and New York City, where 38 percent are Black and 34 percent Hispanic (New York City Board of Education, 1989).

A closer look at the figures shows variable rates of increase among minority groups. Table 1.1 shows U.S. Bureau of the Census (1990c) population estimates by race and Hispanic origin, as well as rate of increase from 1980 to 1989 for each group. This table shows that as of July 1, 1989, African Americans continued to be the largest minority group in the United States, increasing at an average annual rate of 1.5 percent and representing 12 percent of the total population. Second in size was the population of Hispanic origin, increasing at an average annual rate of 3.6 percent and representing 8.3 percent of the total population. The population of Asian Pacific Americans, increasing at an average annual rate of 6.5 percent, represented 2.8 percent of the total population, while the population of American Indians, Eskimos, and Aleuts, increasing at an average annual rate of 2.2 percent, represented 0.7 percent of the total population.

With the exception of the latter group, the rate of increase among non-White groups presents a dramatic contrast to that of the White population, who increased at an average annual rate of 0.8 percent and represented 84.1 percent of the total population.

Table 1.2 shows the components of the average rate of population change, under the categories of natural increase, births, deaths, and immigration. While this table does not offer a breakdown of the category "Other races" into Asian Pacific and Native Americans, the report points out

TABLE 1.1   Change in Population by Age Group, Sex, Race and Hispanic Origin: July 1, 1980 to July 1, 1989

(Numbers in thousands. Includes armed forces overseas.)

Subject	Population on July 1				Population change, 1980–89		Average annual percent change
	1989	% of all residents	1980	% of all residents	number	percent	
Total, all ages	248,762		227,757		21,005	9.2	1.0
Under 5 years	18,752		16,458		2,295	13.9	1.5
5 to 13 years	31,834		31,095		739	2.4	0.3
14 to 17 years	13, 496		16,142		(2,646)	−16.4	−2.0
18 to 24 years	26,564		30,350		(3,285)	−12.5	−1.5
25 to 34 years	44,048		37,625		6,423	17.1	1.8
35 to 44 years	36,584		25,868		10,716	41.4	3.9
45 to 54 years	24,905		22,754		2,151	9.5	1,0
55 to 64 years	21,593		21,762		(168)	− 0.8	−0.1
65 to 74 years	18,182		15,653		2,529	16.2	1.7
75 to 84 years	9,761		7,781		1,979	25,4	2.5
85 years and over	3,042		2,269		772	34.0	3.3
65 years and over	30,984		25,704		5,280	20.5	2.1
Male	121,445		110,888		10,557	9.5	1.0
Female	127,317		116,869		10,448	8.9	1.0
White	209,326	84.1	195,571	85.9	13,755	7.0	0.8
Black	30,788	12.0	26,903	11.8	3,885	14.4	1.5
Other races	8,647		5,283		3,365	63.7	5.5
Asian, Pacific[1]	6,881	2.8	3,834	1.7	3,047	79.5	6.5
Amerindian, Eskimo, Aleut[1]	1,737	0.7	1,429	0.6	308	21.6	2.2
Hispanic origin[2]	20,528	8.3	14,803	6.5	5,724	38.7	3.6

[1]Resident population.
[2]Persons of Hispanic origin may be of any race.
Source: Adapted from U.S. Bureau of the Census (1990c).

that "all immigration to the Other-races population occurs to Asians or Pacific Islanders," since the small exchange of American Indian immigrants among the United States, Canada, and Latin America has not been measured (U.S. Bureau of the Census, 1990c, p. 3). Thus the implication of the figures on Other races is that, between 1980 and 1984, the rate of immigration of Asian Pacific Americans was twice as great as that of Hispanics. While the actual rate of immigration slowed in the period 1985–1989, the same pattern holds, with Asian Pacific Americans immi-

TABLE 1.2 Components of the Average Rate of Population Change, by Race: 1980 to 1989

(Total population including Armed Forces overseas. Rates are per 1,000 mid-period population)

Race and Hispanic Origin	Net change	Natural increase	Births	Deaths	Net civilian immigration
All races:					
1985–1989	9.8	7.0	15.8	8.7	2.7
1980–1984[1]	10.1	7.1	15.7	8.6	2.9
White:					
1985–1989	7.5	5.7	14.7	9.0	1.8
1980–1984[1]	7.8	5.9	14.7	8.8	1.9
Black:					
1985–1989	15.0	13.0	21.4	8.5	2.1
1980–1984[1]	15.1	12.9	21.2	8.3	2.2
Other races:					
1985–1989	48.6	18.9	22.1	3.2	29.7
1980–1984[1]	61.0	20.1	23.3	3.2	40.9
Hispanic origin[2]					
1985–1989	34.2	18.7	23.1	4.4	15.5
1980–1984[1]	38.4	18.7	22.9	4.2	19.6

[1]1980–1984 refers to April 1, 1980 through December 31, 1984.
 1985–1989 refers to January 1, 1985 through December 31, 1989.
[2]Persons of Hispanic origin may be of any race.
Source: Adapted from U.S. Bureau of the Census (1990c).

grating at almost twice the rate of Hispanics. The table also shows that among these two groups the rate of natural increase has been fairly steady throughout the decade and is higher than that of both Blacks and Whites.

The figures in Table 1.1 show that during the 1980s the number of people of Asian origin in the United States increased by 79.5 percent, those of Hispanic origin by 38.7 percent, Native Americans by 21.6 percent, Blacks by 14.4 percent, and Whites by 7.0 percent. While Hispanics are projected to become the largest minority group by the turn of the century (Harrison, Wilson, Pine, Chan, & Buriel, 1990), Asian Pacific Americans are currently the fastest growing group, primarily because of increasing waves of immigrants and refugees from East Asia and Southeast Asia (U.S. Bureau of the Census, 1990c).

With the exception of African Americans, these groups also represent a wide variety of languages. The population of students of limited English proficiency (LEP) is now projected to reach at least 3.5 million by the year 2000; of this group of students, Spanish-speaking students currently constitute about 80 percent of the total (Trueba, 1989).

In light of the current pattern of underachievement among minority students, the educational implications of these figures are immense. Essentially, the American school system is faced with a choice between accepting that at least half of its students may continue to be at risk for school failure and dropout, or else making a firm commitment to examining and remedying this trend. Chapter 3 will be devoted to outlining current thought on the changes that need to be made.

SOCIAL AND EDUCATIONAL STATUS
OF MINORITY GROUPS IN THE UNITED STATES

Tremendous diversity exists within the groups described above. In addition to the racial heterogeneity already indicated, there are several other essential features that may delineate important differences. This section will summarize briefly what is known about all four groups on the dimensions of economic and educational status, since these tend to be the factors on which the American concept of success is built and which, therefore, are influential in the way a group of people may be perceived by the society as a whole. Information on country of origin will also be included. Equally important yet less readily identifiable features, such as psychological/social adaptation and levels of acculturation, will be discussed in a subsequent section.

Figures for White, African, and Hispanic Americans are taken from 1988 and 1989 Bureau of the Census reports on these races. Regarding Asian Pacific Americans, however, the most recent data breaking down information on the specific categories among Asians and Pacific Islanders are from 1980 Bureau of the Census reports. (The more recent data do not distinguish between Asian groups, and they also employ the overall category Other Races, which includes Native Americans.) Thus all observations regarding Asians will be based on 1980 data. Observations regarding Native Americans will also be based on this 1980 data (U.S. Bureau of the Census, 1980).

Country of Origin

Typically, the vast majority of African Americans and Native Americans are U.S. born. Among Native Americans, immigration from other

North and Central American countries is known to exist but has not been measured and is thought to be very small (U.S. Bureau of the Census, 1990c). Among Blacks, however, immigration from other countries, such as the West Indies and Africa, has increased substantially since 1970, accounting for 16 percent of the increase in the Black population in 1988 (U.S. Bureau of the Census, 1989).

There is much greater diversity on this dimension among Hispanic and Asian Pacific Americans. Bureau of the Census figures for 1989 indicate that, among Hispanics, approximately half the growth in population between 1988 and 1989 was through immigration rather than U.S. births. Within the total Hispanic population on the U.S. mainland, Mexican Americans accounted for 62.6 percent, Puerto Rican Americans for 11.6 percent, Central and South Americans for 12.7 percent, other Hispanics for 7.8 percent, and Cubans for 5.3 percent (U.S. Bureau of the Census, 1990a).

For Asian Americans, the 1980 figures showed that, while the majority were foreign-born (62.1 percent), there were wide variations among groups in place of birth, Vietnamese being the largest at 90.5 percent, compared with 28.4 percent of Japanese.

Within Asian groups, Southeast Asian refugees represent the largest group in the U.S. (Rumbant, 1985). Two basic waves of immigration have been identified for these groups—the first from 1975 to 1977, and the second from 1978 to the present time. While official national figures are not currently available for the newer groups within this population, a 3-year study of migration and resettlement of Hmong, Khmer, Lao, Vietnamese, and Chinese-Vietnamese refugees in San Diego County, California (Rumbant, 1985) notes that the second wave includes greater proportions of Hmong, Khmer, Lao, and Chinese-Vietnamese ethnic groups and that 92 percent of the Hmong had come from rural backgrounds, as compared with 53 percent of the Khmer and 5 percent of the Chinese and Vietnamese-Chinese.

Educational Attainment

Minority students' educational attainment continues to lag significantly behind that of Whites. In 1988, 87 percent of Whites had completed 4 years of high school and 24.5 percent had completed 4 years of college or more.

In 1988, 80.5 percent of all African Americans between 25 and 34 years of age had completed 4 years of high school, while 13 percent had completed 4 years or more of college.

Attainment among Hispanics was lower, with 60 percent in the 25 to 34 age range having completed 4 years of high school and about 11 percent having completed 4 years of college. Within this group, 84 percent of Cubans, 77 percent of other Hispanics, 76 percent of Puerto Ricans, 70 percent of Central and South Americans, and 50 percent of Mexicans had completed high school (U.S. Bureau of the Census, 1990a).

Among Asian Americans in 1980, 75 percent had completed 4 years of high school, while 34 percent had completed 4 years of college. Although the college figures place this group as a whole ahead of the White majority, there are wide variations among Asian groups. For example, 82 and 80 percent of Japanese and Asian Indians respectively were high school graduates, as compared with 62 percent of Vietnamese. Similarly, among Asian Indians, 52 percent were college graduates, as compared with 13 percent of Vietnamese.

Among Pacific Islanders, 67 percent were high school graduates and 9 percent were college graduates (U.S. Bureau of the Census, 1980).

Economic Status

One of the central concerns regarding culturally diverse students in the United States is the role of poverty in their lives. This section will offer only the most gross indicator of economic status for White and minority groups, that is, their status in terms of poverty level.

In 1987, 10.5 percent of all Whites were below the poverty level, as compared to 33 percent of Blacks (U.S. Bureau of the Census, 1990b). In 1988, 27 percent of Americans of Hispanic origin were below the poverty level (U.S. Bureau of the Census, 1990a). Within this group, 28.5 percent of Mexican Americans were below the poverty level; 34 percent of Puerto Ricans; 22 percent of other Hispanic origin; 18 percent of Central and South Americans; and 16.5 percent of Cubans (U.S. Bureau of the Census, 1990a).

With regard to Asian Americans, there is tremendous variability on the dimension of poverty. Bureau of the Census figures for 1980 show that 10.3 percent of Asians were below the poverty level, but that within the group, the range was from 4 percent of Japanese to 35 percent of Vietnamese. Among Pacific Islanders, a total of 8 percent lived below the poverty level (U.S. Bureau of the Census, 1980).

The dramatically different patterns evident between the two larger subgroups, Asians and Pacific Islanders, as well as among the many Asian subgroups, indicate that stereotypical statements about economic, educational, or national backgrounds of Asians and Pacific Islanders are particularly inappropriate.

CULTURE, ACCULTURATION, AND STATUS
AMONG MINORITY GROUPS

The figures given above represent what could be called an outsider's view of these culturally different groups. The national backgrounds of people, their numbers in a given community, their level of formal education, and the economic conditions under which they live are all aspects of information that can be easily gained and that give us but a scant introduction to who these people are. This section will attempt to offer a closer view of these four groups, beginning with an explanation of essential distinctions among race, ethnicity, and culture and offering a sense of how groups may vary in terms of levels of acculturation to the United States.

Further, I will discuss dominant theories of how historical origins and social experiences of a people may bring about different psychological and social attitudes toward the dominant culture and may, in turn, affect their attitudes toward schooling and their children's levels of performance in school. A more detailed description of each group's traditional values regarding worldviews, family systems, and social behavior codes will be offered in Chapter 2.

Ethnicity, Race, and Culture

While definitions of culture abound, Wright, Saleeby, Watts, and Lecca (1983) have offered an explanation of the distinctions and connections among race, ethnicity, and culture that is very appropriate to the purposes of this discussion. These authors state:

> There is a difference, conceptually and in reality, between race, ethnicity, and culture. The differences are not simple and clear. . . . ethnic groups will be so defined if they share a common sociohistory, have a sense of identity of themselves as a group, and have common geographical, religious, racial, and cultural roots. The central core of each ethnic group, welding it together with the thread of belief, styles of being and adapting, is culture. Clearly, because of historical contact and intermingling, different ethnic groups share common cultural elements, and it would be nearly impossible to find an ethnic group unsullied by foreign cultures.
>
> Race is, at this point, a dubious biological designation. Unfortunately, though, it has signal social importance. (p. 5)

The intermingling of cultures in response to contact is the process of acculturation—a process of modifying one's original "belief, styles of being and adapting" to those of another culture. In the case of minority peoples, the process is usually one way—a bending of one's traditional patterns in the direction of the dominant culture in which one lives. The level of acculturation is important to the extent that it will mitigate the conflict experienced in cross-cultural interaction. Indeed, the mitigation of such conflict is most often the reason for acculturation. Levels of acculturation vary widely both within and among minority groups, and the process may be expected to differ for immigrant as compared to indigenous groups. Identifying such differences, however, presents an extremely complex challenge.

A basic framework of three levels of acculturation has been described by Ramirez and Castañeda (1974): traditional, dualistic, and atraditional. These authors, in considering Mexican American culture, state that movement from traditional to atraditional tends to correlate with a community's increasing mobility, greater ethnic heterogeneity, urban status, and greater distance from the Mexican border.

Leung (1988) has offered a similar but expanded framework, as summarized below:

1. *Traditionalism:* usually found among older adults who cling to the traditional culture
2. *Marginality:* persons at the juncture of two cultures, accepting neither the old nor the new, and possibly experiencing alienation from both
3. *Biculturation:* a level of efficient integration of both cultures
4. *Overacculturation:* an extreme rejection of the ethnic culture, sometimes shown by young people

Further, Leung isolates six factors that most directly influence acculturation, these being: time in the host culture; proximity to the traditional culture, which, she states, deters the acculturation process; age; birthplace; gender, with females being more open to acculturation than males; and intermarriage. We must also add to this list the variables of social class and educational level, or what Lee (1982) has referred to as professional affiliation and status.

In discussing acculturation among American Indian families, Red Horse (1988) has described a similar picture to that of Leung, with the additional distinction of a "pan-renaissance" group, which tries to "revitalize" traditional views and practices and engage in a kind of cultural revival. A similar process has occurred among African Americans, whose reclamation of their African cultural heritage began in the 1960s. However, the concept of stages of acculturation is more difficult to apply to this group, whose native culture was forcibly undermined by slavery, with no allowance for a period of continuing traditional belief and practice. Among African Americans, therefore, the "pan-renaissance" has the quality of an intense search for a viable Black identity (Jenkins, 1982) and for the reclamation of respect for the African American culture that has been forged through the violent merging of two worlds.

Proximity to the Native Culture

The dimension of immigrant versus indigenous status of minority groups may also provide an additional perspective. While it is true that Native American peoples are the only unquestionably indigenous people in the United States, for the purposes of this discussion we shall consider as indigenous African Americans and many Hispanics from, for example, Mexican American communities that have been part of the United States for many generations. Puerto Ricans hold a unique position, having their own geographical territory yet being American citizens. There are important historical differences among minorities considered to be indigenous to the United States, but a common theme is varying extents of oppression and isolation from the dominant society. For African Americans and American Indians, this experience has been sanctioned by law. For Hispanics it has been less entrenched, although no less powerful in areas such as education and employment opportunities (Ogbu, 1987; Trueba, 1989).

One might expect that the acculturation process should be less intense for groups who are indigenous to a nation than for immigrants since, at least through contact and familiarity, the boundaries of culture ought to be less rigid. This, however, may vary according to the extent of fluidity and contact between indigenous minorities and the majority. For example, regarding Hispanic Americans, it has often been observed that geographical proximity to Mexico and Puerto Rico have tended to strengthen ties to the traditional culture, lessening the likelihood of acculturation for many (Morales, 1986; Ramirez & Castañeda, 1974).

The notion of proximity to the native culture may also be thought of in psychological rather than geographical terms. In the case of American Indians, legally separate homelands and governmental structures would be expected to promote a powerful sense of separateness, maintaining clear boundaries between indigenous native culture and that of the dominant society. For African Americans, while there were no equivalent geographical and political delineations, ingrained racial prejudice, which for centuries legally ensured separate education, residence, worship, and even use of public facilities, has been equally powerful in creating boundaries—indeed, barriers. Yet both these groups have been forced to rely on the larger society for employment and services, so that constant interaction with the dominant society has been inevitable. The extent of acculturation therefore varies widely, and there is no doubt that many such peoples retain strong cultural identification despite a long history of close contact with the dominant society.

Adaptive Strategies

One aspect of the process of acculturation, that of changes in observable social behavior, has been described in terms of the development of "adaptive strategies" that promote the survival and well-being of the group. Harrison et al. (1990) have identified three adaptive strategies common to all minority groups in the United States: family extendedness and role flexibility, biculturalism, and ancestral worldviews. The authors further discuss the influence of these adaptive strategies on the socialization goals of such families and on children's cognitive outcomes. However, the extent to which such features represent adaptive strategies or, rather, preexisting traditional values and practices seems a moot point.

The question of acculturation must also be examined on another level — that of values, beliefs, and psychosocial adaptation. These, I believe, represent a deeper level than "strategies," reflecting the internalization of beliefs and values that may alter the way one sees oneself and one's culture. The following section will outline a much-debated view of this theme.

THE PSYCHOSOCIAL ADAPTATION
OF MINORITY GROUPS

The variable nature of minority groups' psychological and social adaptation has been the focus of much attention by educational anthropologists in recent years. Ogbu's (1978) well-known distinction among autonomous, immigrant, and indigenous or caste-like minorities has been widely cited as a way of explaining differential educational achievement among minority groups.

Indigenous and Immigrant Minorities

Ogbu (1978), in a discussion of cross-cultural issues in education, has made a distinction among three types of minorities, which he calls autonomous, immigrant, and caste-like minorities.

As examples of autonomous groups he cites Mormons or Jews. It seems likely that, in the United States at least, the opportunity for "autonomy" among such peoples relates to the fact that they are considered White within this culture.

Immigrant minorities, he says, have moved to the host society more or less voluntarily and are not deeply affected by the local hierarchical ideology; rather, they tend to use it to achieve their goals. Thus they tend to be more successful because their psychological frame of reference is with their traditional culture, making them less likely to internalize the experience of rejection and discrimination.

Indigenous groups, on the other hand, may often be described as caste-like, operating from a position of low social status and disadvantage within a society that they consider their own. Having no other frame of reference, Ogbu argues, they tend to internalize the rejection of the dominant society and may become psychologically predisposed toward failure. In the United States, Blacks represent a prototypical caste-like minority, and Ogbu argues that many Blacks develop an "oppositional" social identity or frame of reference (Ogbu, 1987) and a "retreatist adaptation" to school (Ogbu, 1978). This results in many Black students' rejection of school values and, consequently, high rates of educational failure.

Ogbu (1987) has made similar observations of other national groups, such as West Indians, who do less well in Britain, where their postcolonial status is more likely to bring them caste-like status, but are much more successful in America, where they come with the psychological advantage of immigrants. The same is also true of the Buraku, a Japanese minority of low caste, who, in their native society, do less well in school than they do as immigrants in the United States (DeVos, 1973).

According to this analysis, Hispanics who are not U.S. born ought to be considered an "immigrant minority"; but Ogbu argues that, to the extent that these immigrants come from countries that hold a politically subordinate relationship to the United States, they tend to function more like caste-like than immigrant groups. He further argues that the caste-like status of indigenous Mexican Americans tends to be generalized to Mexican immigrants (Ogbu, 1987). Thus he concludes that such groups are assigned, and tend to internalize, the status of a caste-like rather than an immigrant minority and tend to demonstrate a similar pattern of low educational achievement.

The overlapping of caste-like and racial minority status provides an additional dimension to this theory. Spener (1988) has emphasized that the racial background of immigrants is important because, after the "outward ethnolinguistic markers" are no longer evident, racial differences are. Consequently children of immigrant racial minorities remain minorities, while the children of White immigrants become part of the majority. The OCR classification system discussed earlier gives evidence of this. Spener argues that non-White immigrants, therefore, are often "lumped" into the same category as caste-like minorities. In addition to the issue of political subordination of their countries of origin, then, the fact that Hispanics are generally considered non-White lends further support to Ogbu's interpretation that many immigrant Hispanics do not benefit from the usual advantage of being in the role of immigrants, but function, rather, like indigenous people of low caste.

Variations in the Status of Immigrants

This taxonomy appears to work well for groups who can clearly be distinguished as indigenous (African and Native Americans) versus immigrant (Japanese and Koreans, for example). It becomes much more complex, however, when looking at groups who defy clear categorization of this dimension. For example, the notion of involuntary minority status is another aspect of the caste-like status of minority peoples who were "originally brought into United States society involuntarily through slavery, conquest, or colonization" (Ogbu, 1987, p. 321). Ogbu argues that later immigrants from Mexico, for example, were assigned the status of the "original conquered group" of Mexican Americans (p. 321). The overlap between immigrant and indigenous status, however, is revealed by the fact that Mexican immigrants cannot be considered "involuntary" minorities, although the oppression they may experience may be involuntary (Trueba, 1989). On the other hand, there are many immigrants whose migration is genuinely involuntary and who may come from countries whose relationship to the United States could also be described as politically subordinate, such as several Central American and Southeast Asian countries. Would these immigrants, then, be expected to function more like caste-like than like immigrant minorities?

Several views of refugees have emerged recently that indicate the variety of situations that may be represented by immigrants. Two common observations are that (1) as involuntary immigrants, refugees may tend to be granted a relatively exalted status because of political considerations, especially if they come from Communist countries; and (2) they may sometimes come from the upper and more educated classes in their countries of origin and tend to acculturate more readily. Both these observations have been made regarding the first waves of Cuban (Morales, 1986) and Vietnamese refugees (Rumbant, 1985). Both these groups are examples of the difficulties of classification, since, while they may have come from the upper classes of their society, they are also involuntary immigrants from countries that have experienced some version of political subordination to the United States. These groups have tended to do well in the United States and have not generally functioned like caste-like minorities; thus it seems likely that class and possibly political values in the host country may have mediated the effects of involuntary status.

Another view of refugees is presented by Suarez-Orosco (1989), whose study of Central American students fleeing war-torn countries and hoping to help family they left behind shows that many of these students exhibit unusually high levels of motivation and relatively dramatic success in the United States. This author also points out that the often-undocumented status of these de facto refugees adds yet another dimension to an already complex picture — the presence of an even greater than usual motivation to succeed. Thus it would seem that political status, social class, and motivational levels may alter the psychosocial adaptation and performance of refugees.

In addition to social class and educational background, the extent of political oppression experienced prior to migration may result in a totally different picture of refugees in the host country. In the case of Southeast Asian refugees, observations so far indicate that while the first wave of Vietnamese students has done quite well in school, more recent refugees have had a more difficult time adjusting. This is especially so among the Hmong and Cambodian groups (Bui, 1983), most likely because of severe trauma in refugee camps, more rural and less educated backgrounds, and the loss of family members.

A study by Rumbant (1985) found that the Khmer had suffered the most severe psychosocial losses, such as loss of family members or inability to locate or communicate with family left behind. The author concluded that these factors led to the Hmong and Khmer groups being at significantly greater risk on affective measures of depression. Despite the ethnocultural diversity among Southeast Asian refugees, Rumbant states that these groups share the "common predicament of involuntary homelessness" (p. 435). This experience predisposes the refugees to conceive of their exile as temporary, viewing themselves in the role of marginal "guests" with significant obligations to their hosts. Such attitudes may be expected to be very different from those of immigrants such as Asian Indians, who are known to have migrated mainly for the purpose of improving their economic and educational opportunities.

Similar observations have been made in Canada regarding the lower academic performance of more recent immigrants (Cummins, 1984), although the reasons for this are not yet known. On the other hand, Cummins also notes that the extremely high level of academic achievement among both Canadian-born Chinese and immigrant Chinese students at all socioeconomic levels seems to challenge the usual assumptions about the predominant influence of social class and family education level on academic achievement. The absence of a correlation between social class and achievement has also been noted by Gibson (1987) among Punjabi students in a California community, who were generally doing well despite the low income and educational level of their parents. This researcher concluded that the students' success was mostly related to their beliefs about the value of formal education and the rigorous pressures for conformity to traditional values imposed by their parents.

Minority Typology:
A Backdrop to Variation and Change

The concept of types of minority groups, then, is important as a general indicator of the likely reasons for differential educational performance between immigrant and indigenous minority groups who conform to traditional conceptions of these terms. Many groups, however, "fall between the cracks" of the theory, leaving it open to the criticism that the categories are so overlapping as to seriously undermine its conceptual framework (Trueba, 1988). Trueba also states that Ogbu's framework is "highly stereotypic" (1988, p. 276) in its inability to account for the success of many members of so-called caste-like minorities.

In this regard it is also essential to note the unique situation of American Indians. The historical fact of the conquering of these peoples and their subsequent low levels of educational and economic attainment would place them in the role of a caste-like minority. Yet the status of these peoples is somewhat different because they are officially considered nations within the United States with whom the U.S. government has engaged in treaties. However, since the autonomy implied by this status only exists within a state, but does not protect the Indian nation from the U.S. federal government, the reality of autonomy is sharply limited (Appleton, 1983).

A final and crucial point regarding the notion that oppressed minorities tend to internalize aspects of their devalued status in the society is that they may simultaneously maintain an enduring preference for many aspects of their own culture. In other words, although a minority group may be aware of and influenced by the fact that the majority group defines it in negative ways, its members may also share their own ways of defining both themselves and the majority culture.

For example, in *Portraits of "the Whiteman,"* Basso (1979) shows how jokes made by Apache Indians about Whites reflect a deep contempt for essential patterns of interpersonal behavior typical of mainstream U.S. culture. The value that cultural minorities place on their own culture is often not perceived, or may be intentionally disguised, because the minority person recognizes that the power is on the side of the majority person. This should not be taken for acquiescence. In a discussion entitled "The Silenced Dialogue," Delpit (1988) indicates the deep chasm in communication that often develops between Black and White teachers regarding different views of authority and power in the classroom. She observes that, when the dialogue is silenced, "Most likely the White educators believe that their colleagues of color did, in the end agree with their logic. After all, they stopped disagreeing, didn't they?" (p. 281).

Further, the contempt of many minority groups for their own members who are perceived to have devalued their own culture by becoming what Leung (1988) has referred to as "overacculturated" is reflected in terms such as "Oreo" among Blacks (as in the cookie, black on the outside, white inside) and "banana" among Asians (yellow/white).

In response to the observation that the caste-like versus immigrant framework is overlapping and/or ambiguous, Ogbu argues that his work is concerned with "the distinctive features of a minority group" rather than with "individual differences" (Ogbu, 1987, p. 321). Indeed, it seems reasonable that a theory of group consciousness should by definition reflect gross rather than individual or idiosyncratic patterns, and provide, thereby, a baseline from which to begin to delineate what factors may contribute to changes in, or deviations from, the overall pattern. The existence of a pattern does not deny either the possibility of changing the pattern for many students or of several individuals doing well in spite of it.

SUMMARY

This chapter has emphasized that the use of the term *minority* in the United States is synonymous with race. The chapter has used the U.S. Department of Education's classification system to identify the four broad categories that, when aggregated, are viewed as minority in contradistinction to White.

The chapter has offered an overall view of the heterogeneity of the four culturally different groups. The main concern was to give an idea of the size of these groups within the United States, as well as their historical, social, economic, and educational backgrounds and the variable effects of these upon minority people's adjustment to life in the United States. Figures from the Bureau of the Census for 1988 and 1989 regarding African Americans and Hispanic Americans indicate that both groups are significantly behind Whites on both educational and economic factors and that, within the Hispanic groups, there are wide variations. Similarly, figures from 1980 for Asian and Pacific Islanders make it clear that generalizations about the educational and economic status of this group are not meaningful and must be replaced by attention to the status of national groups within this category.

The chapter has emphasized the importance of widely ranging levels of acculturation among minority peoples and the strengths and limitations of theoretical generalizations about the psychological effects of minority status. Attempts to classify such groups along dimensions of indigenous or immigrant status can be helpful in offering an overall view of general psychosocial patterns but cannot be applied in stereotypic ways. Professionals need to be aware of what is known about minority groups generally, while attending to the specific, individual situations of all students.

Culturally Diverse Students
and Their Families

It is essential that professionals in the United States understand the tension that exists between an outsider's and an insider's view of minority people's experience: the dimensions of power/powerlessness, traditional/atraditional, cultural pride/cultural shame are intertwined in a dynamic process through which the cultural consciousness of minority peoples evolves. The pride that most minority peoples feel in their traditional culture has continued to thrive despite the widespread promotion of images of cultural deficiency, pathology, and hopelessness.

Wright and colleagues (1983) have offered a "sampler of myths" about child rearing and family life in minority cultures, showing that the stereotypes held by outsiders may be only one side of the coin. For example, stereotypes of machismo among Hispanics and matriarchy among Blacks fail to acknowledge the deep sense of responsibility and authority reflected by these patterns: the ingrained responsibility of the Hispanic young man for his sister and the enduring respect for the mother as the center of the Black family (Eagar, 1986). Wright and colleagues further show how terms such as *the tangle of pathology* used by the Moynihan report (U.S. Department of Labor, 1965) and *cultural deprivation* are built on a misguided notion of superior versus inferior cultures. All cultures, like all languages, are adequate to the needs of the peoples who have developed them, and to suppose that some cultures are inferior, say Wright and colleagues, is to "confuse culture with . . . social tools and resources" (p. 134).

In this chapter I will offer a brief outline of what is known about the general cultural ethos of each of the ethnic groups introduced in Chapter 1, with the primary purpose of demonstrating that values and beliefs related to disability are cultural, not universal, in nature. Perhaps more important than knowing particular features of any one cultural group will be the recognition by American special educators of the cultural base of their own belief system. The Education for All Handicapped Children Act couches its mandate in concepts that are uniquely Western, both in terms of a medical model of disability and of a framework of services derived from a technological culture. The power of this legal mandate and the demand for accountability to it reinforce professionals' tendency to forget the relativity of the concepts, thus delegitimizing all others.

Three provisos are essential to the following outline. First, because the minority group classifications being used are essentially classifications that have been imposed by Western culture, we cannot assume that they are meaningful to these peoples themselves. Second, there is national, cultural, and often racial heterogeneity within each group. Third, further heterogeneity is created in each group by varying extents of acculturation. With regard to the latter, I will use the term *traditional* to indicate what might be expected among peoples least acculturated to Western ways. The outline will highlight underlying commonalities that stand in contrast to the dominant culture of American schools.

In outlining central cultural features of each group, I will first describe the extent to which the group appears to have a cohesive group identity; then outline expressions of traditional culture as they appear in different worldviews, conceptions of family, and codes of social interaction; and finally relate these views to conceptions of disability so far found in each culture.

HISPANIC: A SOCIOPOLITICAL ETHNICITY

In the Chapter 1 discussion of racial classifications used by the Department of Education, it was clear that the concept of Hispanic is not a racial category; rather, it refers to a group whose identity centers on a common language and a history of Spanish American colonial culture. The four choices offered by the 1990 census questionnaire under the umbrella "Hispanic" are Mexican or Mexican American, Puerto Rican, Cuban, or other Spanish, with the opportunity for respondents to specify their country of origin. What does this identity mean to people who claim it? Indeed, the term *Hispanic* is itself controversial; there are many who prefer the term *Latino* because it emphasizes the notion of a Latin American identity.

In a study of Puerto Ricans and Mexicans in Chicago, Padilla (1985) argues that a Hispanic or Latino identity is specific to the U.S. situation. He says that people from the Spanish Americas have cooperated in the creation of this group identity in response to urban pressures, affirmative action, and political activism. He describes their reaction as

> a product of interaction and communication processes among these groups in response to their marginal position in the institutional life of the larger American society. (p. 69)

> Latinismo is political ethnicity, a manipulative device for the pursuit
> of collective, political, economic and social interests in society. (p. 163)

Walker (1987) says that the term *Hispanic* is an umbrella term that may originally have been brought into use at the federal level and "obscures" the many differences among these peoples (p. 16). Partly for political purposes, then, Hispanics seem to have achieved the status of a minority group, despite their tremendous racial and national heterogeneity.

One unquestionably common bond, however, is language. Despite the existence of numerous national and local dialectal forms of Spanish, speakers of the language are essentially mutually intelligible, and an identifiable standard form of Spanish is recognized by all groups. Indeed, this characteristic sets Hispanic groups apart from the other non-English-speaking ethnic minorities in the United States, who may share similar but not common languages. In addition to this commonality, speakers of Spanish have been noted for their commitment to the native language, which seems to stand as an important symbol of their cultural heritage and solidarity (Wright et al., 1983).

Beyond language, what are the identifying features of this group? What is the group's claim to ethnicity and the extent of its cultural difference and/or identity? In addressing these questions, the following outline begins by acknowledging that the racial, national, and social-class heterogeneity of Hispanics, as well as their differing degrees of acculturation to U.S. culture, makes generalizations about this group very difficult (G. Canino, 1982; I. Canino, 1982; Walker, 1987).

There are, nevertheless, several clusters of features associated with Hispanic culture, all of which may appear in different forms and extents among the many nationalities included in this ethnicity. These clusters of values and social behaviors, which cut across the boundaries of Central, South American, and Caribbean Spanish-speaking nations, have resulted from the blending of Spanish culture with the cultures of peoples indigenous to these areas. In the Caribbean territories, in particular, the influence of African cultures and some of the legacies of slavery have also been woven into the cultural fabric.

Worldview in Traditional Hispanic Societies

By the term *worldview*, I mean underlying beliefs about humanity's purpose and place in the universe, beliefs that affect codes of personal and interpersonal behavior as well as attitudes to the health, life, and death of human beings. To discuss culturally based worldviews prior to consideration of attitudes to family and social interaction is simply to set the stage for a full circle, since these three aspects of any society are interrelated; indeed, they are mirrors of each other.

The worldview of Hispanic Americans is based on Catholic ideology, with an inextricable interweaving of the ideologies of native Central and South American views of the universe. In the Caribbean territories, it is mainly African religious beliefs that have been added to a Catholic base.

In a discussion of Mexican Catholic ideology, Ramirez and Castañeda (1974) describe this as "a 'mestizo' religious ideology . . . an amalgamation of European and Indian ideas and practices" (p. 48). The mixed character of religion is equally true in other Spanish American territories, all of which have traditionally been Catholic. In Mexico, Catholicism has been interwoven with traditional Indian beliefs in folk healing; for example, Ramirez and Castañeda quote a student who includes in an explication of his family's Catholicism, a description of his grandmother's ability to heal "susto" (emotional shock), which is essentially a folk, rather than a traditional Catholic, concept.

In the Caribbean territories, Catholicism has also been central to all aspects of society but has been greatly influenced by African folk beliefs. Delgado (1988) has explained that in Cuba and Puerto Rico folk healing may include various forms, such as medicinal treatment by a folk healer or Espiritismo (Spiritism), often taking the form of Santerismo, a mixture of Yoruba (African) religious beliefs and Roman Catholicism, which includes the practice of spirit possession. The greater the influence of African traditions in these territories, the more the perspective tends to reflect an animistic view, in which spiritual influences abound throughout the universe. However, because of the negative evaluation usually attached to African influences in these territories, they tend to be most readily relinquished by Black people who attain higher social status. Thus the retention of distinctly African patterns is generally associated with low social class. Another and more recent influence in the Caribbean and Central America has been various forms of North American Protestantism, in particular those of an evangelical bent (I. Canino, 1982; Suarez-Orosco, 1989).

The notion of worldview is larger than religion per se, in that the religion both informs and reflects a view of humanity's place in the universe. Catholic ideology underscores a view of the human being's superior place within a hierarchy of universal values, an obligation to those who have gone before, and a responsibility to reflect the respect owed to this hierarchy in one's personal and social life.

The interrelatedness of these aspects of Hispanic society has been noted by Ramirez and Castañeda (1974) in their description of Mexican Catholic ideology. These authors quote at length from a sketch of family life written by a college student reared in a traditional Mexican American community, which gives a clear view of the intertwining of obedience and reverence to religion with that which is owed to the family hierarchy. A very brief excerpt from this essay will give an idea of how this is expressed:

> Respeto and obediencia [respect and obedience] were the themes of many sermons and the priests used to stress that just as we obeyed and respected God's law, that we should obey and respect parents and elders because God had given them authority over us. To be disrespectful and disobedient to our parents, therefore, was as if we had done this to God Himself.
>
> As children our parents taught us always to have the greatest respect of our grandparents. We were taught always to kiss our grandparents' right hand whenever we entered their home and to ask for their blessing, which we received while kneeling, when leaving their home. (p. 53)

Culture and Traditional Hispanic Families

The foregoing excerpt illustrates the inextricable bond between religious views and views of the family in traditional Hispanic cultures. Indeed, the centrality of the concept of "familia" (family) is well known in the literature on Hispanic families, regardless of national origin (G. Canino, 1982; Condon et al., 1979; Harrison et al., 1990; Suarez-Orosco, 1989).

Importance of Group Identity. The ideal of "familia" represents an interpretation of self as a reflection of, and contributor to, the larger group identity of the immediate and extended family. In a description of this concept in Mexican American culture, Ramirez and Castañeda (1974) explain that in this value system, "the needs of the individual are considered secondary to those of the family," making repercussions upon family reputation a central consideration in an individual's action (p. 42). These authors point out that close ties among families within traditional communities mean that identification with family is extended to identification with the community itself.

This concept of the role of the family stands in contrast to that of mainstream U.S. society to the extent that it places the importance of the group above that of the individual, as compared to the American emphasis on the separateness and preeminence of the self (Condon et al., 1979; Ramirez & Castañeda, 1974). To fulfill one's role as a member of a group is to place a higher value on cooperation than on individual competition. Thus Trueba (1989) has referred to the dominant mode of U.S. schools as the "culture of competition," to which students from more cooperatively oriented cultures must adapt (p. 37). This is not to say that there is no requirement for cooperation in the U.S. system, but, as Condon and colleagues (1979) have pointed out, the requirement is for an impersonal kind of cooperation—of collaboration with an ad hoc "team" of peers rather than an enduring commitment to one's natural group. Further, Ramirez and Castañeda (1974) point out that the traditional Hispanic emphasis on family and ethnic group is actually discouraged by schools in the interest of Americanization.

Ramirez and Castañeda (1974) cite an earlier study (Ramirez & Price-Williams, 1971) that, they say, "demonstrated the tenacity with which Mexican Americans maintain values related to identification with family and ethnic group" (p. 43). Interviews with Mexican American and Anglo-American mothers of fourth-grade children in Catholic parochial schools in Houston, Texas, revealed that more than twice as many Mexican American mothers felt that relatives are more important than friends and three times as many felt that children who work should turn their money over to their parents. Twice as many Anglo mothers felt that it is good for children to have some friends whose backgrounds are different from their own. The authors point out that these findings were more impressive in that they were observed in a large urban center, where traditional values might be expected to have been significantly eroded.

Family Structure and Roles. The actual structure of the family will vary according to the ethnic history and social class of a given group. For example, in the case of Puerto Rico, 3 centuries of Spanish colonial rule have combined with the legacy of slavery to produce a unique version of Hispanic culture. Several features commonly observed in postslavery Caribbean societies are evident in this society. One of these is the prevalence of consensual unions and mother-based families among Puerto Ricans of lower social status (Bram, 1968; Fitzpatrick, 1987; Mizio & Delaney, 1981). With this comes a flexible family structure in which children of other unions or from the extended family are made welcome within even the most poor or crowded homes (Bram, 1968; Mintz, 1960).

Yet despite a more flexible family structure among some Hispanic groups, family identity and responsibility are highly valued within a framework of clearly defined roles. Against the background of ultimate patriarchal authority (Bram, 1968; G. Canino, 1982; Fitzpatrick, 1987), the mother is generally seen as playing the major spiritual and integrative role in the family, while sibling roles of authority and responsibility are assigned in accordance with age (Ramirez & Castañeda, 1974; Wright et al., 1983). An abiding sense of responsibility for elders continues despite the increase in nuclear families (Mizio & Delaney, 1981).

A description of Puerto Rican families offered by Canino and Canino (1980) is in keeping with what is known about Hispanic families generally:

using Minuchin's (1974) framework of "enmeshed" versus "disengaged" family structures, these authors described Puerto Rican families as falling on the "enmeshed" side of the spectrum, marked by strong identification of individual needs and aspirations with those of the family. This kind of structure has been described by Escobar and Randolph (1982) as a "close-knit extended network with hierarchies" (p. 47).

This model of the family is common in most Hispanic groups and is reflected in other formally sanctioned relationships that impose family-like obligations and loyalties, such as "compadrazgo" (godparenthood), which creates a special bond between the "compadres" (godparents) (Delgado, 1980; Escobar & Randolph, 1982; Mizio & Delaney, 1981; Ramirez & Castañeda, 1974). Through such systems the individual has a network of "ritually sanctioned friends, allies, protectors and confidants" (Bram, 1968, p. 122).

Thus the family, both biological and symbolic, represents for traditional Hispanic cultures the prototype of a "a clearly defined hierarchy of authority" (Ramirez & Castañeda, 1974, p. 90). As the following section will indicate, it is essentially from this centerpiece, rather than from the school, that the individual is expected to become "una persona bien educada" (a well-educated person).

Traditional Values in Social Interaction

In addition to a "mestizo" Catholic ideology and a strong familism, there is a third cluster of values common in Hispanic cultures. This cluster relates to interpersonal attitudes and codes of behavior, along with a marked "esteem for role and status definition" (Ramirez & Castañeda, 1974, p. 46).

Personalism, Respect, and Status. Concepts of "respeto" (respect), "dignidad" (dignity), "personalismo" (personalism), "honor" (honor), and "confianza" (trust) all reflect a tradition of respect for the individual that requires the expression of an explicit deference from one person to another (Delgado, 1980; Diaz, 1981; Fitzpatrick, 1987; Lauria, 1968; Lewis, 1963). In a discussion of Puerto Ricans, Lauria (1968) describes "respeto" as a "quality of self which must be presented in all interpersonal treatment" and without which "no Puerto Rican is considered properly socialized" (p. 43). In reference to Mexican Americans, the same point is reflected in the concept of "una persona bien educada" (a well-educated person) (Ramirez & Castañeda, 1974). Zuñiga (1988) emphasizes that the term does not refer to formal education as such, as it would in mainstream U.S. culture, but rather to an individual who "understands the importance of interacting and relating to other humans with respect and dignity" (p. 75).

While notions of respect are, of course, valued by U.S. culture also, its expressions vary much more widely, are not routinely or ritually required, and are more likely to be tied to respect earned by individual success. The Hispanic version of this value is intrinsically tied to the concept of personalism, which underlies the demand for respect, dignity, honor, and trust. In a discussion of personalism as it expressed in Puerto Rico, Fitzpatrick (1987) describes it as:

> An individualism which focuses on the inner importance of the person. In contrast to the individualism of the U.S. which values the individual in terms of his or her ability to compete for higher social and economic status, the culture of Puerto Rico centers attention on those inequalities that constitute the uniqueness of a person and his or her goodness or worth. . . . [Puerto Ricans are] sensitive to anything that appears to be personal insult or disdain . . . unusually responsive to manifestations of personal respect and to styles of personal leadership by men who appeal to the person rather than to a program or platform. (p. 78)

Lauria (1968) refers to the expectation of a "generalized deference" as well as various particular forms of respect tied to particular social relations, such as respect to be paid to a person of superior authority or prestige. However, Lauria emphasizes that the superior is also "obligated to express his deference to the subordinate's self through the proper symbolic acts" (p. 44). Delgado (1980) emphasizes that the dignity of the individual "transcends social class" and is acquired "through good deeds and the ability to fulfill role expectations of family, friends and neighbors" (p. 28). The latter is very important, because the failure to fulfill these expectations can lead to loss of self-esteem as well as respect from others.

This emphasis on a personalized yet ritualistic respect makes it difficult for an individual from traditional Hispanic culture to be comfortable with North American–style "professionalism," which assumes due respect on the basis of one's possession of specific skills regardless of one's private or personal disposition. For the traditional Hispanic, such a separation of attributes would undermine the trust that could be placed in such a person. Fitzpatrick's (1987) description of the conflict created by these differing perceptions provides a clear summary of how expectations for interpersonal behavior spill over onto broader social concerns:

> It is this personalism that makes it difficult for the Puerto Rican to adjust easily to what Americans call efficiency. For Puerto Ricans, life is a network of personal relationships. They trust people; they rely on people. . . . They do not have that same trust for a system or an organization.

Americans, on the other hand, expect the system to work; they have confidence in the organization . . . Americans become impatient and uneasy when systems do not work. They respond to efficiency. The Latins become uneasy and impatient if the system works too well, if they feel themselves in a situation where they must rely on impersonal function rather than personal relationships. (p. 79)

The attainment of a balance between personalism and respectful deference may be difficult for mainstream Americans to envisage. Falicov (1982) offers an excellent clarification of this in a discussion of interaction between Mexican Americans — a clarification which is equally true for many Hispanic groups:

With Mexicans, initial encounters tend to be formal, polite, and reserved. However, once a relationship is established, hugging or touching and impromptu visiting are common, and over time friendships tend to assume the quality of kinship. Americans, in contrast, are generally casual and friendly — often using first names from the time of introduction. Yet, when social intimacy does develop (usually after a considerable amount of time), individuals customarily continue to maintain a certain distance. (p. 148)

Race and Class in Hispanic Cultures. Considerations of race and social class contribute an additional layer of interpersonal attitudes to the patterns outlined above. The early history of the Spanish Americas is a history of conquest and dominance of European peoples over indigenous non-White peoples and, to varying extents in different territories, African slaves and their descendants. To this has been added, over the past century, the conquest and dominance of Puerto Rico and a large portion of Mexico by the United States. The combined impact of these historical events can be seen in attitudes to race and class throughout these territories.

The importance of social class is an intrinsic feature of most Hispanic societies. In Suarez-Orosco's study of Central American refugees, the contrast between the possibilities for status mobility in their native countries and in the United States was a tremendous motivating factor for these young people, most of whom were from "the underprivileged classes" (1989, p. 98). The author learned from his informants that status positions "were pretty much prescribed by birth into the right family" (p. 99). Thus, he summarizes: "In Central America one made it through family money, or through networks, or through nepotism, or *por apellido* (because of one's last name) and not through effort or knowledge" (p. 99).

The power of social class has, in most territories, been complicated by attitudes toward race — specifically, the devaluing of dark-skinned races, whether of African or indigenous native origin. Thus higher social class has continued to be identified with lighter skin and European features (Bram, 1968; Fitzpatrick, 1987), and in Puerto Rico the intermediary color "trigueño" (wheat-colored) is considered very attractive (Ghali, 1982). At the same time, however, it is also true that the acquisition of higher class through education and/or money may offset the disadvantage of being dark-skinned and may earn an individual a level of social status historically reserved for lighter-skinned groups. Zuñiga (1988), in a consideration of self-concept among Chicanos, gives an example of the extent to which racism toward Indians has been internalized and projected with negative results even within families. She points out that parents may be "grateful for a child who is born light-skinned rather than dark-skinned," and children may be given nicknames accordingly, such as "Hueda" (light one) or "Chocolate," "Inky" or "Prieta/o" (dark one). Zuñiga also cites a very revealing quote from Gibson and Vasquéz (1982):

> One of the first questions usually asked immediately after a child is born is "¿A quién se parece," whom does he/she resemble or look like? Darker children, those with obvious Negroid or Indian features, often become the scapegoats in the family or the objects of pity. (Quoted in Zuñiga, p. 78)

In Caribbean territories, because of the history of slavery, the dominant racial prejudice is toward Blacks. It has been observed that in Puerto Rico many people of color would rather choose to identify with their Indian than their African heritage (Lewis, 1963). The Puerto Rican equivalent to the nicknames quoted above is "Negrito/a" (darkie) for the dark-skinned child. It is true that this term is used among family intimates as a term of endearment, but its existence nevertheless indicates the importance of color even within the family (Thomas, 1967). More telling, perhaps, is the fact that if this term were applied to an individual by someone outside of the intimate circle, it would be considered an insult.

Caribbean attitudes toward people of African descent include important differences from those in the United States, notably a greater fluidity of racial barriers and an approach to racial definition that includes a combination of class and the extent of European/African/Indian mixture in a person's features. This may relate to the fact that in Puerto Rico a less repressive attitude toward slavery allowed for the rapid rise of a free class of people of mixed race, and, along with this, a deep ambivalence to race that can still be sensed in Puerto Rican people's reluctance to discuss race openly and a form of racism based on shade of skin or racial mixture (Lewis, 1963). While the latter has also been observed among U.S. Blacks, this society has pursued an effort to draw an unequivocal dividing line between White and Black, as was evident in the earlier discussion of the OCR racial classifications (Landry, 1987). Lewis (1963) has observed that the Puerto Rican version of racism is more subtle, but no less powerful, than American forms of discrimination.

To conclude this discussion of social relations in Hispanic societies, then, one must acknowledge the tremendous complexities and ambiguities in this essentially heterogeneous culture. The expectations of personalism, with its respect for the intrinsic value of each human being, the high value placed on social status, and the preferential value placed on light-skinned races create a tension that may appear paradoxical to people from more homogeneous cultures.

Attitudes toward Disability

Several threads from the foregoing discussion can be seen to inform traditional attitudes toward disability among Hispanic peoples. The centrality of religion, with its mixture of traditional Catholicism and Native American and/or African folk beliefs, has an enduring effect on beliefs about the causes and treatment of illness. Thus beliefs about causes of mental disorders, which are often not distinguished from developmental disabilities, tend to include both natural and supernatural explanations. While these beliefs have traditionally been held by both lower and upper classes, they do lessen with acculturation to U.S. views of medicine (Adkins & Young, 1976).

The strong familism, with its traditional view of the individual as a reflection of the biological group, makes acceptance of severe disability difficult for many Hispanic parents. Further, the identification of developmental disabilities, such as mental retardation, with mental illness creates additional stigma. Thus family pride has been identified as a major difficulty in Hispanic families who are receiving services for a handicapped child (Adkins & Young, 1976).

Mild disabilities, on the other hand, may be viewed very differently by Hispanic families. In contrasting Hispanic and Anglo-American attitudes to education, Condon and colleagues (1979) include among differing goals of education the greater concern of Hispanic families with the overall development of the child's personality, as opposed to the school's focus on academic achievement. This is not to say that the Hispanic families do not value education, but that the concept of a well-educated person does not necessarily place academic attainment at the top of the value system. The appropriate socialization of a child is considered as important an indicator of the child's overall ability and potential as is academic success. This, along with a belief in the intrinsic value of the individual, can lead to parents' rejection of school tests as a valid measure of a child's potential (Adkins & Young, 1976).

With regard to the special education system, then, it is to be expected that traditional Hispanic families may have difficulty accepting designations that they interpret as bringing stigma to the family, and, in the case of mild learning difficulties, the notion of disability may be considered inappropriate, especially if the child's social comportment meets expected cultural norms. Interaction with special education personnel will, of course, be affected by traditional values of respect and personalism: parents may be constrained in their interactions by an ingrained respect for authority and status, and they may be severely alienated by the absence of personalism inherent in the formalized documentation system on which most special education programs rely. A much more detailed analysis of such patterns will form the substance of the study of Puerto Rican parents presented in Chapters 5 through 9.

ASIAN PACIFIC AMERICANS: GEOGRAPHIC AND PHILOSOPHICAL ETHNICITY

The phrase "East is East and West is West, and never the twain shall meet" reflects an age-old chasm in understanding between two worlds within our world. For us, as Westerners, "the East" is a monolith. Stereotypes of the enigmatic East have thrived perhaps as much because of our unfamiliarity with these cultures as because of any real connections among them. Indeed, our discussion in Chapter 1 of the ocr classifications pointed to the vast racial differences among these peoples. Religious differences also exist, predominantly between peoples of Southeast Asia and Asian Indians. In terms of language, Asian Indian languages have been estimated as not less than 200 (Pattanayak, 1988), while the languages of Southeast Asia surpass this number. Yet it is true that the philosophies and lifestyles of the peoples of Asia share certain commonalities that stand in stark contrast to those of the West.

This modest attempt to outline the essential contrasts will make no pretense of complete understanding of the very real differences among these cultures. For a very helpful overview of Southeast Asians in the United States, the reader is referred to a collection of articles edited by Dao and Grossman (1985). For purposes of this discussion, a recognition of the commonalities, which are becoming evident as increasing numbers of people from Asia come to the West, constitutes a beginning—a place from which to start to become sensitive to differences.

East and West: Worldviews Apart

If the essence of U.S. culture is individualism and competition, the essence of Eastern cultures is collectivism and harmony. These values are reflected in the three religious orientations on which most Southeast Asian cultures are built — Confucianism, Taoism, and Buddhism. Leung (1988) has described these as mutually compatible and has outlined their differing emphases as follows. Confucianism has more of a social and political emphasis, with a focus on ethics as the key to harmony and prosperity and a central concern with the revering and appeasing of ancestral spirits. Taoism, with a more philosophical emphasis, focuses on the cultivation of inner strength, selflessness, meekness, and tolerance, as well as harmony between nature and man. Buddhism is described as having a more personal emphasis, with goals of enlightenment and the attainment of an altered state of awareness that transcends suffering. The most dominant religion of Asian Indians, Hinduism, is actually the source of Buddhism and consequently shares the same essential concepts.

The emphasis on personal and social harmony shared by these worldviews results in certain common principles that govern concepts of family and social relationships. While there may be many versions of these among the nations of the East, the connecting strands contrast dramatically with their Western counterparts. Chan (1986) summarizes the resulting common features as harmony, social order, rules of propriety, filial piety, benevolence, loyalty, cooperation, reciprocity, and obligation, all of which exist within a system of "prescribed roles and relationships which emphasize subordination and interdependence" (p. 39). Chan contrasts these with the Western values of competition, autonomy, self-reliance, and "less well defined, more varied and often ambiguous social/familial roles and expectations" (p. 39).

Chan (1986) also states that a belief in "the supremacy of the universal order over oneself is further manifested in reverence for the past" (p. 39). Thus responsibility and obligation to family extend beyond present members to include ancestors and, ultimately, one's entire race. As in all cultures, these beliefs have a direct influence on family structures and codes of behavior within the family, as well as on codes of social behavior in wider society.

Traditional Asian Pacific Cultures and the Family

One of the most common concepts that appears throughout the literature on traditional Asian Pacific families is the importance of the family's "saving face." This concern reflects the central importance of family cohesiveness, status, and reputation among Asian cultures. Since all individual behavior reflects either positively or negatively on the family, children are raised in the belief that their every act will contribute either to the pride or shame of the family and that severe punishment and loss of face can be expected for failure to fulfill primary family responsibilities (Chan, 1986; Leung, 1988; Morrow & McBride, 1988). While infancy and early childhood are characterized by an extended period of tolerant, nurturing, and relatively permissive child rearing, the growing child is gradually introduced to a system of strict obedience to an "unqualified and unquestioned parental authority" (Chinn & Plata, 1986, p. 20).

The preeminence of the group over the individual necessitates a suppression of potentially disruptive individual feelings in the interest of family harmony, thus placing a high value on reticence, modesty, and self-control among both children and adults (Chan, 1986; Leung, 1988; Morrow & McBride, 1988). In comparison with the U.S. model, relationships between Asian children and parents, especially fathers, have been described as "one-way," with little opportunity for open discussion, particularly regarding such taboo subjects as sexuality (Chan, 1986).

Asian family structures generally have been described as "highly interdependent . . . within a cohesive patriarchal vertical structure" (Chan, 1986. p. 41). Chinn and Plata (1986) observe that while the extent of gender-role hierarchies may vary among national groups, men are generally accorded ultimate authority, while women have authority and responsibility for daily household affairs and older siblings are given responsibility for the younger (see also Chan, 1986). As in other traditional cultures, the concept of family includes extended family members, with great value placed on elders and on the continuing obligation owed to generations past. Further, in some groups, such as the Hmong (Trueba, Jacobs, & Kirton, 1990), the unit of the clan may be of central importance in defining family membership. Within the United States, Asian Indians, like most Asian Pacific immigrants, have been observed to exhibit a strong preference for reliance on kinship networks as well as on informal networks based on religious and linguistic similarities (Baglopal, 1988).

Traditional Values in Social Interaction

The foregoing observations regarding worldview and views of the family set the stage for a description of the emphasis on interconnectedness and harmony in social interaction. Thus codes of social interaction reflect the hierarchical and harmonious goals of these cultures, as well as the essential identification of individuals with family and with extended kinship networks, such as clan or caste.

The emphasis on harmonious interaction results in a reluctance among most traditional Asian Pacific peoples to engage in confrontation or to promote oneself above the group; thus it is considered ill mannered to be boastful about one's accomplishments (Ishisaka, Nguyen, & Okimoto, 1985). While it might be argued that some amount of modesty is also considered polite in U.S. society, the extent of this among many Asian peoples is often construed by Americans as self-deprecating, or may even be taken as a sign of low self-esteem (Leung, 1988; Trueba et al., 1990). In addition, interpersonal propriety requires deference to others, considerable restraint and indirectness in the expression of feelings, and reticence in the discussion of personal information outside of the family (Ishisaka et al., 1985; Leung, 1988; Liem, 1985). The value placed on restraint can be seen even within family interaction, where deeply felt affection is demonstrated more frequently by acts of caring and providing for loved ones than by words or physical acts of endearment (Leung, 1988).

Social roles both within and outside of the family tend to be rigidly prescribed and dictate details of appropriate interpersonal behavior. Because of this, Asian peoples may feel uncomfortable in ambiguous situations where rules of propriety are unknown (Shon & Ja, 1982). These values are reflected in Indochinese languages, which have honorific systems with different pronouns representing awareness of social status and distance as determined by gender, age, education, and social class (Ishisaka et al., 1985). Yu (1985) points out that the Vietnamese language has no second-person pronoun meaning "you" but more than 40 different third-person classifiers specifying the status of the individual. This author offers a telling quote from a Vietnamese person, who exclaimed at the impoliteness of the American habit of calling everyone "you guys!"

Mental Health and Disability

The central concern for harmony within the individual and between the individual and the universe bears directly on many Eastern interpretations of health. Bodily health is understood in terms of attainment of appropriate balance between the five elements of the body and between mind and body (Chan, 1986). Similarly, psychiatric disorders are often interpreted in terms of an imbalance of physiological functions, which creates disharmony among the elements of the body.

An emerging literature on the provision of mental health services to immigrants from these countries mentions as a central concern the impact of the image of the family on individuals' willingness to seek or utilize therapeutic services (Baglopal, 1988; Chan, 1986; Ishisaka et al., 1985; Leung, 1988; Tung, 1985).

With regard to Southeast Asian refugees in particular, the implications of these notions for the provision of mental health services are challenging to traditional Western practice. It has been noted that, despite the tremendous extent of abuse and stress experienced by many of these refugees, they will usually tend to seek professional help only in the most extreme circumstances and will often describe their concerns in terms of factual and physical, rather than psychological, symptoms, with only muted expressions of grief, depression, or anger (Owan, 1985; Tung, 1985). A recognizable posttraumatic stress disorder has been identified particularly among survivors of Cambodia's Pol Pot regime (Kinzie, 1985), as have been patterns of depression and feelings of "severe role and status loss" among many groups (Ishisaka et al., 1985, p. 56).

In a 3-year comparative study of the psychological adaptation to migration and resettlement among Hmong, Khmer, Lao, Chinese-Vietnamese, and Vietnamese refugees in San Diego County, California, Rumbant (1985) noted significant differences among national groups. He concluded that the Hmong and Khmer were at greatest risk for depression and that many refugees showed a pattern of "delayed realization" of their loss of control over their lives. An important aspect of Rumbant's study, however, is the resilience observed among this group of refugees; indeed, the researcher made a point of recording evidence of what he calls "salutogenesis," a very healthy response to difficulties, as well as the expected "pathogenesis," or pathological responses.

With regard to developmental disabilities, Chan (1986) has observed that there are many different terms in Asian languages for specific disorders, which may not correspond in meaning with English terminology. Major handicaps, such as mental retardation or physical or sensory disabilities, have traditionally carried considerable stigma, and parents may tend to be very protective and tolerant of deviant behavior in young children and reluctant to seek help (Chan, 1986). Parents, however, may have quite different attitudes toward milder, school-based difficulties, often interpreting them as "laziness," oppositional behavior, or, possibly, indications that they have not trained their children adequately (Chan, 1986).

Major handicapping conditions have traditionally been interpreted in one of four ways (Chan, 1986; Kinzie, 1985; Morrow, 1987; Owan, 1985; Tung, 1985):

1. Retribution for the sins of either parents or ancestors
2. Possession by evil spirits
3. The result of specific behaviors of the mother during pregnancy
4. The imbalance of physiological functions

Such disorders, therefore, are seen as bringing shame to the family to the extent that they are thought to reflect on the family's behavior, past or present. Further, because of the emphasis on a child's bringing credit to the family through occupational or academic achievements, a disabled child may cause additional embarrassment and shame (Yano, 1986). Parents' response to this may often be one of resignation, with an emphasis on the need for stoicism and dignity, reflecting a fatalistic orientation in which human suffering is seen as part of the natural order (Chan, 1986; Morrow, 1987). Many parents, however, will attempt to obtain a cure through traditional folk healers (Yano, 1986).

In addition to having very different assumptions about the causes of psychiatric or developmental disorders, traditional Asian peoples in the United States often have a concurrent difficulty in accepting help for such problems. One reason is the stigma attached to receiving such services; another is that the emphasis on self-control and the subordination of self means that feelings and emotions are rarely considered proper reasons to seek help (Ishisaka et al., 1985; Kinzie, 1985; Owan, 1985; Tung, 1985). A more subtle reason, according to Ishisaka and colleagues (1985), is that:

> [There is] no traditional role among Indochinese cultures for a person who provides mental health services. Thus for persons raised in societies that maintain an elaborate interpersonal code governing relationships between individuals, the lack of a suitable role to assign to mental health practitioners evokes anxiety about acceptable conduct. (p. 47)

All of these considerations have clear implications for special educators working with Asian Pacific families. Effective practice will require genuine efforts to understand the conceptual framework of disability held by parents and, no less important, to develop modes of communication that respect the traditional values of these cultures while succeeding in achieving collaboration between parents and professionals. Several more specific aspects of this challenge will be addressed in the review of literature on culturally diverse families and special education offered in Chapter 4.

NATIVE AMERICANS:
INDIANS AND ALASKAN NATIVES

As the term *Asian Pacific American* reflects mainly a geographical frame of reference, so do the terms *American Indian* and *Alaskan Native* reflect a historical frame of reference, based on the conquest of these peoples by European settlers over a period of some 4 centuries. This discussion will give preference to the term *Native American peoples*, to indicate the broad conceptualization of the category, and will strive to make only the most universal of statements, acknowledging that it is beyond the scope of this book to begin to address the tremendous variation among the more than 500 tribes or nations (Harrison et al., 1990) and more than 149 languages (Red Horse, 1988) represented by this grouping.

Professionals should bear in mind the need to be aware of specific details of the tribal background of Indian and Eskimo families they work with. In addition, it is important to remember that, while the lifestyles of many Native American peoples are tremendously influenced by life on the reservation, more than half the American Indian and Alaskan Native population do not live on reservations, and many others may have the reservation as their primary base while spending considerable time in metropolitan areas for purposes of employment or education (Attneave, 1982).

To the extent that there can be said to exist a Native American culture in the United States, it must be seen as the product of 3 centuries of contact with U.S. mainstream culture and the imposition of alien forms of government, philosophy, and social organization on varying traditional cultures of Native American peoples. The resultant features of contemporary Native American groups hold certain features in common, which may be, to varying extents, a combination of traditional features, adaptive strategies, and varying levels of acculturation to the dominant culture. These features include an enduring sense of pride in cultural heritage, a belief in the interrelatedness of body and spirit, culturally distinctive communication styles, and a reliance on extended community and kinship networks.

Worldview in Traditional Native American Societies

Two central features of a worldview common to American Indians stand in contrast to that of mainstream U.S. culture: a belief in the equal value of all forms of life in the universe and a holistic view of living phenomena that emphasizes the interrelatedness of spirit and body. The first of these may best be conceptualized in contrast to the Judeo-Christian account of creation, which proposes the existence of a hierarchical framework in which humanity holds a place of honor. Indeed, the biblical description is of man as having been created in God's image and given "dominion over the fish of the sea and over the fowl of the air . . . and over every living thing that moveth upon the earth" (Genesis 1:26–28). This represents a worldview very different from that of Native American peoples. In a comparison of Ute and Anglo cultures, Cuch (1987) states:

Anthropocentrism, the belief that the human species is the center of the universe and that all things on earth are at its disposal, is in direct contrast to the Indian belief that humans are a part of nature — no better and no worse. (p. 72)

This value system is common among American Indian tribes and is evident in the belief that "all creation has a spiritual component"; thus, among many tribes, "thanks and a small gift were given to any animal or plant from which life was taken" (Locust, 1988, p. 319). This emphasis on man's more humble place in the universe can also be seen in the attitude to land common among Native American peoples; although tribes may mark off their territorial boundaries, the belief that man can own land was, traditionally, an alien notion (Cuch, 1987). Similarly, the traditional Indian view of wealth would not be defined in terms of material possessions, but in terms of one's cultural knowledge and role in the tribe (Red Horse, 1988). Red Horse also states that religious beliefs and the extent to which Native American peoples view land as sacred are central features indicating the level of acculturation.

The dramatic contrast between the view outlined above and that of mainstream U.S. culture can be illustrated by a quote from the annual report of the Secretary of the Interior in 1885, wherein the tribal attitude toward property was referred to as "utter barbarism" that needed to be replaced by awakening in each Indian "the desire for the acquisition of property of his own, by his own honest labor" (quoted in Adams, 1988, p. 12).

The second central feature common to views of the world among Native American peoples is an emphasis on the continuity of the life of the spirit and the inseparable interaction among mind, body, and spirit. Locust (1988) explains that traditional interpretations of health and illness among Native American peoples are tied to the notion of harmony or disharmony between these three aspects of the individual. Thus natural unwellness is caused by the violation of a sacred or tribal taboo, while unnatural unwellness is caused by the powers of evil, which may be expressed through witchcraft. Further, Locust states that in some Indian belief systems it is thought that "keeping one's personal energy strong is the best defense against negative energy," and this may be attempted by staying away from situations perceived to be negative (p. 324). The importance of these concepts is underscored by Locust, who suggests that these beliefs "may be identified as the core beliefs of the cultures themselves" (p. 316). Red Horse (1988) focuses on the extent of traditional attitudes toward health behavior as an indicator of level of acculturation.

Culture and the Family among Native American Peoples

It is essential to recognize the variability in social organization and, consequently, in family structure among Native American peoples, as a result of both traditional differences and the impact of social and political subordination by the dominant culture of the United States. Traditionally, differential social and family organization would have been influenced by a number of factors, such as the economic system of the community, whether it was nomadic or relatively permanent, and, possibly, the relative isolation of different tribal groups (Attneave, 1982).

In terms of acculturation, Red Horse (1988) offers a detailed analysis of a spectrum of family systems according to six levels of acculturation: traditional, neo-traditional, transitional, bicultural, accultural, and pan-renaissance. The level of acculturation of a family may be expected to influence certain "modal behaviors" common to American Indian families. Although this overview will not utilize Red Horse's framework as such, the modal behaviors he refers to will provide us with some useful pointers as to crucial values among Native American peoples: these are language of preference, religious beliefs, attitudes toward land, kin system structure, and health behavior. These issues will be addressed in the following discussion as they relate to our framework of worldview, family structure, and social interaction.

An example of traditionally different organization is offered by Medicine (1981), who points out that the existence of clans as an instrument of social organization is found among some, but not all, tribes. This author also emphasizes that, although the principle of family extendedness is commonly found among Native American peoples, patterns of lineage vary widely and may be based on either the mother's or father's side, or on both sides of the family. The type of kinship structure is likely to influence patterns of residence in different ways. With regard to the impact of extended and involuntary contact between Native American peoples and U.S. mainstream culture, Medicine (1981) focuses on the imposition of the model of the nuclear family, which "became the primary instrument to civilize tribal peoples and to obliterate cultural heritages" (p. 14). Thus many variations may represent "different adaptation of the groups to the superimposed administrative policies of education, health, and welfare" (p. 14). Similarly, Red Horse (1988) identifies the extent of kinship organization as an indicator of acculturation.

Against the background of traditional variability and culture contact, Medicine (1981) has offered some basic commonalities of contemporary family dynamics. This author describes "a community-wide web of kinship," often built on flexible alliances between the two kinship groups of marriage partners; the pattern may be envisaged in terms of "concentric circles" that operate reciprocally to support each other (p. 19). Medicine emphasizes that these arrangements are flexible and dynamic, and "foster survival and adaptation to economic and social exigencies" (p. 19).

Cunningham and colleagues (1986) contrast this broader conceptualization of family with the mainstream American "lineal, biological, and paternal" concept of the family. This contrast is particularly illustrated by the fact that, among some groups, clan and/or fraternity membership may be as or more important than blood relationship; this has been noted by studies of traditional family organization among tribes such as the Navajo and the Hopi, in which maternal uncles play an important role in the disciplining of children (Dennis, 1941). Another tradition observed among some groups is that of "a relatively free, informal adoption process," in which a child may maintain a relationship with his or her blood mother while being raised by a clan member who is not related by blood (Cunningham et al., 1986, p. 4). Thus, these authors state, kinship may include a broad range of "culturally defined relatives, any number of whom may temporarily or permanently assume a major or minor part of child-rearing responsibilities" (p. 4). Even today, this structure may allow the child a great deal of freedom, for example, among the Warm Springs Indians, the freedom to stay overnight at the homes of kinsmen without informing parents (Philips, 1983).

Patterns of child rearing are closely connected to the types of social and familial organization outlined above. The traditional emphasis on the supportive responsibilities of tribe and/or clan has been interpreted by Locust (1988) in terms of a "survival instinct" that emphasizes collaborative effort and individual contribution to the welfare of the group. This, Locust says, is reflected in the early responsibilities placed on children to contribute to the group and a consequent "early breaking of the apron strings" (p. 328). This early responsibility, combined with a view of children as basically complete at birth, results in child-rearing approaches that would be considered permissive in contrast to mainstream U.S. culture (Attneave, 1982; Cuch, 1987; Cunningham et al., 1986). Indeed, these patterns have been observed in studies of child rearing within tribes such as the Hopi (Dennis, 1941), the Zuni (Goldman, 1937), the Iroquois (Quain, 1937), and the Ute (Cuch, 1987), as well as more recent studies of the Apache (Boyer, 1979) and the Warm Springs Indians (Philips, 1983). In a consideration of Ute culture, Witherspoon (1961) states:

> The Ute child is viewed as a person in his own right from birth on. He is not viewed as an extension of the parent as the Whites view their children. . . .

In the parent-child relationship, no matter what the age, the parental role is one of advising and admonition and seldom one of force. Children are expected to listen to their parents, but no one is much surprised if children do not heed parental advice. . . .

After advice is given, however, the child has the right to make his own decision. By the same philosophy, Ute parents do not feel called upon to accept responsibility for their child's behavior to the same extent White parents do. (quoted in Cuch, 1987, p. 68)

Parental scolding, ridicule or shaming, and threats of punishment by supernatural powers are noted in the studies cited above as the most typical forms of censure. The use of corporal punishment among most groups is neither traditionally nor currently common. The emphasis on early responsibility for chores and for one's self leads to a pattern of earlier independence than is expected in mainstream U.S. culture. This pattern, along with the flexibility allowed children by the kinship structure, has often been misinterpreted by mainstream social workers as an attitude of parental neglect (Medicine, 1981).

Traditional Values in Social Interaction

Despite wide variations in patterns of social organization and the tremendous influence of the imposition of the reservation structure, certain features of interpersonal behavior have been identified as common to most Native American groups. Central to these is a style of communication that is consistently described in the literature as less verbal and direct than that of mainstream U.S. culture. Attneave (1982) emphasizes that a tradition of noninterference in the affairs of others is a continuing theme in the social interaction of Native American peoples.

A dramatic illustration of the contrast between traditional Native and Anglo-American communication patterns can be seen in Basso's (1979) account of those aspects of the "Whiteman's" social style that provoke ridicule among the Western Apache of Cibeque. Some of the central features emerging from Basso's portraits focus on the Indians' preference for a low-keyed and slower-paced style of discourse in which individuals do not attempt to exert dominance over others, give undue amounts of directions to others, ask for information on personal or family matters, draw undue attention to oneself or to others, address acquaintances in an overly familiar manner, or gaze too directly at others. Basso's close-up, detailed picture of "conflicting ideas of what constitutes deferential comportment" (p. 64) points to some of the most subtle aspects of culture, indeed, to what Philips (1983) has called "invisible culture."

In her study of communication patterns on the Warm Springs Reservation, Philips explains that she uses the term *invisible culture* because "communicative patterns lack the tangible quality of housing, clothing and tools, so that it is less easy to recognize their existence as culturally distinct phenomena" (p. 12).

Many of the communicative features observed by Philips are reminiscent of those described by Basso (1979). In detailing the pace of communication among Indians, Philips notes a more general rather than individually focused manner of addressing others, an absence of interruptions or attempts at verbal control of others, and a tendency to longer pauses with greater tolerance of silence than is common among Anglo speakers. Philips also emphasizes the less frequent use by Indians of both visual and auditory cues to gain another's attention or to indicate one's own attention, for example, speaking more loudly, frequent nodding or gazing directly at the speaker, or using frequent vocalizations such as "yes" or "mmhmmm." Philips concludes that these subtle differences in regulating face-to-face interaction are "culturally distinctive" and may set the stage for mutual misunderstanding between Native peoples and Anglo-Americans.

Red Horse (1988) states that most traditional American Indians are bilingual, but that the native language is preferred in the home, community, and at ritual ceremonies, holding a high value because "language maintenance is intended to avoid intrusions from the outside world, and is necessary to retain and transmit a precise understanding of a sacred past, present and future" (pp. 96–97).

While traditional Native American values emphasize respect for elders, interaction between generations is not rigidly prescribed and social interaction generally tends to be egalitarian, nonjudgmental, and noncompetitive among kinship groups, while being relatively suspicious of outsiders (Red Horse, 1988). Physical touching and other shows of affection are less frequent than in the mainstream U.S. culture (Basso, 1979; Philips, 1983).

Cunningham and colleagues (1986) observe that the traditional Native American acceptance of a variety of sources of authority related to children can also be seen in attitudes toward authority figures or "specialists" who are expected to advise on how to deal with children's health and behavioral problems. Further, it is expected that the appropriate response when interacting with such authorities is a respectful silence. Implications of this attitude for parent-professional interaction will be discussed in Chapter 4.

Attitudes toward Disability

The emphasis on physical and spiritual connectedness, a strong sense of the child as an individual, and membership in larger social groups all have implications for Native American peoples' interpretations of handicapping conditions. The Western emphasis on a strictly medical or biological explanation of severe disabilities, for example, may cause considerable difficulty for parents who are being required to operate within this framework. Locust (1988) explains that, since there is a common belief that a spirit chooses the body it will inhabit, a handicapped body is but the outward casing of a spirit, which is:

> Whole and perfect and capable of understanding everything that goes on in the environment, even when it appears that the physical body cannot comprehend anything. . . . Indians distinguish between a spirit in a handicapped body and the body itself: the causes of a body's being handicapped may lie with the parents (as in the case of fetal alcohol syndrome), and consequently the blame for (prenatal) mutilation of a body falls on the parents; the choice of being in the body, however, remains with the spirit in the body, not the parents. (p. 325)

Locust also makes a point that will be discussed at length later on in this book — that conceptions of handicaps are culturally determined. This is underscored by Locust's observation that most traditional Indian languages do not have words for retarded, disabled, or handicapped and, rather than using such categories, may assign names of individuals that are descriptive of the disability, such as One-Arm, or One-Who-Walks-With-A-Limp. The important factor would be the role that such an individual may play in the community; for example, an individual who might be classified as mentally retarded by the school system would not be viewed in this way by the traditional Native community. Locust says:

> Indian tribes tend to allow each person his or her harmony without forcing absolute conformity to all cultural standards. This custom allows the individuals who are less capable mentally to find a meaningful place in their society in simple physical tasks, such as wood-gathering. (p. 326)

With regard to milder disabilities likely to be diagnosed only in terms of academic learning, the issue of cultural relativity is even more evident, since the Native American conception of education was traditionally action-oriented, with greater value placed on nonverbal communication and a visual orientation (Locust, 1988; Philips, 1983). This issue will provide a central focus for some of the discussion in Chapter 4.

As with other cultural minority groups, professional interaction related to special education assessment and placement must be informed by sensitivity both to concepts of disability and to traditional communication patterns among Native American peoples. The positivistic assumptions of the legal conception of disability are likely to come into direct conflict with Native American beliefs about the spiritual dimensions of disability, while modes of interpersonal communication may be affected by subtle but important differences in pacing, nonverbal behavior, and overall expressive style. Once more, these considerations will be addressed at length in subsequent chapters.

AFRICAN AMERICANS:
RACIAL AND HISTORICAL ETHNICITY

The racial identity of Black peoples is perhaps nowhere so unequivocal as in the United States because of the categorical view of Black and White held by this society. The discussion of racial classifications in Chapter 1 pointed to the U.S. interpretation of White as a pure, unmixed racial group, so that to be, for example, one-quarter Black is to be Black, while a person who is one-quarter White would also be Black. While Latin American and West Indian societies, which also share the history of slavery, have built into their view of race the fact of racial mixture, the U.S. interpretation reflects the enduring legacy of a much more oppressive form of the institution of slavery (Billingsley, 1968; Brice, 1982; Lewis, 1963).

The historical development of differential social status among Blacks was based first on lighter skin color and, more recently, on socioeconomic and professional standing (Landry, 1987). Thus Black communities present a broad array of significantly different social classes (Billingsley, 1968). Further, the specter of skin color and the elitism adopted by many lighter-skinned Blacks were for many years potentially divisive forces within African American society (Landry, 1987). Nevertheless, African Americans have maintained a strong sense of peoplehood, or "historical identification" (Billingsley, 1968). This historical identity, then, is more than a racial phenomenon. Indeed, it has been strengthened by the intense discrimination and oppression experienced by Blacks in the United States until today.

Until the 1960s, the social science literature on the Black community was pervasively negative, rejecting the concept that there was such a thing as a Black culture in America. Glazer and Moynihan (1963) typified this notion with their statement that: "The Negro is only an American, and nothing else. He has no values and culture to guard and protect" (p. 51). These views were strongly rejected by Billingsley (1968) and by several scholars after him. The following sections will outline views currently held regarding worldview, family structures, and social interaction among African Americans.

Worldview among African Americans

The strong religious orientation of African American society is well known. The formal and ritualistic religious traditions of West African tribes, still observable in West Indian territories and in Caribbean pockets of the United States such as New Orleans, were all but obliterated in most Black communities in this country. Thus African Americans are mostly Christian, with a predominance of a variety of Protestant groups. In more recent years, there has been an increase in the number of Black Muslims.

The form of Christianity traditionally practiced by most African Americans, however, has been very different from that of White Protestant America. The spontaneous and emotive quality of Black preaching points to roots in both African and U.S. plantation life (Pipes, 1981). The form of worship emphasizes group solidarity and collectivity, as compared to the much more formal style of White Protestant ritual with its emphasis on a more private and individualistic spiritual life. Indeed, Black churches in the United States have traditionally focused on the group and have played a central role in the social and political life of Black communities. It is known, for example, that in the time of slavery, the church was used as a means of conveying motivation and information regarding plans for escape; meanwhile, in contemporary Black communities, the church continues to function as a powerful support system and focus of social activity (Hill, 1971; Hines & Boyd-Franklin, 1982). This emphasis on the group can also be seen in family structures and social interaction among African Americans, as the following section will show.

African American Culture and the Family

Early views of Black Americans promoted the notion of structureless families and communities that had been decimated by slavery. Frazier (1948), for example, correctly stated that native African religions and languages had been obliterated by slavery and that family structures had been severely undermined by the practice of separating tribal and family groups of slaves. However, Frazier wrongly concluded that this system had also "dissolved the bonds of sympathy and affection between men of the same blood and household," rendering Black communities dependent only on a domineering "matriarchy" and without any functional family structure (p. 15). The view of Black family systems as having been rendered dysfunctional and pathological by history was continued in more recent times by the Moynihan report (U.S. Department of Labor, 1965).

One of the most common indictments against the Black family is the notion of the absent father. Billingsley (1968) and many others have documented the historical dislocation of Black men from their families to serve the purposes of slavery, as well as their powerlessness to protect their families from the abuse of the slave master. Billingsley states that the negative effects of fragmentation on Black families have lasted to the present day, but the literature has continued to emphasize that the identity and functioning of Black men relates to their ability to provide for their families. Hence the stereotype of the absent Black father is tied to economics and class rather than being characteristic of African Americans as a whole (Cazneave, 1981; Frazier, 1948; Hines & Boyd-Franklin, 1982).

Adams (1978), in a review of a spate of studies aimed at contradicting the Frazier/Moynihan view, observes that most of these studies presented the argument that Black families are essentially similar to White ones. Adams states, however, that more recent research agrees neither with the "pathology" nor the "similarity" perspective, but, rather, presents a third perspective—"that there is cultural uniqueness and validity in the Black model" (p. 175).

This view is supported by Aschenbrenner (1978), who states that the Black family has been generally viewed as either "pathological" or "adaptive." The latter view, she says, sees the Black family as "essentially an adaptation to the social and economic conditions in which Blacks find themselves as members of a deprived minority" (p. 182). Both these views, she argues, compare the Black family to an "ideal model of U.S. family life" and see it as "essentially a creature of the American economy" (p. 182). A third view outlined by this author is similar to Adams's view of cultural distinctiveness, in that it examines Black family structure "in the context of a Black cultural tradition, reflecting a framework of fundamental concepts and values which differ in certain crucial respects from those of other peoples in U.S. society and are part of a distinctive heritage" (p. 182).

An example of a feature that, from a mainstream U.S. perspective, may be seen as dysfunctional is the tendency of many Black families to place greater emphasis on consanguineous (blood) relationships than on conjugal ties. In an analysis of African traditional family structures, Sudarkasa (1981) contrasts the European emphasis on the conjugal couple as the center of the family with the African emphasis on the blood family into which a wife or husband marries (depending on whether the structure is matrilineal or patrilineal). This pattern, the author states, was no less stable than that of the European family structure; similarly, where it is observed that some African Americans may give priority to blood rather than marital family, this may be construed as a reflection of the stability of the biological family rather than as a sign of family instability. The notion of instability comes into play only when the family system is measured against the values of the European model.

Shimkin, Louie, and Frate (1978) have supported the concept of a continuing and strong extended family structure among Blacks by offering a detailed study of the Black extended family in Holmes County, Mississippi, which they describe as:

> A genealogically defined, bilateral extended family of some 50–200 members, including spouses and adopted members . . . [which] has been basic not only as a socioeconomic mechanism for rural life but in the facilitation of migration and urbanization as well. . . .
>
> The bilateral extended family can adapt to extreme social and economic marginality. . . . Here, household cooperation and nonreciprocal sharing are basic principles. (p. 140)

Indeed, Shimkin, Shimkin, and Frate (1978) have edited a collection of studies of the extended family in both rural and urban Black communities that demonstrates unequivocally the persistence and viability of this structure. While the debate continues as to the extent to which the values and structure are based on surviving West African tradition or on adaptive changes related to slavery and "plantation culture," Shimkin and Uchendu (1978) conclude that extended family structures are "widespread throughout much of the Afro-American world" (p. 392)

It is evident that, as it exists today, there are identifiable central features of the Black American family that may be modified tremendously by socioeconomic class and rural versus urban location. The values most commonly observed among Black families emphasize a concept of collective rather than individual responsibility, kinship obligation that is extended into the larger community through "fictive kinship," strong parent-child and sibling ties, and frequent fosterage of children.

In summary, Robert Hill (1971) has described the strengths of Black families as strong kinship bonds, with the absorption of subfamilies and children by informal adoption; a strong work orientation, with a historical tradition of working wives, as compared with White culture, in which the housewife has been the tradition; adaptable family roles with egalitarian patterns; a high achievement orientation, with a desire for upward mobility; and a strong religious orientation. Although any of these features may be adversely affected by the negative influences of contemporary urban poverty, professionals should be aware of the centrality of these values among African American communities and families and of many families' potential for combating even the most difficult circumstances. Hill (1971) emphasizes that the fact of significant numbers of single-parent families, headed by mothers, is not in itself a sign of a dysfunctional family, in that "the self-reliance of Black women who are the primary breadwinners of their families best exemplifies the adaptability of family roles" (p. 21). Indeed, a study by Clark (1983) of value systems and personal interaction within low-income families of high- and low-achieving Black high school students argues convincingly that it was the interaction style inculcated by parents, whether in single- or two-parent households, that accounted for the difference in students' school performance.

Traditional Values in Social Interaction among African Americans

Interaction with mainstream society continues to be a source of considerable ambivalence for many African Americans, who, of necessity, have always had to cooperate with and become acculturated to mainstream culture. To some extent, then, African Americans are essentially bicultural, able to switch interaction codes readily in accordance with the cultural situation. Certainly African Americans become increasingly bicultural with higher education and social status.

While biculturality is essentially a positive adaptation, it can also lead to some amount of identity confusion (Pinderhughes, 1982). One example of the difficulties of biculturalism for a devalued minority such as Black Americans is the phenomenon of Black students' needing to develop a "raceless persona"—that is, "acting white" (Fordham, 1988)—in order to be successful in schools. By the same token, many students respond to this perceived demand by withdrawing from the culture of the school and developing instead an exclusive commitment to Black identity, which Fordham also describes as an "oppositional social identity" (p. 55). Among several characteristics of this identity, the use of nonstandard, "Black English" may become a feature highly prized and promoted by Black youth.

Regardless of the extent of biculturality, Black Americans are sharply aware of mainstream prejudice toward their culture and consequently show a marked distrust of mainstream society. Pinderhughes (1982) and Hines and Boyd-Franklin (1982) point out that among low-income Black families, the experience of frequent intrusions by social service workers also contributes to mistrust and unwillingness to cooperate with service providers. Hines and Boyd-Franklin (1982) conclude that this pattern is frequently "a direct, learned, survival response that Black children are socialized at an early age to adopt" (p. 102).

Several writers have also discussed the issue of the changing self-concept of Black Americans and the challenge of developing positive self-esteem in the face of continuing discrimination. Baughman (1971) has argued that the traditional view of the Black child as growing up with low self-esteem because of internalizing the attitudes of the dominant majority is not necessarily true, since most Black children grow up in predominantly Black communities and, in their early years, compare themselves mainly with the standards of the Black community. Similarly, Spencer (1984) has challenged the notion that Black children grow up with low self-esteem, arguing that while Black family life and child rearing are very conducive to the development of healthy self-concept, it is the imposition of mono-cultural values in schools and the wider society that undermines the grow-ing child's self-esteem. Another aspect of self-esteem is the development of assertiveness on the part of Black Americans, which Jenkins (1982) says is often interpreted by Whites as hostility.

Within Black groups, social interaction styles have been observed to be predominantly "humanistic" (Smith, 1981), with a focus on informality, expressiveness, and a strong emphasis on the sense of peoplehood that has resulted from a common history of social oppression and ostracism. This sense of peoplehood provides a protective boundary for African Ameri-can identity, within which members of this minority group, perhaps like others, maintain an intimate bond. There is a common knowingness among Blacks that tends to exclude all but the most trusted of their White compatriots. This point has been neatly illustrated by the writer Alice Walker:

> During childhood I wasn't aware that there was segregation or that it was designed to make me feel bad. White people just seemed very alien and strange to me. I knew that when they appeared everybody sort of stopped having fun, and waited until they left to become alive again. I think as a child you tend to notice that deadening effect on life, more than you would their color. (quoted in Lanker, 1989, p. 24)

Attitudes toward Disability

Research on the attitudes of African Americans toward disability is minimal and so far suggests that, as with many ethnic minority groups, traditional attitudes to severe disability and mental health may be tied to fatalistic and religious interpretations (Hines & Boyd-Franklin, 1982). The extent of this, however, is not known, and a recent study of the reactions of Black, Hispanic, and White mothers indicated that (1) the extent of emo-tional distress and reports of self-sacrificing views were greatest among Hispanic mothers and least among Blacks, and (2) reports of fathers' denial of the handicap were greatest among Hispanics and least among Blacks (Mary, 1990).

With regard to more ambiguous or mild disorders, however, it has been observed that many African Americans have enduring and well-founded concerns about being misdiagnosed and treated inappropriately by mental health services (Hines & Boyd-Franklin, 1982). With regard to school-based disabilities, Black parents are known to be aware of the over-representation of Black and other minority students in special education programs and, consequently, to display considerable distrust of school authorities in this regard (Gillis-Olion, Olion, & Holmes, 1986; Marion, 1980a). Some of the groundbreaking litigation regarding discriminatory treatment of minority students was initiated by Black parents in cases such as *Mills v. District of Columbia* (1963), regarding inappropriate tracking practices, and the well-known *Larry P. v. Riles* case (1972), which led to the banning of the use of IQ tests for school placement in California. Indeed, it has been acknowledged that early practice in special education was marked by the use of separate classes as a vehicle for the continuation of de facto segregation after the implementation of the *Brown* mandate for desegregation in 1954 (Prasse & Reschly, 1986).

Against this background it is imperative that special educators be sensitive to the doubts and challenges that may be presented by Black parents. It is important to remember, however, that factors such as social class and geographical area will allow for widely varying points of view and expectations on the part of such families; Black people in the United States may have shared a common history of oppression, but, like other minority groups, they are found at all levels of the social ladder and, indeed, come in many colors.

SUMMARY:
UNDERLYING COMMONALITIES
AMONG CULTURALLY DIVERSE GROUPS

In a discussion of the interconnectedness among ethnic minority families, Harrison and colleagues (1990) have identified three adaptive strategies common to ethnic minorities in the United States: family extendedness and role flexibility, biculturalism, and ancestral worldviews. The authors also assert that these patterns socialize children for interdependence and a positive orientation toward the ethnic group, which, in turn, result in cognitive flexibility and sensitivity to discontinuities in schooling.

The framework offered in this chapter overlaps with these authors' perspective but has presented the cultural ethos of each group in terms of its views of the individual's place in the universe, in the family, and in society.

The Individual's Place in the Universe

With regard to views of humanity's place in the universe, the discussion in this chapter has highlighted notions of humanity's relationship to universal hierarchies and the effect of these views on societal structures and values. The traditional values of all four groups reflect a belief in the interweaving of the spiritual and physical world, which is tied to a holistic and collectivistic orientation to life. Harrison and colleagues (1990) use the term *ancestral worldviews* to refer to the predominant influence of a spiritual, religious, and philosophical orientation on a group's sense of purpose and fulfillment in life and to the fact that each group's ethnic history is seen as part of the overall pattern. These authors contrast this orientation with the central value of individualism in U.S. culture. They state:

> Further, individualism is incompatible with the ancestral world views of ethnic minorities.
>   The indigenous psychology of ethnic minority cultures differs from the majority culture in how interwoven the interest and well-being of the self is with the ethnic group to which one belongs. (Harrison et al., 1990, p. 353).

As I continue to emphasize throughout this book, such generalizations must not be made into stereotypical classifications, since traditional folkways are inevitably susceptible to modification through proximity to and interaction with mainstream U.S. values and practices. Equally important in our search for underlying commonalities is the observation that to say that different cultural groups may hold similar orientations is not to deny tremendous differences in the innumerable forms in which these orientations may be expressed. For example, the range of expression of a collectivistic view may include greater or lesser extents of egalitarian versus hierarchical elements, such as the noted spontaneity of African American religiosity as compared with the more formal requirements of Hispanic Catholicism. It may also include more or less emphasis on the role of spiritual elements in human health, which very much depends on the extent of admixture with non-Christian belief systems. Thus professionals need to be aware of traditional patterns while simultaneously attending to the broad range of acculturation and adaptation among all groups.

The Individual's Place in the Family

A group's view of the individual's place in the larger scheme of things has a powerful influence on social and familial structures. For Americans, and indeed for most technologically developed societies, the preeminent place of humanity in the universe, and of the individual in society, reflects a history marked by increasing dominance over nature. Further, the primary focus on the individual's right to self-determination is an outgrowth of the essential spirit of Protestantism on which the dominant culture of the United States has been built. An increasingly central feature of this value system has been the delimiting of responsibility and authority to the immediate family.

For the ethnic minorities whose family systems I have attempted to describe, a central theme is that of family extendedness. Regardless of whether this feature reflects adaptive and/or traditional origins, its pervasive existence provides a striking contrast to the mainstream U.S. ideal of the nuclear family.

Once more, it is important to remember that the actual forms that this takes will vary widely from culture to culture on a number of dimensions. For example, patterns of authority within families may vary from strictly hierarchical, with the father as the ultimate authority, as among most traditional Asian Pacific and Hispanic families, to more egalitarian and less prescriptive, as in many Native American and African American families. Similarly, the responsibilities and authority of extended family members may vary widely, as may the authority accorded to siblings. Structural definitions of the family may also vary, being based on the mother's lineage (matrilineal), or the father's (patrilineal), or with equal emphasis on both sides of the family (bilateral).

In addition, traditional patterns in all groups may be affected significantly by acculturation, urbanization, and changes in socioeconomic status. Many of these changes apply to roles within the family. For example, it has been observed among Puerto Rican Americans that the easier access of women to employment may result in a "severe role reversal" (Fitzpatrick, 1987; Ghali, 1982), while African Americans have traditionally adapted to this situation by developing flexible family roles and responsibilities. The impacts of role reversal and changes in family status have also been noted among Southeast Asian refugees (Liem, 1985; Rumbant, 1985).

Another common observation is that strict hierarchical family structures, with their emphasis on children's obedience to those in authority, may be rapidly undermined by the relative permissiveness of American peers and by schools' emphasis on earlier independence for children. On the other hand, the greater freedom and independence traditionally allowed children in Native American families may lead to a clash of values between families and contemporary society (Attneave, 1982).

For families whose home language is not English, significant conflict may arise, pitting pride in the native language against the need to communicate with the larger society; further, communication gaps created by the second generation's bilingualism often lead to conflict between first and second generations (Canino & Canino, 1980; Delgado, 1980; Diaz, 1981; Fitzpatrick, 1987; Liem, 1985; Ramirez & Castañeda, 1974). Overall, changes in the family's relationship to the society are a necessary part of the acculturation process and may be a source of distress to families who find it difficult to accept the authority of the state regarding child-care or child-rearing issues, or even to entrust your children to child-care facilities (Delgado, 1980).

The presence of a moderately to severely handicapped child in the family may be expected to produce distress, but the extent of this may vary according to culturally based interpretations of the meaning of disability and to the level of the family's acculturation to Western interpretations. Existing literature suggests that there is likely to be significant stigma attached to severe disability among traditional Asian and Hispanic groups, where individual ailments are likely to be seen as reflecting upon the family as a whole. Further, there may not be a clear differentiation between attitudes toward developmental disability and those toward mental illness. Mild disabilities are likely to be seen quite differently from the mainstream U.S. interpretation; they may be thought of by some groups as indicating poor motivation or effort on the part of students, or they may simply be accepted as one aspect of the child's aptitude.

The Individual's Place in Society

The collectivist orientation of traditional ethnic minorities in the United States tends to emphasize the interdependence of the individual, family, and society. Thus many scholars observe an emphasis among ethnic minorities on cooperative rather than competitive codes of behavior.

Social interaction styles, however, while being based on collectivist assumptions, are by no means similar among groups. For example, literature on both traditional Native American and Asian Pacific peoples has observed a low-keyed, unobtrusive, and relatively muted personal interaction style, which contrasts sharply with the typically direct, familiar, and very verbal style of Anglo-Americans. Among most traditional Asian groups, personal interaction is firmly prescribed according to gender, age, and social status. On the other hand, while both African American and Hispanic people observe strict requirements for social interaction across generations, they tend to be much more expressive among peers. Hispanics in particular, while requiring a particular respect for social status, are also noted for an expressive, affectionate manner in familiar settings (Falicov, 1982).

Among most ethnic minority groups, views of the family tend to be strongly related to the perceived needs of the larger group. It is also true, however, that for some groups the family may function as a defensive mechanism against presumed or real societal hostilities. Thus, for many ethnic minorities in the United States, trust may be placed to varying extents in the immediate ethnic community, while attitudes toward groups defined as outsiders may be marked by suspicion and defensiveness.

For all groups, an underlying commonality is a frequent discomfort with the informal and egalitarian approach typical of most White Americans. This has very important implications for professional behavior, and a safe assumption for all professionals would be, at least initially, to approach culturally different families in a polite and more formal manner than may be common in working with Caucasian Americans (Falicov, 1982), while striving to create communication that is personal rather than impersonal. The latter point, the need for personalized service, will be discussed at length in subsequent chapters and will be related to a key concept not addressed here, that of "high-context" versus "low-context" cultures (Hall, 1977) — briefly put, the relative value accorded to screening out, as opposed to including, details of the context surrounding human events. This concept will prove tremendously useful in examining the nature of parent-professional discourse in special education.

The central points to be grasped are that all standards for social behavior are culturally derived and that the closer one is to one's original culture, the harder it is to recognize the culturally specific, rather than universal, base of accepted norms for behavior. For example, our discussion in Chapter 4 of the literature on parent-professional interaction will emphasize that the very procedures of special education placement require an approach whose directness may be alienating, even offensive, to people from cultures that require great reticence, modesty, or privacy. The same is true of values: it is difficult for some American professionals to accept that a value such as independence, so enshrined in the mythology of American life, is by no means universally held and that to attempt to impose such a value on a family may be to tread heavily on a cherished ideal of familial interdependence across generations.

One feature that was not mentioned in the description of each group was that of a more flexible orientation toward time than is typical of mainstream U.S. culture (Attneave, 1982; Condon et al., 1979; Norton, 1990). This feature is so commonly observed among all four minority groups that it can safely be considered a commonality among traditional families, with the proviso that it is readily susceptible to change through acculturation. This has serious implications for the way services are conceived, and suggestions for offering more flexible services will be made toward the end of the book.

To conclude, an overriding theme emerging from this overview is that people are committed to their cultures. Cultural pride is an essential part of every individual's self-esteem. People may become acculturated to their environment out of necessity or out of choice, but it is always reasonable to assume that for every change there is a sense of loss. Richard Rodriguez (1982), who describes himself as an acculturated man satisfied with the benefits of his own acculturation, records nevertheless the tremendous sense of loss he felt when his teachers prevailed on the family to emphasize the speaking of English in the home. From his child's eyes, he was losing not just a language, but a way of being—a private world of intimacy and wholeness, which, once invaded by English, would never be the same.

Just as mainstream America is often described as ethnocentric, so should it be expected that people from other cultures will be ethnocentric, viewing the world from the cultural frame that defines their values, beliefs, and day-to-day practices. The challenge for school personnel in the United States is to develop what I have referred to elsewhere as a "posture of reciprocity" (Harry & Kalyanpur, 1991), a genuine willingness to move out of one's habitual frame of reference, in order to build a bridge across which both individuals may pass.

Minority Students
in Special Education

The disproportionately high placement of racial minority students in special education programs for the mildly handicapped has continued to be the topic of controversy in education since Dunn (1968) first called attention to it over 2 decades ago. The attention of researchers to this problem was further fueled by the initiation of litigation in the state of California and by the publication of Jensen's (1969) claim that the poor academic performance of Black students reflected inferior intelligence. In 1973, Mercer's landmark study of Anglo, Black, and Mexican American children in a California community found that socioeconomic and minority status were highly correlated with such placement.

The climate of that period, as Prasse and Reschly (1986) have observed, was one of growing tension between the promise of equal opportunity in the 1960s and the slow fulfillment of that promise. In summarizing the key events of the period, these authors point out that the unwillingness of public school systems to comply with the court-ordered racial desegregation established by *Brown* v. *Board of Education* (1954) had led to allegations of school segregation in San Francisco as early as 1965. Among these, the suit *Johnson* v. *San Francisco Unified School District* (1971) included the allegation that the school district was "dumping" Black children in classes for the mildly retarded. A few months later, the landmark case *Larry P.* v. *Riles* was filed and ultimately led to the state of California decision, 13 years later, to prohibit the use of standardized intelligence tests, which were judged to be racially and culturally biased. The situation on which the case was based was that, while Black students comprised only 28.5 percent of the total student body in the school district, 66 percent of all students in educationally mentally retarded (EMR) classes were Black (Prasse & Reschly, 1986).

The charge of biased assessment also focused on the assessment of children from non-English-speaking backgrounds. The *Diana* case in California (1970) represented Hispanic children, and the *Guadalupe* case in Arizona (1972) represented both Hispanic and Native American children.

These cases charged that placement decisions were made on the basis of English-language testing of bilingual and, in some instances, monolingual Spanish-speaking children, with no effort to assess adaptive behavior. The defendant school districts and state departments of education did not defend their programs in court but agreed to the reforms required by the consent decrees; these included less emphasis on IQ tests, the use of nonverbal tests with bilingual minority students, and the inclusion of assessment of adaptive behavior (Reschly, 1988).

While the focus of litigation has continued to be on the issue of linguistic and cultural bias in standardized intelligence testing, several writers have pointed to an equally crucial issue, that of the effectiveness of placement in special education programs. Reschly (1988), for example, observed that there is no objection to the overrepresentation of Black students in Head Start or Chapter I programs, since these do not carry the stigma attached to being mentally retarded and are presumed to be effective programs. Additional reasons for the acceptability of overrepresentation here must also be that these programs are based entirely on the choice of parents, while special education is not, and since they are targeted to populations in poverty, it is inevitable that minority students will be highly represented. All of these reasons make compensatory preschool programs less vulnerable to criticism than are special education programs.

The point about the effectiveness of programs is salient, since students are referred from regular to special education because they are not achieving well in the regular program and special placement is recommended as a solution. The report of the National Academy of Sciences Panel on Selection and Placement of Students in Programs for the Mentally Retarded (Heller et al., 1982) emphasized this point, and my discussion of the problems of disproportionate placement will refer in more detail to the recommendations of this report. The present section will highlight trends in the most recently available data on the racial distribution of students in special education programs.

The fact that the Department of Education's Office for Civil Rights (OCR) monitors enrollment in what are known as the "judgment" categories (the more ambiguous, "mild" handicapping conditions) reflects awareness that the civil rights of students may be violated by inappropriate classification and placement (Chan & Kitano, 1986). Thus the OCR does not include information on more objectively based conditions, such as sensory- and health-related disabilities or multiply-handicapping conditions. The following discussion is not intended to relate to these students, since the issue of equity in special education placement refers, in the main, to students whose learning difficulties are first identified in school. In the words of several of the Puerto Rican mothers whose views comprise Chapters 5 through 9 of this book, these are the children who "were doing fine until they went to school."

PATTERNS OF OVERREPRESENTATION OF MINORITY STUDENTS

In examining patterns of representation of various groups in special education, it is essential to attend to the details of different disability classifications as well as national aggregates. For example, Reschly (1988) has stated that, at the national level, the phenomenon of overrepresentation of minority students is true mainly for the EMR category and that, based on the 1978 figures given by Heller and colleagues (1982), when all special education categories were considered, "there was little or no overrepresentation" (p. 30).

Aggregating the figures, however, does not deny the importance of the imbalance, especially in view of the state-by-state analysis of the National Academy of Sciences report figures, offered by Finn (1982). This analysis showed that while Hispanic and Native American students' rates of placement in special education did not reflect any disproportion when figures were aggregated at the national level, this was not true at the state level; Finn pointed instead to an important pattern—that both these groups tended to be overrepresented in states where they accounted for a substantial amount of the population and to be underrepresented or proportionately represented in states where their numbers were small. Specifically, Finn stated that as enrollment rises from 10 percent to 70 percent of the student population, so does the rate of disproportionate placement in special education. This pattern is also true for Black students, although their rate of placement is almost always high.

Further, in the most recent data available from the U.S. Department of Education's Office for Civil Rights (1987), projections of survey data from 1986 showed an even more extreme pattern for Black students than was evident in earlier reports—that, nationally, they were overrepresented in the educationally mentally retarded (EMR) category by more than twice their numbers in the total school system and in both the severely emotionally disturbed (SED) and trainable mentally retarded (TMR) categories by more than one and a half times their total enrollment.

Table 3.1 shows the rate of enrollment by race in special education programs for the nation as a whole and in selected states. The seven states were selected on the basis of variable population sizes of each minority group in order to show four trends.

(continued on pg. 64)

TABLE 3.1 Percentage of Students in Disability Categories by Race

NATION

	American Indian	Asian	Hispanic	Black	White
Total Enrollment in School System	1	3	10	16	70
Special Ed Classifications:					
Gifted & Talented	0	5	5	8	81
Educable Mentally Retarded	1	1	5	35	58
Trainable Mentally Retarded	1	2	10	27	60
Speech Impaired	1	2	8	16	73
Severely Emotionally Disturbed	1	0	7	27	65
Specific Learning Disability	1	1	10	17	71

ALABAMA

	American Indian	Asian	Hispanic	Black	White
Total Enrollment in School System	1	0	0	37	62
Special Ed Classifications:					
Gifted & Talented	0	1	0	11	88
Educable Mentally Retarded	0	0	0	65	35
Trainable Mentally Retarded	0	0	0	57	43
Speech Impaired	0	0	0	36	64
Severely Emotionally Disturbed	0	0	0	31	69
Specific Learning Disability	0	0	0	27	72

ALASKA

	American Indian	Asian	Hispanic	Black	White
Total Enrollment in School System	25	3	2	4	66
Special Ed Classifications:					
Gifted & Talented	15	4	0	2	79
Educable Mentally Retarded	44	3	2	4	47
Trainable Mentally Retarded	35	2	0	0	63
Speech Impaired	33	2	1	5	59
Severely Emotionally Disturbed	26	1	1	7	65
Specific Learning Disability	38	1	1	7	53

ARIZONA

	American Indian	Asian	Hispanic	Black	White
Total Enrollment in School System	6	1	26	4	62
Special Ed Classifications:					
Gifted & Talented	3	3	12	2	80
Educable Mentally Retarded	6	0	35	12	46
Trainable Mentally Retarded	7	1	27	7	58
Speech Impaired	6	1	27	3	63
Severely Emotionally Disturbed	5	1	16	6	73
Specific Learning Disability	8	0	30	5	57

TABLE 3.1 *Continued*

CALIFORNIA

	American Indian	Asian	Hispanic	Black	White
Total Enrollment in School System	1	9	27	9	54
Special Ed Classifications:					
Gifted & Talented	0	15	12	5	68
Educable Mentally Retarded	1	4	35	19	41
Trainable Mentally Retarded	0	8	32	15	45
Speech Impaired	0	6	27	9	57
Severely Emotionally Disturbed	0	3	16	18	63
Specific Learning Disability	1	3	28	13	56

HAWAII

	American Indian	Asian	Hispanic	Black	White
Total Enrollment in School System	0	72	2	2	23
Special Ed Classifications:					
Gifted & Talented	0	71	1	1	27
Educable Mentally Retarded	0	80	2	2	16
Trainable Mentally Retarded	0	74	0	1	25
Speech Impaired	0	66	3	3	27
Severely Emotionally Disturbed	1	59	5	2	33
Specific Learning Disability	1	69	4	2	34

NEW JERSEY

	American Indian	Asian	Hispanic	Black	White
Total Enrollment in School System	0	3	11	17	69
Special Ed Classifications:					
Gifted & Talented	0	5	4	10	80
Educable Mentally Retarded	0	1	14	39	46
Trainable Mentally Retarded	0	3	14	29	55
Speech Impaired	0	3	12	14	72
Severely Emotionally Disturbed	0	0	10	30	59
Specific Learning Disability	0	1	10	19	71

NEW YORK

	American Indian	Asian	Hispanic	Black	White
Total Enrollment in School System	0	3	12	17	68
Special Ed Classifications:					
Gifted & Talented	0	6	8	14	71
Educable Mentally Retarded	0	1	4	22	72
Trainable Mentally Retarded	0	1	5	31	62
Speech Impaired	0	1	4	8	87
Severely Emotionally Disturbed	0	0	18	53	29
Specific Learning Disability	0	0	3	9	87

Source: Adapted from U.S. Department of Education, Office for Civil Rights (1987).

1. While placement of Black students is generally high in most categories, and severely so in EMR, SED, and TMR programs, rates of placement increase further as the number of Blacks in the total student population increases.
2. While disproportionate placement of Hispanic and Native American students varies widely from state to state and from category to category, the rate of placement also rises as the number of these students in a school system increases.
3. Asian Pacific students are generally underrepresented in disability categories and overrepresented in gifted and talented (G&T) programs.
4. White students are consistently overrepresented in G&T and specific learning disability (SLD) categories.

What follows is a more detailed summary of these patterns for each group and, subsequently, a discussion of possible interpretations of these patterns.

African American Students

The table shows that in Alabama, where Black students comprise 37 percent of the student body, they are represented in EMR programs at one and three-quarter times the rate of their enrollment in the school system as a whole and in TMR programs at approximately one and a half times the rate. In Alaska, where Blacks comprise only 4 percent of the student body, their representation in EMR programs is proportionate, but they are represented in the SLD and SED categories at one and three-quarter times the rate of their overall enrollment. In California and New Jersey, placement of Black students in EMR and SED categories occurs at twice the rate of their overall numbers. In the G&T category, Black students are always underrepresented; indeed, nationally they are enrolled at half the rate of their numbers in the total student body.

Hispanic Students

For Hispanic students there is more variability in special education placement. While national averages show that these students comprise 10 percent of all students, and between 5 percent and 10 percent in the various categories of special education, figures from individual states reveal variability. Table 3.1 shows, for example, that in Alaska, where Hispanics account for only 2 percent of all students, their placement in special education programs is not disproportionate. In California, however, where they account for 27 percent of all students, Hispanics represent 35 percent of students in the EMR category; similarly, in Arizona, where they represent 26 percent of all students, they account for 30 percent of the SLD category. In New Jersey, where Hispanic students account for 11 percent of all students, their placement in EMR, TMR, and speech-impaired (SI) categories is also disproportionate.

Overall, national figures are not very telling with regard to Hispanic students. Finn (1982) summarizes this in stating that, at the national level, there is a "small Hispanic/non-minority difference," but that this is really "an average of many sizable disproportions in both directions" (p. 368).

Native American Students

Native American students with handicapping conditions may be served either by the public school system or by the Bureau of Indian Affairs (BIA). With regard to students served by the BIA, the placement pattern has shown a shift from EMR to SLD classification; in the 6-year period from 1977 to 1983, numbers of handicapped Indian students served by the BIA increased by 31 percent, with the categories SLD and SI accounting for almost all of this increase (Ramirez, 1987).

The figures in Table 3.1 reflect only data from public schools, where this group also displays the general pattern of special education placement increasing with numbers of the minority group. Table 3.1 shows the contrast between no disproportion in California, where these students account for only 1 percent of the total, as against Arizona, where, with a 6 percent Native American population, disproportion is evident. (This increasing pattern can also be seen in other states not shown in the table, including Montana, New Mexico, and North and South Dakota, where the Native American population ranges from 5 percent to 9 percent of all students.)

In Alaska, where Native American students account for 25 percent of all students, the rate of overrepresentation rises dramatically in all but the SED category. The greatest rate of placement is seen in EMR programs, where their presence is one and three-quarter times greater than in the overall population. The increasing placement in EMR programs evident in Alaska, however, is not uniformly typical of states with high placement of Native American students, since some states have shown a shift toward the SLD category.

With regard to the G&T category, Native American students are typically underrepresented.

Asian American Students

The pattern shown by Asian American students is very different from that of the other minority groups. With regard to disability, most state figures typically show an even pattern of proportionate representation of Asian students in the TMR category and a pattern of underrepresentation in other categories.

A unique picture is offered by Hawaii, however, the only state where Asian students are in the vast majority (72 percent). Here these students are overrepresented in the EMR category (80 percent). The population of Hawaii includes many Asians as well as indigenous Pacific Islanders, but the OCR data do not distinguish between Asians and Pacific Islanders in these figures.

Table 3.1 shows that the most striking pattern among Asian Pacific students is that, like White students, this minority group is consistently overrepresented in G&T programs.

Interpretations of the Placement Patterns

The controversy over disproportionate placement in programs for students with mild disabilities is now almost 2 decades old. While precise figures and patterns of placement have changed, the fact remains that African American, Native American, and Hispanic American students continue to swell the ranks of special education programs for students with mild disabilities. Reasons for this, and for the patterns noted by Finn (1982) in the National Academy of Sciences report, have not, so far, been verified, but the facts do give rise to several possible interpretations.

Variability According to Size of Minority Group and Program. Heller and colleagues (1982) have observed a correlation between disproportion and the overall size of a particular program in a district; that is, the larger the program, the greater the disproportion of minority students. In attempting to interpret this observation, the authors point out that it presents a chicken-and-egg dilemma: while large numbers of minority children may lead to a perceived need for more special education programs, it may also be that the greater availability of programs encourages increased placement of minority children. This, along with the noted trend of higher rates of placement as minority group size increases, suggests two possible underlying factors that are by no means mutually exclusive: (1) the continuing influence of prejudicial preconceived notions about minority students' abilities, which may become more marked as their numbers increase, resulting in greater bias in judgment, and (2) the presence of real difficulties experienced by minority students, who may, for varying reasons, be as ill prepared for the agenda of the school as the school is for serving them.

The point to be borne in mind here is the distinction that has been made by many writers between cultural difference and deficit; that is, while it is evident that the students are experiencing serious difficulties in school learning, the assumption cannot be made that this necessarily reflects within-child deficits or that the same students would not be more successful under more appropriate conditions. These possibilities will be discussed in more detail in a subsequent discussion of current thinking on assessment and instructional practices.

Variability in Specific Classifications. While high rates of placement continue for Black, Hispanic, and Native American students, there is clear evidence of a shift in the specific categories. Early observations of disproportion were concerned mainly with placement of students classified as EMR (Dunn, 1968; Mercer, 1973). While the highest rate of disproportionate placement still occurs for Black students in EMR classes, the SLD category has the greatest proportion of students in special education on a nationwide basis. For Hispanics, the rate of placement in SLD programs is higher than in EMR and occurs in greater proportion than for White students. Once again, however, there is great variability among states as to whether Hispanic students are placed mostly in programs for EMR, SLD, or SI (Finn, 1982; U.S. Department of Education, 1987).

In some cases, this variability seems to depend on the preference of individual states for particular labels or, perhaps, on different societal concerns or circumstances from one state to another. For example, a comparison of the SED label between New York and the nation as a whole in Table 3.1 shows that Black and Hispanic students in that state tend to be labeled SED at twice the national rate, with Hispanics accounting for 18 percent and Blacks for 53 percent of all students in the SED category. A look at the EMR label in New York, however, shows that its use is in line with national figures.

It is widely thought that a shift to greater placement of ethnic minorities in the SLD category reflects greater social acceptance and more ambiguous criteria for classification (Argulewicz, 1983; Tucker, 1980). It is still true, however, that the SLD category continues to be assigned more frequently to White than to minority students. In an insightful analysis of the effects of the way learning disability has been defined, Collins and Camblin (1983) point out that by excluding environmental disadvantage as a possible explanation of learning disability, the definition effectively excludes many poor children and hence many minorities.

Where numbers of minority students in the SLD category have increased, however, the most common explanation relates to widely cited court decisions delimiting the use of inappropriate evaluation tools, such as in the *Larry P.* v. *Riles* (1979) and *Diana* v. *State Board of Education* (1970) suits mentioned previously. As a result of these decisions, it has been observed that "special education theory, research and practice are moving towards alternative classification schemes and a wider variety of programming options" (Prasse & Reschly, 1986, p. 343).

Classification of Limited-English-Proficient Students. With regard to the placement of limited-English-proficient (LEP) students, research has offered another important interpretation of the increased assignment of the SLD category. This argument reflects the complexity of second-language acquisition in academic learning and in the referral and assessment process. In a study of 334 LEP students in special education programs in three large urban school districts in Texas, Ortiz and Polyzoi (1986) found that 83 percent were labeled learning-disabled (LD). The authors conclude that the referral and assessment process did not pay sufficient attention to the language needs of students, including inadequate native language testing. Interpreting the "main source of error" as a weakness in "the state of the art of bilingual special education," the authors state:

> The results of this study suggest a lack of understanding of how to identify learning disabilities among language-minority students and how to distinguish behaviors which are indicative of a true handicapping condition rather than normal second language development. (p. 31)

A growing body of research supports the argument, at least for Hispanic students, that the LD label is being applied to students whose difficulties really arise from a normal process of second-language acquisition. This research has been summarized in the October 1989 issue of the journal *Exceptional Children*, which was devoted to the multicultural needs of Hispanic students in special education (Figueroa, Fradd, & Correa, 1989a). The overall indictment of the inadequacy of special education processes emerging from this literature is displayed in Figure 3.1, the editors' summary table of the findings of the two research institutes on Hispanic students (Figueroa et al., 1989b).

The majority of the research in the United States regarding special education of students from limited/non-English-speaking backgrounds has been conducted on Hispanic students. Literature on Asian Pacific and Native American populations, however, is emerging and, so far, points to similar concerns regarding the efficacy of prereferral instruction, assessment, and special education instruction, with a particular emphasis on the

FIGURE 3.1 Summary of Findings from the Texas and California Handicapped Minority Research Institutes

Assessment

1. Language proficiency is not seriously taken into account in special education.
2. Testing is done primarily in English, often increasing the likelihood of establishing an achievement or intelligence discrepancy.
3. English-language problems that are typically characteristic of second-language learners (poor comprehension, limited vocabulary, grammar and syntax errors, and problems with English articulation) are misinterpreted as handicaps.
4. Learning disability and communication handicapped placements have replaced the misplacement of students as educable mentally retarded of the 1960s and 1970s.
5. Psychometric test scores from Spanish or English tests are capricious in their outcomes, though, paradoxically, internally sound.
6. Special education placement leads to decreased test scores (IQ and achievement).
7. Home data are not used in assessment.
8. The same few tests are used with most children.
9. Having parents who were born outside the United States increases the likelihood of being found eligible for special education.
10. Reevaluation usually led to more special education.

Instruction

1. The behaviors that trigger teacher referral suggest that English-language-acquisition stages and their interaction with English-only programs are being confused for handicapping conditions.
2. Few children receive primary language support before special education; even fewer, during special education.
3. The second and third grades are critical for bilingual children in terms of potentially being referred.
4. Prereferral modifications of the regular programs are rare and show little indication of primary language support.
5. Special education produces little academic development.
6. Individual education plans had few, if any, accommodations for bilingual children.
7. The few special education classes that work for bilinguals are more like good regular bilingual education classes (whole-language emphasis, comprehensible input, cooperative learning, and student empowerment) than traditional behavioristic, task-analysis driven, worksheet-oriented special education classes.

Source: Figueroa, R.A., Fradd, S.H. & Correa, V.I. (1989b).

role of language proficiency (Johnson, 1987; Kitano & Chinn, 1986; Sharp, 1983).

Asian Pacific students comprise a disproportionately small proportion in special education programs in most states, which leads some researchers to fear that students may not be receiving services they do need. For Native Americans, Hispanics, and Blacks, the concern is that many are being wrongly identified as handicapped.

A point to be noted, however, is that the percentage of Asian Pacific students placed in EMR and TMR programs increased between 1978 and 1986. Chan and Kitano (1986), quoting OCR figures from 1978 surveys, state that these students accounted for 2.2 percent of all students, while in special education, they accounted for 0.5 percent of EMR, 0.4 percent of SED, and 1.0 of SLD enrollment (p. 7). In the 1986 OCR surveys, national figures displayed in Table 3.1 show that the percentage of Asian students had increased to 3 percent of all students and accounted for 1 percent in EMR, 2 percent in TMR, 1 percent in SLD, and 0 percent in SED programs. With the exception of the latter category, the percentages have increased slightly while still signaling underrepresentation. It is not yet clear whether newly arrived immigrants, such as refugees with traumatic social and individual histories, might be having more difficulties in schools than did previous Asian Pacific immigrants. For example, Trueba and colleagues (1990) have described the painful transition of Hmong children in a California community and the role of the school in some of their difficulties, but no comparisons with other Asian Pacific groups have so far been made.

Chan and Kitano (1986), in discussing possible reasons for the low representation of Asian students in special education programs, suggest three explanations:

1. Some students' difficulties may be interpreted not as learning problems but as language difference, and such students may inappropriately be placed in bilingual rather than special education programs.
2. Some genuinely disordered behavior, such as withdrawal, may be misinterpreted as culturally induced.
3. Parental attitudes toward the stigma of disability and family shame may lead to refusal of testing or keeping children at home.

Leung (1988) also suggests that such parental attitudes may lead to underidentification in behavioral disorder categories, while the need to save face, combined with philosophical/religious beliefs, may lead to underidentification of physical handicaps. This author also adds that students may be underidentified because of this cultural group's emphasis on achievement and the consequent high expectations of families and professionals.

On the other hand, the possibility of inappropriate identification as handicapped is not ignored. Leung (1988) also observes that some Asian students may be wrongly identified because of their traumatic history, language difference, or inadequate prior schooling; they may be in need of language and counseling services rather than special education. Indeed, the National Association for Southeast Asian Students with Special Needs has drafted an action plan to address difficulties in assessment, instruction, and parent support (Dao & Grossman, 1985).

With regard to the overrepresentation of Asian students in G&T programs, Chan and Kitano (1986) state that these students tend to show a "heightened motivation" toward educational success because of firmly inculcated parental beliefs that "education leads to equity" (p. 10). M. K. Kitano (1986) further suggests that:

> Although APA [Asian Pacific American] cultures differ in many ways from the majority culture, the Asian values of educational attainment and obedience to authority clearly support achievement in American schools. Hence, the assessment procedures designed to identify high achievers are consistent with Asian Pacific values, and, in fact, may be biased in favor of Asian minority students. (p. 54)

M. K. Kitano also refers to H. Kitano's (1969) observation that some Asian children may attain gifted status by virtue of tremendous pressure to conform to teacher expectations.

The latter observations logically bring us back to the question of underrepresentation of Asian Pacific students in disability categories. If students can qualify as gifted by virtue of a strongly entrenched value system and rigorously applied familial and societal pressure to succeed, then it is reasonable to assume that such circumstances could also account for many Asian Pacific students' succeeding rather than failing in the regular classroom. Students from cultures that do not provide these supports and pressures, then, might be more readily overwhelmed by the cultural incongruities and prejudices of American schools and more likely to fall into failure and, ultimately, become classified as handicapped. Nevertheless, even if it is true that some aspects of Asian cultures are more conducive to students' success in school, this does not lessen the responsibility of schools to provide the optimum opportunities for all students to learn. Several considerations about ways that this can be accomplished will be presented in the following section.

IS DISPROPORTIONATE PLACEMENT A PROBLEM?

The foregoing discussion has illustrated the dominant patterns and issues in the placement of minority students in special education programs. The question of whether special education placement is effective for these students may still be asked. If disproportionate numbers of minority students are having difficulty in mastering academic material, why should special education placement be a problem? Is the fact of disproportionate representation in special education classes a problem per se, or under what conditions is it a problem?

This question received extensive consideration in the report of the National Academy of Sciences (Heller et al., 1982), which offered three guiding criteria for answering the question:

> Disproportion is a problem (1) if children are invalidly placed in programs for mentally retarded students; (2) if they are unduly exposed to the likelihood of such placement by virtue of having received poor-quality regular instruction; and (3) if the quality and academic relevance of the special instruction programs block students' educational progress, including decreasing the likelihood of their return to the regular classroom. (p. 18)

Thus the report highlights assessment, prereferral instruction, and special education class efficacy. Although the authors of the report begin with the notion of "invalid" assessment and placement, the focus of their argument is not on whether a child so placed is "really" retarded, but rather the implications of that decision; that is, whether the special education placement has resulted from poor instruction in the first place, and whether it will help or hinder the child's future academic career. The following sections will use the report's three guidelines as a framework for outlining current thinking on the implications of disproportionate placement of minority students in special education programs.

Assessment Practices

The question of bias in standardized testing has been the dominant issue in the controversy over disproportionate placement. The legal mandate for nonbiased and native-language assessment (P.L. 94–142) came into effect only a few years after Mercer's (1973) study, giving urgency to the search for solutions. Research has focused on the validity of standardized testing in an attempt to identify the presence of linguistic and/or cultural bias (Figueroa, 1983; Jensen, 1980; Jones, 1976).

While it has been demonstrated that assessment tools inevitably reflect cultural as well as school learning (Cummins, 1984), the "invisible" quality of many central aspects of culture (Philips, 1983) makes the identification of cultural bias a challenging task. It is easy, for example, to see that testing an LEP student in English would be unfair, but it is less obvious to many that standard English testing can be equally unfair to speakers of nonstandard varieties of the language, for example, speakers of Black English. Wolfram (1976) and many other sociolinguists have observed that dialect speakers may appear linguistically retarded simply on the basis of dialect differences.

Even more subtle are aspects of the actual conditions of testing, which may have varying effects on culturally different students. Fuchs and Fuchs (1989), in a meta-analysis of the effects of examiner familiarity on children's test results, observed that while Caucasian children were not affected by familiarity, Black and Hispanic students scored "significantly and dramatically higher with familiar examiners" (p. 306). Similarly, Leung (1986) observed that Asian Pacific students may be more stressed and tense than Anglo students because of their experience in Asian countries, where, because of limited resources, tests are typically used to exclude many students from educational services. Leung emphasizes that there are no available instruments that are totally appropriate for Asian LEP students, since Asian students are not appropriately represented on standardized norming samples. Leung recommends administering tests in a "non-standardized manner, using test-teach-test techniques and avoiding the application of inappropriate norms" (p. 32).

With regard to nonnative English speakers, an important issue is the difficulty of assessing whether a child is sufficiently capable in English to be tested in English. Cummins (1980a) stated that it may take a non-English-speaking immigrant child up to 5 years to approach native norms in conceptual and literacy skills in the second language. This leads to a strong caution against assuming that proficiency in oral fluency means that a child is ready to be tested in English.

Yet more than a decade after the introduction of the law, Ortiz and Polyzoi (1986) and, later still, Figueroa, Fradd, and Correa (1989b) concluded that many school districts were not adequately observing the legal mandate for assessment in a child's native language and that the total process of identification, referral, and assessment is loaded against the student with limited proficiency in English.

Classroom Practices

Heller and colleagues (1982) have emphasized that questions about appropriateness in special education placement must attend first to the prereferral experiences of the student, because, for the majority of students in mild disability programs, it is in the regular classroom that their difficulties first become evident. These experiences will include a number of aspects: the overall attitude of the school and classroom teachers toward students from culturally diverse backgrounds, in particular such children who are also poor; the language in which instruction is offered; and the cultural congruity and efficacy of instructional procedures and curriculum.

School Climate and Racial/Cultural Prejudice. Studies too numerous to mention, but perhaps best typified by Rist's (1970) classic study of the prejudicial organization of a first-grade classroom, have documented the power of teachers to stigmatize students. Rist's study, which detailed the social-class prejudices that were evident in the behavior of a Black middle-class teacher in an urban ghetto school, concluded that it was not by coincidence that, within the first week of school, the children least able to meet middle-class standards of hygiene, dress, and manners were relegated to the lowest reading group, where, for the most part, they were given minimal instruction and remained until the third grade. The issue here was not race, but social class. Given the already powerful bias of schools in favor of middle-class norms and values, it seems inevitable that, in a country where minority races have traditionally been identified with poverty and low social status, mainstream teachers will be even more susceptible to prejudicial behavior toward racially and/or culturally different working-class students.

In a recent study of Hmong children in California, Trueba and colleagues (1990) charge that a prejudicial school environment led to the isolation of ethnic children. The authors state:

> Racial prejudice about the ability of Indochinese children in La Playa, whether conscious or unconscious, is deeply rooted in the misperception by mainstream teachers and peers that these children are academically incompetent because they have an inferior intelligence or an inferior culture, not because they have a different set of experiences leading to different values and cognitive system. (p. 103)

In such an emotional climate, children are set up for failure. Indeed, within this same study it was evident that children made much better progress in the classrooms of teachers who made them feel welcome and comfortable. The authors placed primary importance on this feature, emphasizing the central role of "a personal relationship with adults or knowledgeable peers who help children in attacking cognitive tasks which are seemingly decontextualized and meaningless" (Trueba et al., 1990, p. 87).

A considerable body of literature supports the belief that racial bias is built into the behavior of many teachers. Studies of teachers' impressions of hypothetical case studies have shown that teachers expected special class placement significantly more frequently for Mexican American than for Anglo students (Aloia, 1981; Prieto & Zucker, 1981). More telling have been observational studies of teacher-student interaction that showed higher rates of teacher attention and praise to Anglo children (Buriel, 1983; Jackson & Cosca, 1974) or negative teacher attitude toward non-English native speakers (Laosa, 1979).

Cultural Incongruity in Instruction and Curriculum. Arguments concerning the role of cultural discontinuity in the failure of ethnic minorities in schools emphasize that children learn better when provided with opportunities to learn and express themselves in culturally familiar ways. For example, the language-learning style of Black working-class children has been described as less linear and factual, more imaginative, and less adult-directed than that of their White counterparts (Heath, 1983; Houston, 1973), while their cognitive style has been described as more contextual and personal (Hale-Benson, 1986). Some researchers have noted that the traditional approach to learning among Native American peoples shows a strong preference for nonverbal interaction, with an emphasis on the visual mode, and on learning that is accompanied by doing (Macias, 1987; Philips, 1983). These modes contrast with the typical analytical, verbal style of mainstream U.S. classrooms. Further, the cooperative rather than competitive orientation of many minority communities is also a source of conflict in mainstream classrooms for many students who have been trained not to promote themselves over their peers (Delgado-Gaitan, 1990; Philips, 1983; Trueba, 1989).

Perhaps the best-known studies of learning style are those focusing on the concept of field dependence or independence (LeCompte, 1981; Ramirez & Castañeda, 1974) with the observation that many children from traditional cultures are more dependent on a contextually based cognitive style than are mainstream American children. There have been some challenges to this theory (Cazden & Leggett, 1981; McDermott & Gospodinoff, 1981), as well as the objection that it may tend to support stereotyping of Hispanic children as passive or lacking in analytic skills (Escobedo & Huggins, 1983). Whatever the theoretical validity of this concept, however, many students from culturally different backgrounds learn best when information and academic skills are presented "under conditions of high context" as opposed to "behavioristic, task analysis drive [*sic*], work-sheet oriented approaches" (Figueroa et al., 1989b, p. 176). Similar comments have been made by Cummins (1984), Ruiz (1989), Trueba (1988), and many others.

Other aspects of children's learning styles relate to the attempt to include culturally familiar verbal and interaction styles in the teaching of basic academic skills. The success of the Kamehameha Elementary Education Program (KEEP) in Hawaii provides a prototypical example of the meaning of this principle. This project incorporated into its reading program a traditional, oral, group narrative style known as "talk story." Using this approach, the school succeeded in raising reading achievement scores for urban Hawaiian children from very low levels to national norms and higher (Au & Jordan, 1981; Boggs, 1985; Tharp & Gallimore, 1988).

The complement of learning style is teaching style, and several ethnographic studies have observed the effective communication attained in classes where teachers use culturally typical interactional styles. For example, such observations have been made concerning the creative and comfortable use of Black nonstandard speech by "artful" Black teachers with their students (Piestrup, 1973), and concerning the much greater "cariño" (affection/caring) displayed in the personal style of a Mexican American teacher as compared with her Anglo counterpart in a first-grade classroom (Cazden, Carrasco, Maldonado-Guzman, & Erickson, 1985). Boggs (1985) observed that Hawaiian children from low-income backgrounds responded best when they were allowed to exercise their preference for initiating and pursuing activities without the involvement of an adult.

Perhaps best known are studies of certain characteristic behaviors of Native American teachers that are congruous with the typical style of the communities from which the children come (Mohatt & Erickson, 1981; Philips, 1983; Van Ness, 1981). The characteristics most frequently noted in these studies include slower pacing of verbal exchanges during lessons, less teacher-directed and more peer-directed cooperative activity, greater self-determination of students' behavior, and a low-keyed style that does not "spotlight" individual students.

A classic example of the cultural mismatch theory is the detailed account by Heath (1983) of the differences in verbal style between working-class Black and White families in the Carolinas. This study gave dramatic illustrations of the differences in the ways Black preschoolers spontaneously "learn how to talk junk" while Whites "are taught" to talk factually, as well as the much greater emphasis on structure and individual space among Whites as compared with Blacks.

The most dramatic point made by the study, however, is that middle-class ("townspeople") status brought the patterns of both Blacks and Whites into the mainstream of national U.S. norms, values, and behavior. Thus the extent of structure in the lives of these families and the emphasis on conversational skills in child rearing were virtually identical among the two groups. The preschool experiences of the children of the townspeople were absolutely congruous with the style and expectations of the school. White working-class preschoolers, on the other hand, had been schooled in question-answer routines and structured behaviors similar to those of the school, but without the school's requirement for analytical skills, while Black working-class students were prepared with neither, bringing instead an oral and personal interaction style that emphasized complex verbal play and imaginativeness. Heath's study shows, in sum, the complex interplay between traditional cultural patterns, social class, and schooling. Equally important, the study shows the tremendous mainstreaming effect of higher social class.

There is the possibility of genuine incomprehension between teacher and student. A dramatic example of this is given by Michaels (1981) in her study of "sharing time" in a racially integrated primary classroom. Michaels identified two culturally based narrative patterns in children's stories: a linear, topic-centered style used by White students and sanctioned by the teacher, and the branching, topic-associating style of Black students, whose stories were usually mistakenly construed by the teacher to be pointless and lacking logic. This study highlights a crucial point regarding African American students: although the designation "language minority" is typically applied to students from non-English-speaking backgrounds, native English speakers may use varieties of English that differ in important ways. One central aspect of this is the likelihood that nonstandard English use by a native speaker is likely to be stigmatized because of attitudes supporting the "correctness" of the standard form and the association of nonstandard speech with low socioeconomic background and racial/ethnic difference.

Teachers' attitudes toward vernacular Black English (VBE) have been illustrated in studies showing the extreme emphasis placed on correcting errors in the speech of Black children. A study by Collins (1988) showed that teachers often responded to VBE speakers in an oral reading task by correcting their speech, while they responded to students who spoke standard English by discussing the meaning of the text. Similar observations have been well documented by other studies (McDermott, 1976; Piestrup, 1973). Indeed, Labov's (1972) pioneering work on African American speech emphasized the salient distinction between language difference and deficit as it applied to nonstandard speakers.

Moll and Diaz (1987) have demonstrated that when native Spanish-speaking children's reading ability in Spanish was ignored in an English reading class, the students' true abilities were grossly underestimated. The authors challenge teachers to view students' abilities as a "cultural resource" in their education. The following story from Houston (1973) offers a powerful illustration of the point that when students' cultural and linguistic knowledge is rejected in the classroom, their competence to express themselves is genuinely impaired in that setting. Houston reports that in a rural area of northern Florida, teachers' complaints and the evidence of videotapes of Black children pointed to limited and inferior language skills, as described below:

> The Black children tended to give one-word or one-sentence replies to their teachers' questions. They spoke slowly, with marked stress and intonation peaks. Their sentences had very simple content and limited expression of feeling. The children looked anxious and constrained, their gestures and postures tense and uncertain. (p. 45)

In dramatic contrast to this picture, Houston recorded the following story, told to her by a Black 11-year-old outside of school, in a relaxed atmosphere. The excerpt is only a sample, and the reader is urged to read the entire story as told in Houston's article. There is no doubt that this child's linguistic style could be used as a valuable "cultural resource" in the classroom:

> This story about three lil pigs. One day, the lil pigs went out to play. They made lil house. One made a dog house an one made a hog house. One made a pen. . . .
> [The wolf] came to the big house. And the wolf say, "Let me in!" And [the pig] say, "no, no, no, my shinny shin shin!" He huff, and he puff, and he tough, and he rough, but he couldn't knock the house down. . . .
> He went an got [some] greens and put 'em out, and then when the ol fox came, he say, "Lil pig! You ready?" He say, "No! I done got my greens! You smell it? The hot water still aboilin!" And ol wolf say, "I'm a jump down you chimney!" And that ol pig put some water on the fire till when you could jump in it, and the lil pig had cook the greens. Yeah, he fool him! He jump in the hot water, and the pig, he had greens and wolf! Greens and wolf! (Houston, 1973, p. 46).

One final point: McDermott and Gospodinoff (1981) state that, while there is abundant evidence of the presence of cultural mismatch between schools and culturally different students, "ethnic differences do not cause irremediable miscommunication" (p. 214). These authors argue that trouble with cultural differences originates not in disparities in interaction per se, but in the disparity in the relations between teachers and children and the use by both parties of a communication event to reinforce their differences or, as these authors put it, to turn cultural boundaries into barriers. In their words: "The problem is not ethnicity, but ethnic differences made into borders for political reasons" (p. 217).

Language of Instruction: Bilingual Education.   The question of whether limited/non-English-speaking students will be taught in their native language or in English continues to be a point of controversy throughout the country. Bilingual education is not new to the United States. Until the end of the nineteenth century, the challenge of other languages was met by native language and/or bilingual schooling through both parochial and public schools in several German, French, Scandinavian, and Dutch communities (Baca & Cervantes, 1984; Cordasco, 1976; Lewis, 1980; Stein, 1986).

The turn of the century saw a rising nationalism, described by Stein (1986) as a "crusade for Anglo-conformity." This led to the practice of

English-only instruction for non-English-speaking children and the punitive repression of any native-language use in schools. This practice, often referred to as the "submersion" approach, is seen as a detrimental "sink-or-swim" approach by many scholars (Baca & Cervantes, 1984; Cordasco, 1976; Cummins, 1979, 1980b; Ovando & Collier, 1985; Stein, 1986; Walker, 1987).

Cordasco's (1976) summary of the effects of this approach is typical of the critics of "submersion":

> With English as the sole medium of instruction, the child is asked to carry an impossible burden at a time when he can barely understand or speak, let alone read or write the language. Children are immediately retarded in their school-work. . . . Since the curriculum is in English, the child must sink or swim in English. . . . A program that prematurely forces English on children can guarantee their eventual illiteracy in that language. (p. 92)

The English as a second language (ESL) approach, introduced into schools in the 1950s, represented an improvement over "submersion." ESL offers a structured approach to the direct teaching of English, instead of expecting students to "pick it up" incidentally.

What Stein (1986) has called the "reinventing of bilingual education" began in the early 1960s in response to the influx of Cuban refugees to Miami. Stein reviews the impact of subsequent events such as the Bilingual Education Act of 1968, which allowed for bilingual-bicultural programs, and the landmark *Lau* v. *Nichols* decision in 1974, which emphasized that there is no equality of opportunity if students do not understand the language of instruction.

The implementation of the Bilingual Education Act has been varied and controversial, reflecting the central question of whether the purpose of bilingual education is to help students make a transition from one culture and language to another, or to help them gain an additional language and culture while retaining that of the home. "Transitional" models are by far the most popular and reflect the U.S. Department of Education's growing emphasis on the mastery of English as the express purpose of bilingual education (Ovando & Collier, 1985; Spener, 1988). In recent literature on the topic, ESL is consistently recommended as an integral part of, rather than an alternative to, bilingual programs (Cordasco, 1976; Lewis, 1980; Ovando & Collier, 1985).

Lewis (1980) has given a comprehensive summary of the rationales for bilingual education. This summary shows how sociopolitical rationales are tied to pedagogical concerns. A large body of current research indicates that students who learn to read and write in their primary language will learn these skills in a second language much more quickly and effectively than students who are taught to read in their second language only (Collier, 1987; Cummins, 1980b; Krashen, Long, & Scarcella, 1979; Skutnabb-Kangas, 1981). These authors argue that oral fluency, or "basic interpersonal communicative" proficiency, in a second language does not mean that a child has the "cognitive and academic" proficiency to learn to read in that language. If it is true that children who have oral fluency in their second language may not be ready to learn to read in that language, this must be even more true for children who do not yet speak English.

If, as Cordasco (1976) says, "submersion" in a language they do not understand is going to lead to students' eventual "illiteracy," what will be the social and political implications for this group of students? Both ESL and transitional bilingual programs have been interpreted as serving political ends. Critics argue that these approaches are usually conceived of as "compensatory" or "remedial," in that the students' native language is perceived as unequal and undesirable and the aim is to replace it with English. This approach, it is argued, serves two specific sociopolitical aims: to assimilate culturally different individuals into the mainstream by alienating them from their native language and culture and to prepare them for low-status roles (Cordasco, 1976; Lewis, 1980; Ovando & Collier, 1985; Spener, 1988; Stein, 1986). These arguments reflect the "social reproduction" theories of minority underachievement, which argue that schools, rather than changing the social order, serve to reproduce it, thus keeping low-status populations at the bottom of the socioeconomic ladder (Bowles & Gintis, 1976; Ogbu, 1978).

The future of bilingual programs is very much in question. Almost a decade after the passing of the Bilingual Education Act, Cordasco (1976) observed that bilingual education was still a "luxury," with Title VII having become a "highly selective program." By 1985, the U.S. Department of Education had restricted funding of bilingual education projects to those districts that could demonstrate the ability to continue the project after federal funding expires (Spener, 1988). This will work against districts with limited resources.

Efficacy of Special Education Placement

The third criterion offered by Heller and colleagues (1982) for deciding whether disproportionate special education placement is a problem is the extent to which, once placed in such programs, students are provided with adequate opportunity to progress and, ultimately, return to the mainstream of education. This section will look at four aspects of what happens when students are placed in special education: labeling, the efficacy of special class instruction, bilingual special education, and the actual decision-making process concerning placement.

Labeling. It is crucial, for the purposes of this book, to recognize that constructions and interpretations of the concept of disability are culturally relative (Bogdan & Knoll, 1988). This does not mean that biologically evident deviations from normative bodily health do not exist, or that the competence of individuals in various areas may not be thereby constrained. What it does mean, however, is that the extent to which a biological difference will disable a person depends to a great extent on what a person expects to do and what society requires one to do. Further, whether or not a noticeable difference in functioning will be stigmatized also depends on many factors within a society, such as the presumed causes or results of the condition. In the case of mild learning and behavioral differences with no clear biological basis, the construct of disability is certainly moot. Thus the meaning of disability will vary according to the array of roles available to individuals and the values attached to the condition.

Among many examples of this relativity is that given by Groce (1985) in a consideration of the acceptability of deafness in a New England community where its incidence was very high. In this setting, where "everyone spoke sign," deafness was not a disabling condition. Similarly, Locust (1988) points out that the prevalence of a congenital hip deformity observed among the Navajo is not considered disabling, while surgery to correct it may create a disability because it tends to make riding a horse uncomfortable.

The same principle is true of mental disabilities. While there is no doubt that severe impairment in this area severely restricts one's functioning, there may be a wide range of activities still available to such individuals, and the value placed on their contribution will reflect the values of the society as a whole. Locust (1988) gives an example of a mentally retarded boy who was the water carrier in a Hopi village until the Bureau of Indian Affairs insisted he go to a school in the city. There Bear became homesick and violent, spending the rest of his life in an institution for the criminally insane. Locust concludes: "Bear was in harmony in his village carrying water. His retardation was part of his harmony; the state hospital was not" (p. 322).

In the case of mild disabilities, which tend to be identified mostly in schools, the importance of these difficulties is also related to the importance of formal education to the society. Thus it is not surprising that weakness in this area is readily interpreted as a "disability" in technological societies, which place a high premium on literacy and analytic skills, while in less technologically advanced societies it may not be so interpreted (Dexter, 1964; Ginzberg, 1965). Edgerton (1970), in a study of mental retardation in non-Western societies, has challenged this assumption, pointing to nonliterate societies where people who are retarded are stigmatized and concluding that there are wide variations both in the extent to which mental incompetence is recognized and to which it is positively or negatively valued. However, since Edgerton also acknowledges that his analysis does not include a "cross culturally viable definition of mental retardation" (p. 555), it cannot be assumed that persons classified as mildly mentally retarded in the United States would be so designated in developing societies. Regardless of designation, it certainly seems reasonable to assume that there would be a wider range of occupational opportunities available to such people in a society less dependent on literacy.

There are two important implications of this for culturally diverse peoples living in the United States. First, parents from less technologically developed societies are likely to be confused by the interpretation of academic weakness as a disability, especially if it is cast along the same spectrum as more severe disabilities that may, as observed in the previous chapter, be severely stigmatized in some cultures. For some groups, this is the case with the construct of mild mental retardation. Second, since the designations mildly mentally retarded, learning-disabled, and emotionally disturbed are all relative not only to the society but to the definitions given them (Polloway & Smith, 1988), one cannot assume that such designations are valid (Cummins, 1989).

Arguments against the current classification system are no less than 20 years old (Dunn, 1968; Mercer, 1973) and have continued to gain momentum (Gardner, 1982; Reynolds & Lakin, 1987) with regard to both the mild mental retardation construct and learning disabilities. One recommendation for change has been a call for new designations, such as "educational handicap" (Reschly, 1988) or "educationally delayed" (Polloway & Smith, 1988), reflecting the fact that students' difficulties are largely related to academic learning. Indeed, Reschly (1988) acknowledges that the classification "mentally retarded" tends to carry connotations of stigma even within mainstream U.S. culture and argues that students classified as mildly retarded are "inappropriately stigmatized by implicit use of the same continuum for all levels of mental retardation" (p. 37). Another recommendation has been to label programs and services rather than students (Reschly, 1988).

To conclude, the commitment of the special education system to the practice of categorical labeling is alienating and confusing for people from different backgrounds because of the cultural relativity of terms and meanings. Further, where assessments do not reflect the true abilities of a child, the classification system becomes grossly unfair.

Locust (1988) has summarized the outcome of the special education labeling system for Native American children. Acknowledging that there have always been children who learn more slowly than others, the author continues:

> Only when formal education came to the Indian Nations were labels applied to the differences between children. Public Law 94-142, the Education for All Handicapped Children Act (1975), was a two-edged sword for Indian people. On the one hand, it provided educational opportunities for severely disabled children who were once institutionalized off the reservation by the Bureau of Indian Affairs, but on the other hand, it caused multitudes of children to be labeled mentally retarded or learning disabled who up until that time were not considered handicapped in their cultures. (p. 326)

It is true that children from nontechnological societies, once in the United States, will need to succeed within the requirements of this culture. Delpit (1988) has argued strongly that minority people do not want inferior standards for their children; they do not want their children to be "passed through" the system and emerge incompetent by mainstream standards. But neither do they want their children to be unfairly classified as disabled and unnecessarily stigmatized. They want their children to be fairly assessed and appropriately instructed.

Special Class Instruction. While there have been some mainstreamed models of special education service, these have been more experimental than typical, and the two most common forms of special placement continue to be the separate class and the resource room. Typically students labeled EMR or TMR are placed in the separate class, while those labeled SLD or SED may be placed in either.

Research on the effectiveness of the separate class as compared with regular class placement has failed to show that students make better academic progress in either setting (Heller et al., 1982; Polloway & Smith, 1988). While some comparisons of the resource model with recent mainstreaming models suggest that the latter may be more effective if instruction is appropriately individualized (Wang & Birch, 1984), there is considerable debate concerning this research. Further, the research on effective schools suggests that effective instructional practices and school environment as a whole contribute more to student performance than do particular types of settings (Bickel & Bickel, 1986; Edmonds, 1986). Similarly,

Comer's work (1980) on "school power" demonstrates the power of ghetto schools to reverse an entrenched pattern of failure through a schoolwide commitment to flexible organizational responsiveness to students' needs.

With regard to approaches to the teaching of reading and writing in particular, an earlier reference to the findings of the Texas and California Handicapped Research Institutes (Figueroa et al., 1989b) highlights a theme now very current: the criticism of "reductionistic" methods typically used in special education. Cummins (1984), like many critics, has severely criticized the reliance on "disembedded or context-reduced 'learning tasks' that are unrelated to [minority children's] lives and interests outside of school" (p. 223). Cummins states that students who are doing well can tolerate the "ritual and nonsense" better than those who do not understand what these activities are all about. The latter, Cummins states, are "most vulnerable to the distortions of drills and tests and most need the guidance and security of meaningful encounters with written language" (1984, p. 240).

In a consideration of direct instruction models such as DISTAR (Direct Instruction Strategies for Teaching and Remediation), Cummins emphasizes that these approaches have little transfer of learning, do not contribute to vocabulary or syntax development, and do not generalize to nonacademic situations or academic tasks requiring higher cognitive skills. Although there is research showing that they are effective in promoting the desired learning outcomes, Cummins argues that what is usually assessed are "lower-level mechanical skills, such as decoding or computation" (1984, p. 252). These are precisely the methods most frequently used in special education classes.

Heller and colleagues (1982) argue that if neither special nor regular class instruction is demonstrably superior, it is likely that the separate class has the disadvantage of evoking lower expectations by placing students with a disability label together and offering an unchallenging curriculum. Since there is doubt as to the benefit of special education placement, a conservative approach to such placement would be appropriate. If minority students are being placed in special education classes in disproportionate numbers, this should be considered a problem since many of these students are already at a social and economic disadvantage.

Bilingual Special Education. Students who qualify for special education services and are also limited in English proficiency present a dual challenge for the system. Baca and Cervantes (1984), in a comprehensive consideration of bilingual special education, point out that while no laws specifically mandate bilingual programs in special education, bilingual exceptional children, regardless of the level of their handicap, qualify for both sets of services. For exceptional children who are learning to read and write, the arguments about first-language literacy are no less true than they are for students in regular education. For students with severe disabilities, whose curriculum may be more functional, the need for the language they are accustomed to is crucial (Baca & Cervantes, 1984; Bernal, 1977).

Baca and Cervantes (1984) outline an "interface design for bilingual special education" that emphasizes native-language instruction, cooperative program planning between bilingual and special education personnel, and an administrative structure that ensures that these programs are part of the "mainstream" of the school, as opposed to being seen as "compensatory" or "marginal." These authors note that the concept of "least restrictive environment" is often ignored in decision making about LEP students.

Baca and Cervantes emphasize the need for an individualized approach in which the cognitive, affective, and social needs of students should be met by a bilingual/bicultural educational process. The aim of this process is to prevent unnecessary special education placement and offer an appropriate education to those who are so placed.

Making Decisions about Placement. Whether bias is mediated through the rejection of students' native language, teacher-student interaction, or culturally inappropriate curriculum and instruction, and whether it is based on socioeconomic, cultural, or linguistic prejudices, the result is a high rate of referral of African American, Hispanic, and Native American students to the special education placement process. It seems that the answers to students' difficulties in the regular classroom are all too often sought by attempts to refer students to special education rather than seeking to improve the quality of regular education (Maheady, Towne, Algozzine, Mercer, & Ysseldyke, 1983). Once students have been referred, the likelihood of special education placement is very high (Mehan, Hartwick, & Meihls, 1986; Ortiz & Polyzoi, 1986).

What are the checks and balances to the high rate of referral of minority students? It seems certain that the requirement for input from several professionals as well as from parents, and for a formal, uniform placement process, may not work as objectively as it ought to.

In an ethnographic study of the placement process, Mehan and colleagues (1986) have shown that many potential placement or service options were not included for consideration and that the process of reporting and decision making that occurred in formal placement meetings did not necessarily follow a model of "rational" decision making. In addition, official channels of decision making were routinely circumvented by the use of informal procedures. In the actual placement meetings, decisions were heavily influenced by individuals of higher status within the professional team, notably psychologists, whose reports were often presented in such as way as to make it difficult for other team members, and certainly parents, to understand the information and to form or express an opinion on the reports. Mehan and colleagues (1986) concluded that "placement outcomes were more ratifications of actions that had taken place at previous stages of the decision-making process than decisions reached in formal meetings" (p. 164).

The role of parents and advocates becomes crucial here. The requirement in the Education for All Handicapped Children Act that parents consent to every step of the process reflects not only the notion that parents can be helpful in planning, but also that they can protect their children against biased decision making. Current literature on parent participation promotes an ideal of a parent-professional "partnership" in decision making (Turnbull & Turnbull, 1986) that goes far beyond mere consent. In practice, however, the formal meeting is often parents' only opportunity to participate in or influence a decision. Without adequate information and the opportunity to build the confidence to advocate for their children in a setting dominated by a large group of professionals, parent participation may be reduced to mere consent of the least informed nature (Shevin, 1983). A detailed discussion of the role of parents will be reserved for Chapter 4.

SUMMARY

This chapter has outlined and discussed the continuing disproportionately high placement of African American, Hispanic American, and Native American students in programs for students with mild disabilities. Illustrations from the Office for Civil Rights' (U.S. Department of Education, 1987) most recent data reveal a consistent pattern of increasingly disproportionate placement of these students, in various categories, in districts where their numbers are large. Continuing efforts to explain these patterns by indicting the general cognitive potential of whole races and cultures have no basis in fact and, indeed, are meaningless in the light of the extreme extent of biracialism and biculturalism among Hispanic Americans, African Americans, and Native American peoples.

While there are, to date, no verifiable explanations of the patterns observed in minority overrepresentation, a speculative interpretation is that prejudice against people who are racially and/or culturally different may tend to increase as their numbers increase and that, in the light of continuing inappropriate assumptions about curriculum and instruction, schools' unpreparedness to address students' differences exacerbates the pattern of student failure.

In response to the challenge that disproportionate special education may be appropriate or acceptable if it reflects real needs of students, this chapter has outlined three essential aspects of the importance and implications of disproportionate placement.

The first of these is the issue of whether assessment was valid in the first place. The opinion of the courts has emphasized the negative effects of culturally and linguistically biased assessment procedures. While researchers have continued to debate the complexities of this process, it is agreed that standardized tests do not measure the construct of intelligence as some innate characteristic of individuals, but rather the extent to which individuals have learned certain culturally based information (Cummins, 1984). Thus it has been recommended that professionals must attend carefully to the overall picture of a child's background and performance and must not assume that oral language proficiency in English indicates a nonnative-speaker's readiness to be formally tested in English (Cummins, 1984). Professionals are also advised to consider the effects of the conditions of testing on minority students (Fuchs & Fuchs, 1989; Leung, 1986). The requirement of the law, of course, is that the testing procedure must include a variety of tests, given in the native language of a child who is not English dominant, and must also assess students' adaptive functioning.

The second implication of disproportionate placement is the recognition that assessment cannot be complete without an understanding of whether prior instruction has been adequate and appropriate. There is reason to believe that this has not been so. Several studies have pointed out that there is considerable teacher bias against children from different cultural and linguistic backgrounds, of which many teachers, deeply entrenched in ethnocentric assumptions, may not be consciously aware. Besides bias, teachers may often be unaware of how incongruous the style and emphasis of the school is with those of the cultures from which students are coming. This, along with several mistaken assumptions about the way children learn, often leads to reductionist instructional practices that teachers believe are necessary for children who display limited mastery of basic skills. This approach emphasizes students' weaknesses, making them seem more incompetent than they are.

Further, bilingual instruction is strongly recommended, but it has not been the norm for LEP students who have not yet learned to read and write in their native language. While the fact of tremendous linguistic diversity may make bilingual instruction impossible in some circumstances, researchers have pointed to the value of using the cultural and linguistic resources of children to maximize their potential, rather than insisting on an English-only approach, which ignores students' strengths and undermines the perceived value of their native language and culture.

The third aspect of placement that has been emphasized is the efficacy of special education programs themselves and the extent to which they provide for a return to the regular stream. The record of special education in these regards is markedly weak, and one of the central controversies of the field currently is the issue of greater cooperation, collaboration, and, possibly, integration of regular and special education services. Researchers have called for more holistic and community-referenced curricula and instruction for culturally diverse students.

Underachievement in regular education is the point at which regular and special education meet. The special education net is wide, pulling in many children from what has been referred to as the "mental withdrawal–grade retention–drop-out syndrome" (Stein, 1986, p. 107). One of the saddest findings of Trueba and colleagues' (1990) recent examination of the situation of Hmong students in a California school was the observation of increasing deterioration in some of these children's motivation, self-esteem, and cognitive skills. Regarding the process by which these students were officially declared "handicapped," the authors conclude:

> It did not matter that the testing took place in English, a language the children did not understand, or that the information leading to teacher referral was not accurate, or that the child's performance in domains such as art or mathematics was above average. (p. 105)

The tenet that failure breeds failure is so widely recognized as to be virtually a cliché — but sometimes it is the clichés that bring us back to basic truths. If we want students to succeed in schools, we must arrange learning in such a way as to make that possible.

The argument that many students respond to the cultural and racial hegemony of schools by rejecting the values and goals of the school is well documented (Fordham, 1988; Ogbu, 1974), but this does not mean that schools cannot bridge this gap by commitment to more appropriate approaches. Nor does the success of several researchers and teachers in remedying patterns of failure (Comer, 1980; Macias, 1987; Moll & Diaz, 1987; Ruiz, 1989) negate the fact that many students do withdraw under deleterious circumstances. What is needed is a recognition of the devastating effects of forcing children to choose between the culture of the home and that of the school in order to succeed. As Moll and Diaz (1987) have said, the culture of students must be seen as a resource on which schools can capitalize, rather than as a deficit to be rejected and replaced.

4

Culturally Diverse Families and the Special Education System

The Challenge of Building Trust

The notion of parent participation in school affairs reflects the logical progression of a century-old social reform movement whose roots in the 1887 formation of the National Congress of Mothers (subsequently the National Parent-Teachers' Association) came into full bloom as one of the "progressive" educational experiments of the 1920s (Schlossman, 1983). The dual thrust of this movement was toward the education of parents in "effective" parenting strategies as well as the cultivation of parental influence in children's educational careers.

The underlying assumption of the parent education and participation movement has been the belief that parent involvement affects the cognitive, affective, and social development of children (Bronfenbrenner, 1979). Indeed, many well-known studies have concluded that family environments are more influential in children's school achievement than the input of schooling itself (Coleman et al., 1966; Gordon, 1979; Marjoribanks, 1979).

Gordon (1977) has identified three basic models of parent involvement: the parent impact model, which emphasizes the school's having a beneficial impact on the home; the school impact model, in which parents exert influence on the school to be more responsive to their needs; and the community impact model, which recognizes the interrelatedness of home, school, and community and allows for mutual responsiveness and flexibility. In a comprehensive review of studies of the effects of parental participation on children's academic performance, Leler (1983) concluded that positive outcomes were reported for 70 percent of the studies of parent impact models and for all of the community impact model studies.

With regard to the specific functions that parents may serve, Keesling and Melaragno (1983) have identified the following:

1. Governance (primarily defined as decision-making)
2. Education (as instructional paraprofessionals or volunteers, or as tutors of their own children)
3. School support (both tangible and intangible)
4. Community-school relations (referring to communication and interpersonal relations)
5. Parent education (personal learning experiences). (p. 223)

While the initial target group of the parent education and participation thrust was essentially middle-class families, and the practice of participation was entirely voluntary in nature, the advent of antipoverty and compensatory education programs in the 1960s introduced the concept not only of educating low-income parents in effective parenting techniques but also of including them in governance and policymaking functions of federally funded programs. Keesling and Melaragno (1983) point out that federally funded programs have concentrated mainly on governance and educational functions. The impetus for this came from the Community Action Program of the Economic Opportunity Act (EOA) of 1964, which called for "the maximum feasible participation" of persons served (Keesling & Melaragno, 1983, p. 234) and resulted in the inclusion of parents on policymaking bodies of Head Start programs. Similar requirements were subsequently initiated to varying extents in programs under Title 1 of the Elementary and Secondary Education Act (ESEA) of 1965, Title VI of the ESEA (also referred to as the Emergency School Aid Act), and Title VII of the ESEA, more commonly known as the Bilingual Education Act. Keesling and Melaragno studied the extent of parental participation in these programs and concluded that programs with a stronger legal mandate and incentives for parental participation, such as Follow Through, succeeded in attaining higher levels of participation.

The developments outlined above present two concerns that are central to the discussion of this book: first, the difficulty of imposing value judgments regarding effective parenting in a culturally diverse society, and second, the fact that, because of the central role of the federal government in certain educational programs, parent participation in the affairs of schooling has come to exist within a distinctly legalistic framework. The following sections will address the implications of these concerns.

CULTURAL DIFFERENCE, DEFICIT, AND DYSFUNCTION

The link between parent participation and compensatory education for young children from low-income backgrounds has clear implications for the way parent programs are conceptualized. Most programs have typically reflected the assumption that beneficial family environments are those that incorporate mainstream American values and behaviors (Laosa, 1983; Ramirez & Cox, 1980). Thus the home environments of working-class and culturally different families have generally been viewed as needing to be replaced by desirable qualities represented by the school.

This approach to parent education is based on a deficit model that posits the inherent inferiority of lower-class and culturally different socialization styles (Laosa, 1983; Cochran & Woolever, 1983). Laosa (1983) states that this view emerged from the contention of several scholars that lower-class parenting styles tended to emphasize the arbitrary and direct expression of authority, using a "restricted" linguistic code, in contradistinction to the "elaborated" and more rational code of middle-class parents; the notion of deficit, Laosa argues, reflects the assumption that the parenting styles of White, middle-class families represent the standard against which "good" parenting should be measured.

It is also important to keep in mind that the influences of culture and social class can be quite distinct. In a review of studies of cultural differences in child rearing, Laosa (1981) pointed to the tendency of the literature to confound "purely cultural factors with differences in educational level and socioeconomic status" (p. 148). In a study of forty-three Chicano and forty Anglo-American mothers of young children, Laosa (1980) illustrated the influence of both culture and educational level on child-rearing practices. The study found that the Anglo mothers used inquiry and praise strategies more frequently than Chicano mothers, while the latter used modeling, visual cues, and directives more frequently than did Anglos. These differences, however, "disappeared entirely" when the researcher controlled for level of formal schooling (p. 764). Further, since the strategies of Anglo mothers were characteristic of those typically used in schools, Laosa concluded that the more educated mothers were likely to use the academic style of the classroom, thus mitigating the mismatch between home and school styles.

The point that difference is not equivalent to deficit has been neatly illustrated by Delpit (1988) in her discussion of the direct expression of authority used by Black mothers and teachers, as compared to the "veiled commands" more typical of the White middle class. Delpit gives the example of a Black mother's directive to her 8-year-old son—"Boy, get your rusty behind in that bathtub"—in contrast to "Would you like to take your bath now?" Delpit points out that there is no less love or mutual understanding in either style and that both may be representative of true power. A similar point has been made by Boggs (1985) regarding Hawaiian children's ability to distinguish between parental commands they must obey and those they need not, despite the apparently authoritative manner of their parents.

While recognizing that cultural difference does not constitute a deficit, it is crucial to acknowledge that, regardless of culture or class, dysfunctional family patterns do exist. Laosa (1983) gives the example of abusive parenting, whose existence is seldom a cause of disagreement among social scientists, since there is a recognizable "normal range" of parental behavior in each sociocultural group (p. 337). This is a particularly sensitive and difficult issue, since some traditional cultures accept corporal and psychological punishment of children to an extent that would seem severe by mainstream American standards (Chan, 1986; Chinn & Plata, 1986; Falealii, 1986). Families who rely on culturally appropriate forms of corporal punishment, however, should not be considered to be dysfunctional.

Literature on traditional Asian family environments has also addressed the issue of distinguishing between cultural difference and dysfunction. Ishisaka and colleagues (1985), in discussing professional interaction with Southeast Asian families, advise professionals to seek information from a wide range of informants in order to determine "which behaviors are cultural in origin and which are symptomatic of disorders of functioning" (pp. 54–55). For example, it is frequently observed that culturally appropriate acquiescent or self-deprecating behavior on the part of Asian parents should not be interpreted as indicative of weak ego identity (Chan, 1986; Ishisaka et al., 1985; Leung, 1988); however, it is also pointed out that the habitual reticence of Asian peoples may make it difficult for professionals to recognize pathological depression where it does exist (Kitano & Chinn, 1986). Similarly, the tradition of family extendedness and parental authority among Asians may encourage dependency of children far beyond what would be normative for mainstream Americans, but this does not imply pathological dependence (Baglopal, 1988; Chan, 1986; Gibson, 1987). A similar point has been made by Condon and colleagues (1979) regarding the relative dependency of children in traditional Hispanic families. On the other hand, professionals in special education may need to strike a balance between the traditional protective tolerance allowed a young handicapped child and the commitment of the special education system to maximizing independence and growth for such a child (Chan, 1986).

The challenge involved in facing such issues is essentially a challenge to the ethnocentrism of American professionals. Styles of child rearing, like styles of participation, will continue to vary with the extent of tradition versus acculturation in families. It is the job of professionals to respect these differences while introducing culturally different families to the expectations of the special education system and the rights accorded parents within that system. It is a question of balance: just as it is unacceptable for us to assume the superiority of mainstream American approaches, so is it unacceptable for us to evade our responsibility to parents by allowing them to remain unaware of their rights and authority within the system. People cannot choose unless they are aware of the choices that exist.

SOCIAL CLASS AND PARENTAL PARTICIPATION

Implicit in the foregoing discussion is the overlap between racial minority and social class. Indeed, dominant theories of the 1960s offered negative views of working-class family environments that were closely tied to deficit theories of ethnic cultures (Wright et al., 1983). The term *tangle of pathology* was used by the Moynihan report (U.S. Department of Labor, 1965) in reference to the environment of poor Black families and is commonly associated with notions of "culturally deprived" (Reissman, 1962) and "socially disadvantaged" (Deutsch, 1967) children. A central assumption in these ideas has been that poor and/or minority parents do not value education for their children.

A recent ethnographic study by Lareau (1989) offers an in-depth view of the reasons for the greater effectiveness of upper-middle-class as compared to working-class parents. Lareau's study concluded that greater educational competence, social status, income and material resources, view of work, and social networks all constituted a significant advantage for upper-middle-class parents. With these advantages, and the warmer welcome given their intervention by school personnel, these parents achieved what Lareau refers to as "customized or individualized" educational careers for their children. In contrast, working-class parents were able to gain only a "generic," undifferentiated educational path for their children.

Contrary to the position that has been supported by earlier researchers such as Deutsch (1967), Reissman (1962), and more recently Dunn (1988), Lareau (1989) emphasizes that class differences in the educational activities of families cannot be accounted for by differences in "values and concern" (p. 170). Parents in both groups in Lareau's study valued and desired education for their children, but, the author concludes, "social class . . . provides parents with unequal resources and dispositions, differences that critically affect parental involvement in the educational experience of children" (p. 171).

For most working-class parents in Lareau's study, school was "an alien world" (1989, p. 112) that parents assumed to be out of the realm of their influence. Upper-middle-class parents, on the other hand, assumed and readily acted on the right to intervene in school matters. It seems reasonable to assume that the sense of alienation would be even more intense for culturally diverse working-class parents from low-status racial or language minority groups.

Notwithstanding the convincing arguments of researchers such as Lareau, it should not be assumed that such influence is only available to parents who possess the cultural capital that makes them comfortable in dealing with schools. That influence is harder to come by among working-class parents does not mean it is impossible. Indeed, the fact that many students from poor homes do succeed raises the question of what factors enable some families to defeat the patterns described above.

The work of Reginald Clark (1983) effectively addresses this question. Clark contends that the much-quoted work of researchers such as Coleman and colleagues (1966) and Jencks (1972) shows statistically significant relationships between family background and school achievement but examines only sociodemographic characteristics such as family size, income, and ethnic background, paying no attention to the "psychological orientations and activity patterns" of family interaction (p. 7). Clark's in-depth interviews with ten low-income Black families demonstrate distinct parent-child dynamics and an "implicit pedagogy" in the homes of high-achieving students, regardless of income level and family constellation.

Similarly, Trueba and Delgado-Gaitan (1988) found that the role of parents as "academic mentors" was the salient variable distinguishing the families of Hispanic and Anglo students who finished high school as compared with those who dropped out. Even though parents in this ethnographic study were generally "unwelcome guests" in the schools, the study showed that socioeconomic level did not determine which parents were confident enough to confront the school system. The potential for some low-income parents to effectively advocate for and support their children suggests that collaboration between more and less successful families could be an important strategy in parent empowerment.

Two crucial factors emerge as essential to the attainment of parental influence. First, working-class parents must depend more on group influence, since they have less individual power; within this thrust, collaboration and mutual support play a central role. Second, it is certain that they will be in need of instruction in their rights and in strategies for interacting with the school system. Indeed, studies of efforts to empower working-class and/or culturally different parents point to the role of group support, increased self-esteem, and conscious acquisition of skills in dealing with schools (Ada, 1988; Cochran, 1987; Curtis, 1988; Delgado-Gaitan, 1990; Warren, 1988). Delgado-Gaitan (1990) summarizes the process of empowerment that occurred in her study of working-class Spanish-speaking parents: "Parents learned that skills and procedures to help their children were acquired abilities. This dispelled the isolation of powerlessness. . . . This process empowered them and influenced structural change" (p. 167).

COMPETING INTERESTS
AND THE RENEGOTIATION OF AUTHORITY

At the heart of parent-professional relationships lie considerations of power and authority. While parental influence may be mediated by social class, parental knowledge and skills, or group influence, there continue to be certain essential differences between the interests of parents and teachers that make this relationship very complex.

An example of this tension is offered in a study by Warren (1988), who compared parent-teacher relationships in a rural German village, an Anglo middle-class neighborhood in northern California, and a bilingual program in a lower-middle-class Mexican American neighborhood in southern California. He found that although parents and teachers in each setting shared common socialization norms and values, relationships between the two groups were essentially "complex, tentative and stressful" (p. 157). Warren concluded that the sharing of common values is not sufficient to overcome the "basic conflict between parental interest in the progress and life chances of a single child and teacher interest in the successful management of a group enterprise" (p. 157).

Of particular interest to our discussion is Warren's report of a language-maintenance bilingual-bicultural program whose commitment to affirming the value of Mexican American ethnicity resulted in "virtually ideal conditions" for parent-teacher collaboration, through the medium of advisory committees for both Title I (compensatory education) and Title VII (bilingual education) programs, as well as a traditional PTA. Warren (1988) concluded that this commitment and structure led to a "dramatic increase in parent involvement in school life" yet had "ambiguous results because they intrude on traditional alignments of authority and interaction between parents and teachers" (p. 153). Thus the commitment functioned as "both a powerful unifying force in parent-teacher relations and a source of tension and conflict" (p. 156).

This brings us to an issue that is central to the topic of this book: the question of what happens when traditional patterns of authority are challenged, either unilaterally by parents or through mutual agreement in an attempt to fulfill legal requirements for parent-school collaboration. In Warren's study of the bilingual-bicultural program, the advisory committees fulfilled requirements of the funding for bilingual and compensatory programs and offered parents more "entrée" to administrative issues than did the traditional PTA. Thus, Warren observed, the bilingual-bicultural program and its concomitant ethnic values

> present parents and teachers with fundamental questions of cultural affirmation and transmission. The questions are within a context of historic

and changing accommodations between the dominant culture and minority ethnicity. The questions are not resolved in the broader society but are nevertheless projected into the school to be mediated within a maze of judicial, legislative, administrative, organizational, and curricular factors. For parents and teachers, responding cooperatively to such questions is difficult. (1988, p. 155)

Such "historic and changing accommodations" as are required by Title I, Title VII, and, as will be seen in the next section, Public Law 94-142 represent gradually arrived at yet radical changes in the longstanding tradition of school authority. How these legal requirements are carried out will, of necessity, reflect cultural assumptions, values, and conflicts current in real-life settings. Further, the very fact that the impetus for collaboration derives from legal mandate sets the stage for a legalistic framing of parent-school discourse, which is not only likely to describe the relationship in adversarial terms but also means that those already in power will be the ones to define the dimensions, structures, and avenues by which the mandate is implemented. That parents are, by definition, respondents in this process does not make it impossible for them to play a role in its development, but this role may prove hard to achieve.

Bowers (1984), in a discussion of what he calls the "relativizing of traditional forms of cultural authority" (p. 5), describes this as a process of making explicit, and thereby questioning, the assumptions on which traditional values and practices are based. Bowers emphasizes that, in this process of change, there exists "a moment in social and conceptual time when the individual experiences the temporary openness of liminal space" — a moment of being "betwixt and between accepted definitions," and at which "new definitions can be presented, and the conceptual foundations of authority renegotiated" (pp. 6, 7). Bowers states that while those who possess "greater skill in using (and manipulating) the language system" will tend to dominate and control the process of redefinition, others who possess adequate "communicative competence" will be able to counter this (p. 28). Communicative competence, Bowers argues, requires an "explicit and rational knowledge of the culture that is being renegotiated" and the resulting ability to challenge taken-for-granted beliefs and customs (p. 29).

The process of parents and schools renegotiating traditional patterns of authority in response to legal mandates provides us with an example of Bowers's (1984) rather theoretical discussion. The situation described in Warren's study can be thought of in terms of what Bowers has called the "liminal space" in which power may be renegotiated and patterns of discourse redefined. The study showed that while parent advisory committees

(PACS) provided an avenue for parent influence, parents were not represented at faculty meetings, while there was provision for one faculty member to attend PAC meetings held at the school. Thus the structures provided for decision making reflected a modified separate-but-equal notion, with faculty retaining the balance of power. The result was separate decision making on topics that really required collaboration and, consequently, considerable friction when parents would challenge decisions made unilaterally by faculty. Nevertheless, in each of the study's examples of such challenges parents' point of view prevailed. The picture that emerges is of a gradual process of renegotiation of power, with the parents' role being steadily strengthened. Indeed, Warren (1988) observes that while controversial issues proved hard for teachers to discuss in faculty meetings, "parents approach[ed] them with increasing skill and aggressiveness" (p. 156). In Bowers's terms, we could say that the lower-middle-class parents in this study were in the process of gaining the communicative competence necessary to challenge the traditional power of school personnel.

The power attained by parents in the face of traditional resistance by school authorities can, however, be tenuous and fragile if it is not actively maintained by parents. A study by Curtis (1988) of a group of Mexican American parents' acquisition and subsequent loss of influence in the parent advisory committee of a bilingual program showed that despite the observance of minimal legal requirements for parental participation, the parents' role was severely undermined by the pervasive negative social attitudes of school district administrators.

Nevertheless, the presence of a legal mandate is both essential and powerful, as demonstrated by Keesling and Melaragno's (1983) comparative study of parent participation in federally funded programs. These researchers emphasized that "the language of the enabling legislation," and the extent to which compliance was monitored and evaluated, directly influenced parents' roles (p. 248). In particular, figures on participation of parents in management activities revealed that in Follow Through programs, which had the most specific requirements, parents maintained a high level of involvement—between 86 percent and 100 percent participation—in various activities, while Title I, Title VI, and Title VII programs showed a range of parent involvement from 21 percent to 100 percent in the same activities.

In sum, current mandates for parental participation in schools represent a gradual movement from notions of parent education to a thrust toward redressing the imbalance of power between schools and those populations who traditionally have been the least likely to be influential, that is, low-income and minority groups. The extent to which this thrust is likely to succeed is constrained by the fact that those who define the implementation of the law are those who already hold power; yet the potential for parents to participate in the creation of the new order, rather than merely respond to it, is inherent in the process of change.

PARENTS AS PARTNERS IN SPECIAL EDUCATION

Handicapped students constitute yet another minority group in education. The following section will examine the vision of parental participation developed for this group, the role of the law in this vision, and the response of parents.

Legal Advocacy and the Parental Role

The parent participation movement has found what might appear to be its most resounding expression in the special education mandates of the past 2 decades. In 1968, the Office of Special Education Programs (OSEP) made family involvement a requirement for funding of projects under the Early Childhood Assistance Act. This act resulted in over 200 demonstration programs, generally known as the Handicapped Children's Early Education Program (Karnes, Linnemeyer, & Myles, 1983). In 1975, P.L. 94-142 of the Education for All Handicapped Children Act (EHA) not only required parental permission for the entire process of referral, evaluation, and placement of handicapped students, but specified that program planning should include parental agreement to an individualized education plan (IEP) for each student. In 1986 P.L. 99-457 reauthorized and amended the EHA to include a family-focused early intervention discretionary program that makes stringent demands for an individualized family service plan (IFSP).

The growing emphasis on the rights and expertise of parents can be seen in a unique grant program, under P.L. 98-199, to support organized parent-to-parent information and training activities for parents of children with special needs. The result of this has been 50 parent training and information (PTI) centers across the country, which offer a variety of parent-to-parent support services (Ziegler, 1988). More recently, an increasing number of parent-to-parent projects have targeted low-income, minority, or geographically isolated families ("Programs Serving," 1988).

All of the above constitute important breakthroughs in societal attitudes toward the rights of handicapped children to education. Indeed, the law itself represents the culmination of parent advocacy that began with the early efforts of the National Association for Retarded Citizens in 1950 and the increasing role of parents in litigation, such as *Pennsylvania Asso-*

ciation for Retarded Citizens v. *Commonwealth of Pennsylvania* in 1971 and many others (see Pizzo, 1983, for a comprehensive summary of parent advocacy during this period).

Nevertheless, the definition of parents' roles under P.L. 94-142 places parents essentially in the role of respondents; that is, the law requires that parents grant permission for the various steps of a process that is conducted under the authority of experts in disability and that parents participate in individualized planning for the child. This is certainly much more than is required of parents of children in regular education programs, but it is also much less than is required of parents of children in compensatory programs such as Follow Through or bilingual programs, where parents are cast in roles of potential influence regarding project governance and policy (Keesling & Melaragno, 1983). The Education for All Handicapped Children Act includes no equivalent of the parent advisory committees in bilingual or compensatory programs, although the law calls for state advisory panels that must include parent representation. In special education, then, parents' input is envisaged in terms of discrete events related to consent and partial participation in planning. The implementation of this mandate includes written parental consent to evaluation and placement, as well as an invitation to parents to attend annual and triennial review meetings with the multidisciplinary team and an annual individual planning meeting with a child's teacher.

The language of the law itself makes it clear that its services are conceived within a medical model that casts students in the role of patients, and parents in the role of consumers of services delivered by experts who determine the truth about their children's learning potential and performance. The following section will outline what is known about the outcome of the mandate for parental involvement within this system.

Participation of Minority Parents: The Meaning of Passivity

Questions about culturally diverse parents' views and potential for participation and advocacy are particularly provocative if one considers several studies showing that, while parent participation is "widely accepted" and parents express general satisfaction with services, their role is largely passive in nature (Turnbull, 1983). Studies have focused on participation in IEP conferences, and their findings emphasize a distinction between attendance at meetings and genuine participation (Gilliam & Coleman, 1981; Goldstein, Strickland, Turnbull, & Curry, 1980; Lusthaus, Lusthaus, & Gibbs, 1981; McKinney & Hocutt, 1982; Schuck, 1979). Reasons cited for low participation include logistical difficulties such as transportation and child care (Pfeiffer, 1980; Thompson, 1982); professional perceptions of the relative unimportance of parents' role in meetings (Gilliam & Coleman, 1981; Mehan et al., 1986; Yoshida, Fenton, Kaufman, & Maxwell, 1978); professional time constraints (Price & Goodman, 1980; Safer, Morrissey, Kaufman, & Lewis, 1978); and lack of parental understanding of the school system (Strickland, 1983; Turnbull, Winton, Blacher, & Salkind, 1983).

While it is true that some parents may not particularly want to participate (Turnbull & Turnbull, 1982), it is essential that parents be sufficiently informed to choose their level of participation and to give meaningful consent (Shevin, 1983). Studies testing the impact of intervention strategies have succeeded in increasing parental participation by strategies such as using the school counselor as a parent advocate (Goldstein & Turnbull, 1982) and training parents in conference skills (Malmberg, 1984; Thompson, 1982). The success of these interventions suggests that it is safer to assume that parents do not know how to participate effectively than that they do not want to. Further, for some parents with limited education or proficiency in English, written materials may do little to provide essential information. For example, Roit and Prohl (1984) analyzed the readability of P.L. 94-142 written materials for parents and concluded that the sixth-grade reading level of the materials may be beyond the skills of many native and nonnative English speakers.

The participation of minority parents in special education programs stands out as even less involved and less informed than those of the mainstream. The following list summarizes the most common features in both empirical studies and conceptual discussions (Bennett, 1988; Chan, 1986; Connery, 1987; Figler, 1981; Leung, 1988; Lowry, 1983; Lynch & Stein, 1987; Marion, 1979, 1980a; Sharp, 1983; Smith & Ryan, 1982; Tran, 1982):

1. Lower levels of involvement than White counterparts
2. Less awareness of special education procedures, rights, and available services
3. An expressed sense of isolation and helplessness
4. Low self-confidence in interaction with professionals
5. Stressful life circumstances that overwhelm parents
6. Need for logistical supports such as transportation, child care, and respite
7. Culturally based assumptions of noninterference on the part of parents in school matters
8. Professionals' implicit or explicit discouragement of parents' participation in the special education process.

What is the meaning of this pattern of passivity that seems to characterize the participation of minority parents? While it is common to hear practitioners exclaim that "these parents just don't care about their children's education," several writers have attempted to probe beyond such preconceived notions. One common thread emerging is that professionals directly or indirectly discourage the participation of minority parents. Sullivan (1980) has charged that there is a pervasive attitude among professionals that "poor people just don't want anything" and can "accept any evaluation of children as being accurate and final" (p. 3). In a similar vein, Marion (1980a) states that many professionals deliberately withhold information "under the assumption that culturally different parents are not sophisticated enough to grasp the material" (p. 619). Lynch and Stein (1987) found that professionals interpreted parents as apathetic and disinterested, while the parents cited poor communication with staff and logistical problems.

Further, the contribution of professionals to the creation and maintenance of barriers can be quite explicit. In a carefully controlled study of 355 referrals in an urban school system, Tomlinson and colleagues (1977) found that school psychology personnel made significantly more contact with the parents of majority versus minority students (mostly Black and Native American). Parents of majority students were offered a wider range of alternatives, such as program placement, counseling, social groups, and attitude-change programs, while the minority group was limited to decisions about program placement.

Even where no prejudicial practices exist, the responsibility of school personnel must go beyond simply following the letter of the law. The work of Comer (1980) in transforming both the school climate and the academic performance of Black students in low-income urban neighborhoods has cited a willingness to share power with parents as one of the central tenets of the program's success. Indeed, to propose that it is up to the parents to bridge the gaps created by ethnicity, poverty, exceptionality, and language is to engage in a process of blaming the victim. Parents are the indirect recipients of services, and while it may be argued that they should develop a "consumer approach" to evaluating these services (Strenecky, McLoughlin, & Edge, 1979), the research cited below will show that this is particularly difficult for parents who are at economic, linguistic, and cultural disadvantages.

Perhaps the strongest call for school responsibility in creating a parent-professional partnership has come from Herman (1983), who advocates a proactive stance in which schools provide for the sharing of power with such parents and in which the courts would extend to poor, minority parents of exceptional children the status of a "suspect classification . . .

which signals the court to extend heightened concern and protection" (p. 59).

The most common research interpretation emerging from documented empirical studies has been that many minority parents tend to place their trust in the school and do not expect to play an influential role. Studies of Hispanic families by Figler (1981) and Lynch and Stein (1987) point to a traditional trust in school authorities and to families' expressed satisfaction with services. Figler used single but lengthy, home-based, semistructured interviews in Spanish to ascertain the views of Puerto Rican families with and without handicapped children. The study found that traditional respect for school authorities was a deterrent to parental participation. Parents preferred to stay away from the school, and while those with handicapped children were required to attend conferences, they maintained a "passive stance . . . and an implicit and explicit trust in the school and school staff" (Figler, 1981, p. 12).

Similarly, Lynch and Stein (1987), using single, questionnaire-based interviews, found that while Mexican American parents expressed greater satisfaction with educational decisions than did Black and White parents, their level of participation in and awareness of that process was considerably less. Like Figler, these researchers concluded that cultural attitudes such as trust in and respect for educational authorities, as well as difficulties in communicating and identifying with the dominant culture, have a negative influence on parents' interaction with the school system. Indeed, Lynch and Stein observe that participation may carry a different meaning for parents holding traditional Hispanic cultural values.

With regard to Native American parents, the pattern of low awareness and expressed satisfaction is described in a study by Connery (1987), who interviewed twenty-two Anglo and nineteen Navajo parents in a rural school district. Anglo families had an average of 5 more years of education and an average income almost three times greater than Navajo parents. The study found a common low level of awareness of rights and educational processes among both groups, but there was a significantly greater awareness among Anglos of the existence of special education laws. Anglo parents attended twice as many meetings as did Navajo parents, showed more familiarity with school procedures and personnel, and were better able to describe their children's handicaps. The study offered two implicitly contradictory observations: while Navajo parents expressed greater satisfaction with services, significantly more of them considered the testing for special education to be culturally biased. The author offers the speculation that such suspicions may have led Navajo parents to communicate less with school personnel. It seems reasonable to assume that it may also have led to reluctance to express dissatisfaction with services. The author also observes that almost half the Navajo parents offered suggestions at the end of the interview and speculates that they may have needed more time to "become comfortable with the interview process" (Connery, 1987, p. 131).

Research Constraints. The foregoing observation underscores the crucial importance of the interview process in attitudinal studies (Briggs, 1986; Glaser & Strauss, 1967; Spradley, 1979). If interviews are circumscribed by constraints on time or language, such as monolingual interviewers using interpreters, and if the study is perceived by informants as being identified with school authorities, either by the way it is introduced or by the use of a school-related location, findings should be viewed with caution. For example, in the Lynch and Stein (1987) study, the authors pointed out that interviews were conducted in a community near the Mexican border at a time when there was considerable anxiety on the part of the Spanish-speaking population regarding immigration authorities. Although interviewers were trained Spanish-speaking parents of handicapped children, the political climate and the fact that the study was introduced by the local education authorities suggest that parents' comments about their satisfaction with and trust in educational services should not be taken at face value. Similar constraints were evident in Connery's study, which consisted of single, questionnaire-based interviews in a study introduced by school authorities and conducted by a monolingual English speaker using an interpreter.

Studies of parents' attitudes will be more reliable if they utilize a recursive, open-ended approach by an interviewer who is perceived to be separate from the educational powers that be and who is to some extent familiar to parents (Blakely, 1982). Given all that is known about power relations between dominant and subordinate cultural groups, it should always be assumed that respondents' initial answers to judgments about the educational system may not be reliable. This is particularly important in interviewing parents, who, as Bennett (1988) observes, may be afraid that adverse comments may result in victimization of their children.

In addition to probing interviews, the use of other procedures and sources of information can provide a balance that qualitative researchers refer to as "triangulation" (Patton, 1980). This is nicely illustrated in a study by Sharp (1983) of factors affecting services to rural and urban Papago students. In-home interviews with parents, conducted by a bilingual Papago interviewer, revealed that urban parents expressed significantly greater satisfaction with services and knowledge of special education laws than did rural parents. The study was also supported by case studies, however, and these data did not corroborate parents' belief that prescribed services had been implemented and copies of IEPs received. In view of the low level of parents' awareness, it is possible that they may have been unaware of the contents of the IEP or of the requirement that these contents must be strictly adhered to.

Trust versus Deference.   It is not the intention of this chapter to challenge the well-established observation that some minority groups, notably traditional Hispanics and Asians, hold schools in reverence and trust (Chan, 1986; Correa, 1989; Figler, 1981; Gibson, 1987; Lynch & Stein, 1987; Tran, 1982). It is important to recognize, however, that a very different dynamic may occur when such people become the recipients of educational services in a society in which they feel like outsiders, and in cases where their children are in danger of being stigmatized by the system. Trust may rapidly be undermined if parents do not understand the system to which they must, legally, entrust their children and if they feel that they are not understood by its representatives. A culturally ingrained habit of respect for and deference to school authorities, however, may hide parents' real concerns.

Mainstream practitioners and researchers cannot afford to underestimate the power of history to dominate and undermine even the best-intentioned efforts at cross-cultural communication between dominant and subordinate groups. This is particularly so for groups who have historically been accorded caste-like status (Ogbu, 1978). The painful truth of this is revealed in the following observations by Sharp (1983) regarding research methods used with Papago parents in her study:

> Many parents of handicapped children are reluctant to contact agency officials because they fear their child will be taken away from them and placed into an institution or boarding school as happened so frequently in the past. . . . (p. 26)
>
> From an historical point of view, it was considered unrealistic and culturally inappropriate for non-Indians to attempt formal interviews with Papago parents of handicapped children. . . . Any investigator must know the cultural influences and gain acceptance by the persons to be interviewed. Direct questioning of traditional families is culturally inappropriate. (p. 29)

The observation regarding direct questioning points to differences in culturally determined aspects of interpersonal style that are applicable to both researchers and practitioners. In a discussion of relationships between Hispanic parents and special educators, Condon and colleagues (1979) state:

The very directness of Anglo-American style parent-teacher consultation is apt to create serious obstacles to the resolution of problems experienced by Spanish children. . . . The school's emphasis on immediacy in decision-making may secure agreement but this apparent concurrence may conceal a world of resentment, resistance and downright opposition. (pp. 71–72)

Condon and colleagues (1979) conclude that parents' resulting "polite transparent excuses intended to convey a negative answer without offending the listener" often lead to conferences ending in frustration (p. 71). Similarly, Chan (1986) states that for Asian parents who hold a traditional attitude of deference, noninterference, and delegation of authority to the school, the mandate for parental involvement "may be both alien and threatening" and may even be interpreted as meaning that the child's problems are so severe that the school has transferred accountability to the parents (p. 46). Further, parents may be reluctant to express preference for fear of offending school officials. The point has also been made by Leung (1988) and Condon and colleagues (1979) that provision must be made for input from influential family members other than parents if decisions are to be meaningful.

This combination of trust, respect, deference, and withdrawal can make collaboration an elusive goal for special educators. This point is eloquently summarized by Leung (1988), who states that while Asian parents can be expected to be cooperative:

Attention and affirmation may only mean courtesy and propriety; parents do not wish to contradict the authority figures and cause them to lose face. Therefore a "yes" is not equivalent to a promise of adherence to the counsel or direction, especially if it is at odds with the Asian's knowledge base or belief or value system. (p. 94)

Yu (1985), in a discussion of methodology in transcultural research, has referred to the above patterns of parental response as "courtesy bias" or, in a more cynical vein, "sucker bias," which may occur when informants do not yet trust the researcher and when researchers are not aware of the cultural inappropriateness of certain approaches. Ethnographic methods can be successful in countering these difficulties for two reasons: first, the researcher assumes that his or her main job is to understand meaning from the cultural perspective of the respondents; second, such methods seek changing information over time through observations of various settings and recurring interviews with a wide range of participants. In addition to revealing a more holistic picture, these methods also capture the dynamic process by which relationships are constructed (Lofland, 1971).

Views from Ethnographic Studies.   Recent ethnographic studies have targeted the cross-cultural dynamics that underlie minority parents' failure to participate in their children's education (Ada, 1988; Bennett, 1988; Delgado-Gaitan, 1990; Trueba et al., 1990). Although only one of these focuses primarily on special education, implications for this system can be extrapolated from the findings of all.

Bennett's (1988) microethnographic analysis of meetings between Hispanic parents of deaf children and professionals in a private special education program points to the power of school authorities to structure and define the limits of parent-professional discourse in such a way as to limit effective parent participation. Bennett offered a conclusion so emphatic that it is worth quoting at length:

> In a general sense, school staff engaged in a number of practices which tended to position parents in a stance of noninvolvement. These could include such practices as reducing big issues to smaller ones, localizing problems within individuals, particularly the children, and isolating those problems from the school context; actively maintaining a non-sharing of information; limiting the areas of concern that parents could legitimately have a voice in; assuming the prerogatives of allocating times, places, participants, formats and agendas for meetings between parents and staff; and isolating categories (both concepts and social roles) from each other and from their contexts, thus obscuring relationships between them. (p. 127)

Bennett also points to the role of deference in parents' behavior. Even parents who expressed severe criticism of the school in interviews with the researcher nevertheless "presented the face of respeto (respect), which often took the form of a seemingly respectful silence as school staff did their thing" (p. 150). The author observes that this withdrawal further contributed to the continuing boundaries between parents and the school.

To date, the most dramatic example of cultural dissonance in parent-professional interaction is the following story from Trueba and colleagues' (1990) study of Hmong students in a California community. The story points to two sources of parents' inability to participate "American style": first, their sense of inadequacy in educational matters, and second, a cultural style whose emphasis on deference and modesty may be incomprehensible to American professionals. Trueba and colleagues (1990) state:

When asked for questions at the end of the parent-teacher conference, the most frequent Hmong reply is "Kuv ruam ruam." The translation is, "I am stupid," and, alternatively, "I am mute." Explaining why he had no questions, one father went on to say: "I don't know anything. I can't do anything to help my child learn at school. Tell the teacher thank you for helping my child and please to continue to help. I leave everything to the teacher." (p. 56)

In addition to the humility and trust expressed by such parents, the authors point out that for Hmong parents it is always culturally appropriate to be modest about children's abilities and that this can be mistakenly interpreted by school personnel as a sign of low self-esteem. Ishisaka and colleagues (1985) have also made this point regarding modesty among Southeast Asian parents, while Chan (1986), too, has emphasized the deference to authority typical of Asian families.

It seems clear that if parent-professional interaction is cast in a framework where power is loaded on the side of professionals, genuine communication with parents from such backgrounds will be virtually impossible. When the rules of interaction are changed, however, the process of parent empowerment may begin. Delgado-Gaitan's (1990) study of low-income Mexican American parents demonstrates that the intervention of the researcher enabled parents to surpass their own expectations of themselves and, through collaborative planning and action, to discover their own potential for influence. These parents, whose habitual lack of participation reflected a deep sense of shame at their poverty and lack of education, soon discovered that "la vida es una escuela" (life is a school), and, as they gained confidence, they gradually also gained the attention and response of the school administration. Delgado-Gaitan (1990) emphasizes that it is skills in "social competence and social literacy" that empower parents to participate (p. 58).

Ada (1988) reports similar success with rural, predominantly Mexican American families in the Pajaro Valley in California. Parents with little schooling, many of whom had never read a book, participated in a project to promote literacy activities. The program, which emphasized writing and reading their own stories to each other and to their children, resulted not only in increased literacy among the group of sixty to a hundred parents, but also in an upsurge of pride in their own and their children's abilities. The moving comment of one mother at a meeting illustrates the power of negative evaluations to influence the self-perceptions of minority people: "What is happening to us is that no-one has ever told us [before] that our children are worth something, and no-one has ever told us that we are worth something" (Ada, 1988, p. 227).

REACHING OUT TO MINORITY PARENTS

This review of literature has so far emphasized two features that are central to interpretations of parental participation: the influence of culture and social class in the interactions between parents and professionals and the framing of parent participation in such a way as to preclude genuine communication. The following section will briefly summarize current thinking on specific strategies through which some of these difficulties might be overcome.

Minimizing Cultural Dissonance

One aspect of cultural dissonance most frequently discussed is interpersonal style. We are often not aware of how our cultural style is perceived by others. It is difficult, for example, to explain the difference between the "direct" style characteristic of Americans and a slower-paced, more generalized approach that may be more successful with many minority peoples. In discussions of mental health services to Puerto Rican families, Mizio and Delaney (1981) and McGowan (1988) both describe this in terms of more informal, slower-paced, supportive approaches as compared to a "highly rational, efficient, 'quick-fix' approach" (McGowan, 1988, p. 62). Yet these authors also emphasize the need to offer practical problem-solving support in a manner that respects people's discomfort with direct questioning. The same point is made in the literature on services to Southeast Asians (Chan, 1986; Ishisaka et al., 1985; Murase, Egawa, & Tashima, 1985; Yu, 1985). Professionals are advised to use a more indirect approach, supported by a willingness to listen to "tangential" issues (Chan, 1986), or to develop a relationship with clients that includes elements other than direct service issues (Cassidy, 1988; Murase et al., 1985).

In addition to sensitivity to cultural style, there are two key issues that may appear to be merely logistical but that are essential in establishing trust: decisions about the use of interpreters and the route by which professionals gain access to families.

Two absolutely unacceptable approaches to non-English-speaking families have been noted: first, attempts to communicate without an interpreter if the parent speaks a little English, and, second, reliance on children to interpret. The need for interpreters even when parents can speak some English is illustrated in a report by Trueba and colleagues (1990) that the absence of interpreters at a conference with Hmong parents led to incorrect reporting of a child's history and the misinterpretation of a Hmong parent's modest reference to a child as "dumb" to mean that the child was retarded. With regard to the use of child interpreters, these authors note both the inadequacy of their English to the technical vocabulary of medical or educational services and the unfair responsibility placed on child interpreters to mediate with adults on behalf of their parents.

Several discussions of the issue of interpretation with Southeast Asian refugees have emphasized the importance of using interpreters who are not only fluently bilingual but also bicultural, able to understand the subtle nuances of language, interpersonal behavior, and social status as well as the expectations of American human service systems (Blakely, 1982; Chan, 1986; Chinn & Plata, 1986; Murase et al., 1985; Owan, 1985; Tung, 1985; Yu, 1985). The question of whether interpreters should also be community members overlaps with the issue of how best to gain access to traditional families. The point has been made that while access through a trusted community member is often essential (Blakely, 1982; Chan, 1986; Ishisaka et al., 1985, Leung, 1988; Yu, 1985), it is crucial to attain a balance among cultural and personal familiarity, the need for confidentiality, and the need for impartiality (Chan, 1986; Tung, 1985). The importance of using kinship and informal social networks in working with Asian Indian families has also been emphasized by Baglopal (1988). In sum, Leung (1988) concludes that the central characteristics needed for the establishment of trust with such families are "acquaintance, credentials and sensitivity" (p. 94).

A special comment must be made regarding the issue of participation and trust among African American parents. Despite the deep mistrust held by many such parents regarding any systems that represent White authority, African Americans have traditionally held education as the route from poverty to social status (Hill, 1971) and were traditionally both active in and supportive of school matters (Marion, 1981). Marion, however, has pointed out that this pattern underwent significant change with the desegregation of schools and the subsequent struggle for the acceptance of Black students in previously White school systems. Black parents' growing mistrust was exacerbated by the pattern of overrepresentation of Black students in special education programs and the controversy over nondiscriminatory evaluation, as well as by low levels of information regarding their rights within special education (Lowry, 1983). Marion (1979) has recommended strategies appropriate to Black and other minority families that emphasize a respectful and personalized approach.

All these observations reflect the concern with achieving a balance between personalism and professionalism that was identified in an earlier discussion. Indeed, Murase and colleagues (1985) state that the often-heard call for personalism with Mexican American families is equally needed for work with Southeast Asian families. Most writers observe that without this, trust is hard to attain.

Advocacy Training

Our discussion of the role of social class pointed to the need for collaboration and training for working-class and culturally different parents. In special education, the difference between the reality of passive parent participation and a state-of-the-art vision of parent-professional partnership has resulted in advocacy training becoming a central aspect of many parent support programs. The emphasis is on parents becoming aware of their rights under the law, understanding basic tenets of special education, and developing skills for effective and confident interaction with professionals (Anderson, Chitwood, & Hayden, 1982; Gorham, 1975). Most of these programs have tended to attract middle-class parents. Gliedman and Roth (1980), in a discussion of the imbalance of power between parents and professionals, observe that traditional advocacy training strategies presuppose "cultural traits, tastes and abilities [that] are perhaps most frequently approximated by the tiny fraction of parents who are well-to-do and well educated" (pp. 185–186).

Difficulties such as these have prompted parent training programs to include a specific outreach component to meet the needs of minority parents. Marion (1979) has outlined a model for improved participation that emphasizes professionals' cultivation of respect for Black parents and their culture and the implementation of a personalized style. Similarly, Baca and Cervantes (1984) have developed a model for parents of bilingual children, while parent support programs (Sour & Sorell, 1978) and advocacy training have been developed for Hispanic parents in particular (Riley, 1978; Tessier & Barton, 1978). Parent training for limited/non-English-speaking Asian and Latino parents has been developed and tested with positive results by Chan, Lim-Yee, and Vandevier (1985). Another approach to improving service to parents has been through training professional personnel, in programs such as the one at the University of Texas (Marion, 1980b), which requires student teachers to gain extensive experience with minority parents through field placements and research, or at Georgetown University, which has published a manual for professionals working with culturally diverse groups (Roberts, 1990).

Recommendations for outreach programs and actual reports from such programs for various minority groups offer the following similar strategies (e.g., Cassidy, 1988; Florida Department of Education, 1988; Grippo-Gardner & McHugh, 1988; Moore, 1986):

1. Establish personalized, individual contact with parents.
2. Disseminate information, and gain access to parents through traditional community supports such as churches or ethnic organizations.

3. Educate community leaders in the central issues facing parents of children with disabilities.
4. Recognize that issues of survival may have to be given precedence over educational concerns, and be willing to assist parents in such matters.
5. Seek and respond to the expressed needs of parents regarding scheduling, transportation, child care, and other logistical concerns that may hinder their participation in training.
6. Establish peer support groups, with parent-to-parent training.

THE STRUCTURE OF PARENT-PROFESSIONAL DISCOURSE IN SPECIAL EDUCATION

The foregoing review of literature on the participation of minority parents reveals the power of underlying cultural assumptions and values to structure the entire process of interaction. The special education system, in its attempt to fulfill legal requirements for parental input, has built channels of communication by which parents receive information, give their consent, and meet with professionals to review children's progress and participate in decision making regarding program placement and content. These systems are designed to be internally consistent — that is, ensuring that all parties concerned exchange relevant information in a way that can be documented.

The assumptions on which any system is built inevitably determine the design of its structure. The special education system is conceived within the framework of a medical model that calls for disabled children to be sought, found, evaluated, and treated by experts who hold the keys to truth regarding the conditions and needs of such children. The law calls for the inclusion of parents both to further inform professionals and to protect the interests of children. The law, however, can be likened to a suit of armour, whose tight demarcations serve to constrain as well as to protect. Thus the legal mandate itself influences the way in which this participation is designed.

Philips (1983) has used the term *participation structures* to refer to the unwritten rules of discourse by which participants regulate their interaction. When this notion is applied to discourse that has been mandated by law, it seems reasonable to expect that its patterns will become even more ingrained and inflexible. Indeed, Hall (1977) has used the concept of "high- and low-context" cultures to describe the potential of the law in various societies to address human issues in a more or less personalistic manner. Hall concludes that American law is, in comparison to that of many other countries, markedly "low-context" in its reliance on positivistic criteria for truth and in its tendency to exclude and treat as irrelevant the complexities of human perception and personal interaction. Thus Hall sees the American system of justice as a "low-context edifice in which it is extraordinarily difficult to guarantee that the proceedings can be linked to real life" (p. 106). Hall further describes this tendency as a reflection of the Western commitment to the "new religion" of science, whose emphasis on positivism has resulted in an attempt to screen out as much context as possible.

What Hall refers to as the "overbureaucratization" of our education system is but an example of the Western tendency to frame organizations in terms of many discrete categories and linear patterns of interaction, in accordance with our preference for low-context systems. The high value placed on this is evident in the very language of the special education system, which seeks to objectify the work of special education by using language that is low in context and high in level of abstraction. For example, the term *service delivery system* offers no connotations of the personalism or ambiguity inherent in the work of the field; rather, it intends to convey an image of a precise package that can be delivered in a predictable fashion through prescribed routes and channels. Indeed, it is not facetious to say that the term is more likely to conjure an image of a delivery van doing its daily round than of a complex pattern of personal interaction.

This preference for low-context language and tools makes the concepts of the system particularly susceptible to reification. Bowers (1984) has described this as a process of "externalizing" ideas and values in such a way as to "transform what was a subjective reality into an objectified, socially shared reality" and, in so doing, losing sight of the human authorship of an idea (p. 60). Bowers observes that the very act of putting ideas into language tends to lead to reification because of "the inadequacy of our language to communicate context, intentionality and subjective meaning" (p. 61). Bowers gives as examples of common reifications in public education such phenomena as standardized tests, degree requirements, theories of learning such as behaviorism, and the various roles prescribed for individuals, such as student or teacher.

One of the implications of this for parental participation is the difficulty that parents from high-context cultures may experience in trying to participate within essentially low-context structures. For example, the American view of "professionalism" tends to focus only on characteristics directly related to one's field of expertise, while for many minority people, judgments about professional competence would tend to be based on much broader and more inclusive criteria. This kind of dissonance may be thought of as being at the level of personal style.

More far-reaching are systemic reflections of dissonance, which exist for mainstream parents and even more so for culturally different parents.

For example, the very task of communicating with a parent about the learning difficulties of a child is by nature a high-context activity; that is, an activity in which all aspects of the discourse are dependent on subtle, often imprecise personal and cultural information—and therefore open to interpretation. To approach such a task with low-context tools such as standardized tests of language, intelligence, or academic skills, or with a chain of communication that relies on the most low-context of all communication tools—the written word—is to set the stage for failure.

Yet these are precisely the tools that dominate the discourse that occurs between parents and special educators. Reliance on these tools reflects the field's concern with objectivity and accountability. Closely tied to this is the belief that these features, reflecting the internal validity of a tightly structured system, somehow ensure "truth." The work of post-structuralists such as Cherryholmes (1988) emphasizes that even the most internally valid structure is based on a subjective value system. Thus discourse is never objective, but rather reflects the power structures inherent in every activity. Cherryholmes uses the work of the French theorist Michel Foucault and others to show that the patterns of discourse within a given structure are neither apolitical nor value-free, but are negotiated in accordance with dominant values:

> The rules of a discourse govern what is said and what remains unsaid. They identify who can speak with authority and who must listen. They are anonymous because there is no identifiable author, nor do they have a clear-cut beginning. (1988, p. 34)

Such rules, Cherryholmes contends, gradually come to be seen as constituting "truth" and to reflect meanings that are fixed rather than relative. Cherryholmes argues that one means of attaining this image of stability is to appeal to a "transcendant idea that rises above the text or discourse" (1988, p. 32).

The study that will be presented in the following five chapters of this book illustrates the impact on culturally different parents of two transcendent ideas that undergird the practice of discourse in special education. The first is the concept of disability, which, because of its base in the highly esteemed science of medicine, has been given transcendant status by a law that calls for disabled children to be sought, found, evaluated, and treated by experts who hold the keys to truths regarding the conditions and needs of such children. The second is the notion of parental participation, which, designed within the constraints of a legal mandate, has tended to take on the low-context character of the law and the dominant postivistic values to which modern education subscribes.

The study will show that the system devised for parent participation is not merely a value-free conduit for communication between parents and professionals, but rather a body of discursive practices whose framework determines what will emerge as the meaning of participation. The language of the law regarding parental participation is, in reality, minimalist, while the rhetoric of the state-of-the-art in the field envisages a full-fledged collaboration between parents and school authorities. Between these two extremes fall the real-life efforts of both parents and professionals to give meaning to the legal mandate.

It is true that special educators are faced with the dilemma of how to implement state-of-the-art practice with parents who may see themselves as inadequate to the task of collaboration with professionals, who may perceive this task as inappropriate or intimidating, whose low participation may appear to reflect lack of interest, and whose life circumstances may be so overwhelming as to make educational concerns a low priority.

Before citing these as barriers to collaboration, however, as professionals we must first ask what barriers exist on our side. The literature shows that one set of barriers may reflect personal values. Do we see culturally different parents as unreachable or too difficult to communicate with? Do we assume that they are somehow different from mainstream parents in their concern for their children or their willingness to support them? Do we expect them to value education less than do mainstream parents? Do we find ourselves recoiling from racial, cultural, or linguistic characteristics that are unfamiliar or that have traditionally carried the stigma of social inferiority? Do we believe, although we may never say so, that parents whose speech is different, whose dress is different, and who have minimal formal education really have little to offer to educational planning for their children?

Equally powerful are systemic barriers that treat culturally based beliefs as reality and create systems and procedures that effectively preclude genuine participation of all but the most culturally literate parents. In this regard we must ask whether our systems are designed for communication or for control, for questions or only for answers, to empower or to disempower students and their families.

This is where professionals must begin: we must examine and eliminate the barriers we ourselves have erected, while creating opportunities for culturally and racially different parents to learn about the special education system and to exercise their rights within it. The study that follows delineates the views of one group of parents on the creation and maintenance of barriers, as well as the efforts of professionals to dismantle these barriers within the constraints of the legal framework of special education.

5

A Study of Puerto Rican American Parents' Views of Special Education

Background and Method

The first four chapters of this book presented the issues and challenges that provided the impetus for this study. A great deal of research has placed the burden of responsibility for minority students' failure and disproportionately high placement in special education programs at the feet of an overly ethnocentric school system that provides students and their families with culturally incongruous communication, assessment procedures, and instructional methodologies. Inherent in the system is the message that cultural difference is equivalent to educational deficit.

Previous studies of Hispanic families' interaction with the special education system have focused either on Mexican American (Lynch & Stein, 1987) or Puerto Rican families (Condon et al., 1979; Diaz, 1981; Figler, 1981). A recent study by Bennett (1988) has targeted a more heterogeneous group of parents from Caribbean Hispanic backgrounds. The discussion in the previous chapter pointed to the common observation among these studies that a tradition of trust in the school combines with cultural differences and communication difficulties to create a pattern of relative passivity and noninvolvement among Hispanic parents.

This study seeks one group of parents' interpretations of children's school failure and special education placement as well as their views of the dynamics of communication between themselves and school personnel. The findings of the study tell twelve families' side of the story of low parental participation.

RESEARCH METHODS WITH CULTURALLY DIVERSE FAMILIES

Participants in the study were twelve Puerto Rican American families whose children had been placed in special education programs in a small, inner-city school district in the Northeast. The language of all the homes was Spanish, and only one mother, born on the mainland, was a fluent English speaker. All the other parents were born and raised in Puerto Rico and were predominantly or solely Spanish-speaking. The children to whom the study related had all learned English as their second language and had all been placed in mild disability categories.

The Methodology

The method of the study was driven by what is known about traditions of respect and personalism in Latino cultures — in particular, what Bennett has referred to as "the face of respeto" (respect) (Bennett, 1988) that Hispanic parents traditionally show to school authorities. Given this knowledge, it seemed clear to me that formal, preplanned interviews would only yield information of a stereotyped nature as opposed to more informal, open-ended interviewing (Glaser & Strauss, 1967; Spradley, 1979).

Another powerful influence in my thinking was Mehan and colleagues' (1986) study of the process of decision making in special education, which demonstrated that parent participation really amounted to cooperation with a system that was beyond parents' influence. This made it clear that naturalistic observation would be the most effective complement to interviews, and I was particularly influenced by Becker's (1970) persuasive argument that the power of participant observation lies in the fact that subjects are seen responding to the typical demands of a naturalistic context rather than to the presence of a researcher or a contrived setting. Since the real-life situation is far more important to participants than the views of a researcher, one need not be unduly worried about one's presence influencing the outcome of events.

Further, I was impressed by Trueba's (1983) statement that "process-oriented research and ethnographic close-ups tend to fulfill that function in educational research of searching for understandings and explanations which other types of research must let go" (p. 409). I felt that the traditional questionnaire approach used in previous studies had had to "let go" of many important understandings that could be offered by parents. Bennett's (1988) ethnographic study of parent participation was not yet published, and there were as yet no studies that combined both interviews and observation of Hispanic parents' interaction with the special education system.

The Dilemma of Subjectivity

The concern with subjectivity in research, and perhaps more so in naturalistic, qualitative methods, has been explored by several writers (Patton, 1980; Peshkin, 1988). Such discussions typically address the question of researcher awareness of subjectivity and efforts that can be made to minimize negative effects of this.

I believe that I brought to the study a reasonable balance of personal identification with and distance from the culture and perspectives of the participants. Although I am a native speaker of English from the English-speaking Caribbean, my identification with Latino language and culture came from what is referred to in Jamaica as the "Pan-Jam" connection — a history of migration of Black West Indians to Panama for the purpose of employment on the canal; my father's family had taken this route, and his side of the family is still "Panameña a los huesos" (Panamanian to the bone).

When I embarked on this study, my Spanish was more than rusty, but a strong sentimental attachment to the language and my previous fluency convinced me that it would come back in the course of the research. As it turned out, the participants responded positively to my limited vocabulary and bad grammar and readily assumed the role of tutoring me. In terms of race and culture, I was also in a position to be readily accepted, since I am of a racial mixture similar to many Hispanic people from the Caribbean. Indeed, visitors to the homes of the study participants would routinely address me in Spanish and express surprise when my Spanish told them that I was not "Puertorriqueña." Further, I found that my background as a Caribbean person equipped me with certain ingrained habits in interpersonal behavior that were consonant with those of my participants — in particular, an intuitive understanding of what constitutes "personalismo" (personalism), a quality so commonly referred to as central to interaction in Latino cultures. On the other hand, the fact that I am neither Puerto Rican nor a native Spanish speaker gave me sufficient cultural distance from the people whose views I was studying that I constantly had to seek clarification of cultural assumptions and meanings.

Another advantage was the fact that I was not only a student but a "foreign student" with no roots in the city, which led participants to the reasonable and correct assumption that I was not a person of influence in the community. More important, my research was independent of any authority related to the families and was in no way affiliated with the school or any public service system; I was introduced to the families by neighborhood voluntary agencies trusted by the families.

That I approached the study with an implicit bias in favor of the vulnerability of parents of handicapped children was probably inevitable because I have been such a parent. I certainly approached the study with the assumption that poor, minority parents would be triply vulnerable to the exigencies of a heavily bureaucratic system that reflects mainstream American values.

Qualitative research methods include a number of strategies intended to ameliorate the effects of preconceived assumptions and the subjective leanings of what Peshkin (1988) has referred to as the numerous "I's" (ideological personas) of the researcher that may be activated in the course of research. In this study I utilized several of these, including:

1. Three basic data collection strategies: interviews, participant observation of both school-based and community events, and review of students' records
2. A recursive interview process in which a minimum of three interviews with each parent allowed me the opportunity to review and clarify information as well as to probe issues that I suspected may have been too sensitive to elicit honest responses the first time around
3. Sharing with the participants my initial interpretations of events I had observed, such as special education meetings, in order to compare their impressions with mine
4. "Triangulation" of data (Patton, 1980) by interviewing all professionals frequently cited by participants, so as to find out the school's views of events and persons, as well as to understand school district policies regarding special education placement and parent participation in the process.

RESEARCH DESIGN

The study was based on in-depth interviewing, participant observation, and reviewing of records over a period of 9 months. All names of groups, schools, and individuals in the study have been changed.

Overall, the study aimed to discover these Puerto Rican parents' views of special education placement in order to recommend improvements in (1) educational services for these children and (2) the attainment of effective home-school interaction and parent advocacy. The study was guided by the following questions:

- What does the identity "Hispanic/Puerto Rican" mean to these parents?
- Do they think that their children's identity as "Hispanic" or "Puerto Rican" plays a role in special education placement?
- Do parents agree with the school's view of the child as having a "disability"?
- What meanings do parents attach to the particular disability classification ascribed to the child?

- How satisfied are parents with the special education services received?
- To what extent do parents understand the workings of the special education system?
- To what extent do parents participate and wish to participate in decisions regarding special education for their child?
- What factors facilitate or obstruct parents' effective participation?
- How do educational personnel and personnel in advocacy organizations see the issues raised by parents?

Recruitment of Participants

In this northeastern city of approximately 170,000, the Hispanic population totals about 15,000, of which some 5,000 live on what is known as the West Side. The Hispanic residents of this area are predominantly Puerto Rican Americans of low income. The predominance of this group is reflected in the fact that the school district uses two classifications of Hispanic students: "Puerto Rican" and "Spanish surname." The school district has a total of approximately 21,000 students, of which 436 are designated "Puerto Rican" and 65 "Spanish surname." In special education there is a total of just over 2,400 students, of whom 48 are designated "Puerto Rican" and 10 are "Spanish surname."

Puerto Rican Families with Children in Special Education. I asked two voluntary agencies in the neighborhood to introduce me to Puerto Rican families in the community. The Latin American Association (LAA), an advocacy organization located in the heart of this area, employs only Hispanic personnel and serves the local Hispanic community. Neighborhood Services (NS), located on the same street as the LAA, offers various educational and social welfare services for residents of the area and employs three Spanish-speaking social workers.

The Spanish-speaking personnel at both these agencies initially agreed to introduce me to parents of children placed in special education. However, the LAA was at the time experiencing a change in personnel and found it impossible to assist.

The school district at the time had fifty-eight Hispanic students placed in special education. Personnel at NS informed me that their records showed forty families with at least one child in a special education program. Hispanic social workers at this agency contacted and introduced me to eleven of these families. Selection of these families was based on personal judgments by the social workers as to which families they felt would be most accessible and most willing to participate. The families were not chosen on the basis of knowledge of any particular experiences with the educational system. One participant in the study introduced me to a twelfth family who were friends of hers. I will discuss the implications of the recruitment method in a subsequent section on generalizability of findings.

Personnel at NS subsequently sent letters to the remaining twenty-eight families listed as having children placed in special education, informing them that the study had already begun and inviting them to participate. None of these families responded to the letters.

Agency personnel introduced me to parents on the understanding that, after the initial introduction, the conduct of the research would be entirely up to me and the participants. In the interviews, all the participants described themselves as "Puerto Rican" or "Puerto Rican American."

Recruitment Dilemmas.   Recruiting participants through introductions by community agencies has the limitation that volunteer participants might be in some ways different from the larger population; for example, they might be more aggressive, better educated, or have a particular axe to grind. Further, the families who seek services from these agencies may not be typical of the larger Hispanic population. Thus the generalizability of the findings could be limited since there can be no claim to randomness in selection.

An alternative way of recruiting could be by letter through the school district, since all families are served by the school. I felt, however, that this would have been less effective for two reasons: one, the formality of a letter-only invitation would lack the personal touch that I believed would be crucial in gaining parents' participation; second, such an approach would present me to parents as an affiliate of the school and lend the research a quality of formality that would alienate many parents.

Overall, I think that the nature of this research makes it impossible to gain a "captive audience," since parents are under no obligation to agree to participate. In explaining the project, I was careful to present all information in an objective and neutral manner in order to avoid the impression that the study was to be a forum for disenchanted parents in particular. I believe that the depth of information I obtained through this methodology offered a balance to any limitations placed on generalizability.

Further, since the purpose of the study was to make recommendations based on parents' stated opinions and my own observations, what is important are the lessons that can be learned from the data, not the notion that the information might be true for most or all Hispanic parents. Patton (1980) offers a thoughtful discussion of the relevance of generalizability to qualitative data and concludes that the great strength of qualitative data lies in the provision of perspective and of information that can lead to action. Generalizability may be important when one is trying to demonstrate some law of cause and effect or of correlation between events, but is not necessarily relevant to the study of human perspectives.

Professional Personnel. I interviewed a total of twelve professionals: three Hispanic social workers from the two agencies, three Spanish-speaking liaison workers employed by the school district, the district's only Spanish-speaking psychologist, one Spanish-speaking middle school teacher, one middle school special education teacher, the chairman of the district's speech and language task force, and two senior administrators at the school district's central office.

Most of these selections were made on the basis of information from participants in the study as to persons they perceived as being actively involved in educational issues facing their own children or those in other Hispanic families. Others were made on advice from the school district office as to which educational administrators could inform me on demographic and policy data.

Interviews, Observations, and Review of Records

In many instances interviews and observations overlapped, since interviews were held in participants' homes and afforded many opportunities for me to observe/participate in informal discussions and activities. Information from students' records also contributed to the data.

For the most part, parent interviews were accomplished during the first 7 months of the study, and those with professionals were done in the eighth and ninth months, with the exception of two professionals whom I met frequently in the course of observing meetings. Interviews with all but one parent were conducted in Spanish, or, in a few cases, in a combination of Spanish and English. Interviews with professionals were conducted in English.

Upon meeting parents I explained the goals and procedures of the study and asked them to sign a consent form before beginning. Interviews were held at the participants' homes and were unstructured and informal, in the tradition of the ethnographic interview (Bogdan & Biklen, 1982; Spradley, 1979). Indeed, Oakley (1981) has referred to interviewing women as a "contradiction in terms" because of most women's preference for a reciprocal style of communication. I found this to be true of my interviews, which were more like chats in which I used my interview guidelines extremely flexibly, introducing questions at whichever point they seemed appropriate and adjusting the interview agenda in response to information volunteered by the participants and very often in response to questions posed by them to me.

I have called this a study of parents' views, although it is true that the bulk of my information came from mothers. While Hispanic culture is described as "patriarchal," it is also true that the responsibility for children's activities typically falls to the mothers (Delgado, 1980). Indeed, this is also the norm for mainstream American families. This was evident in the fact that, in all but three families, it was the mothers who attended school meetings or dealt with correspondence from the school. Further, four of the twelve mothers were single.

I interviewed the three fathers who did participate in school matters and have referred to them in the study. However, I must note that there were two constraints to my access to fathers: one, as a woman, it would not be culturally appropriate for me to spend a great deal of time interviewing the men or to ask personal questions, such as questions about feelings, which I could easily ask of the women; second, the men were seldom home on weekdays, which was the time that was most comfortable for myself and the mothers. On the occasions that I visited families on weekends, there were usually friends or relatives also visiting, including several children, which made interviewing difficult. These visits were useful to me mainly for observation rather than for verbal information from families. In ten of the families, I met the children; I discussed special education with four of them.

With the exception of one family who returned to Puerto Rico soon after my first interview, I held conversations with each family on at least three occasions, in visits that lasted from 2 to 3 hours. While the vast majority of interviews were taped, I made decisions about whether or not to tape on the basis of my judgment as to whether taping might interfere with a participant's level of comfort in speaking openly on sensitive matters and whether the noise and activity level of the household would make taping feasible. With all families I taped at least one interview, and with some families I taped at as many as four interviews.

In addition, many conversations were held on the way to meetings or other activities or on the phone. Where tape recording was not possible or appropriate, I recorded field notes immediately after the interviews. The verbatim quotations from participants reported in the text are taken from transcriptions of taped interviews; I have paraphrased those conversations that were not taped.

There were four participants whose homes I also visited on a friendly basis and with whom I participated in activities unrelated to my explicit research purposes, such as going to the supermarket, collecting children from preschool, or running other errands. The most special occasion was attending the wedding of one of the participants. These activities contributed a great deal to my understanding of important family and community values and helped to provide a background to information more directly related to my research.

Most district personnel were interviewed once, but the liaison worker attached to special education students was interviewed on three occasions. The two Hispanic social workers who introduced me to families accompanied me on the first visit to each home, so there were several opportunities for conversation with these informants in addition to formal interviews. Formal interviews with professional personnel were taped and typically lasted from 1½ to 3 hours.

In addition to casual and spontaneous observation of several events and settings as mentioned above, participant observation consisted mainly of my attendance at a total of seven special education meetings held for five families: five were annual review meetings between parents and the Committee on Special Education (CSE), one was a parent-initiated meeting with the teacher, and one a parent-initiated meeting with the bilingual psychologist.

I attended all meetings at the invitation of a parent but made it clear that my role was not that of advocate for the family. (While the validity and impact of intervention research with Hispanic families has been powerfully demonstrated by Delgado-Gaitan [1990], this was not my intention in this study.) On one occasion a parent asked me to act as interpreter, since the person who had agreed to interpret canceled at the last minute. Generally, my predominant style was that of "observer as participant" (McCall & Simmons, 1969), participating in meetings only enough to dispel any impression of myself as a "cold" researcher; I felt this was important for the comfort level of both professionals and parents. Meetings were not taped and I recorded field notes immediately after all observations.

Seven parents showed me whatever documents they had regarding their children's placement in special education. One of these also showed me documentation of her income benefits from Welfare and SSI. Five others said they could not find their records.

THE FOLLOW-UP STUDY

Two years after completion of the research I decided to conduct a brief follow-up to update the study and to check once more on the validity of my interpretations of the initial data.

Over the course of 2 months, I visited all but the three families who had since moved away from the city. I talked informally with all parents, gaining their permission to publish the findings of the study and summarizing the main points I intended to make. I taped more lengthy interviews with five of the mothers and succeeded in receiving a taped monologue from one mother who had moved away. I was not able to locate the other two families who had moved. In addition, I interviewed a mother who was emerging as an unusually vocal and effective advocate for her child and was being considered for possible appointment as a family liaison worker in the coming year. I also held a lengthy interview with the family liaison worker who had been a key informant from the professionals' point of view.

In addition, I observed four events:

1. A teacher training workshop organized by the family liaison worker, which emphasized the role of cooperative learning and "sheltered English" for Spanish-dominant students
2. A workshop for Latino parents in early childhood development
3. A meeting of a recently formed Latino community advocacy organization at which members were being addressed by the Bureau of the Census with regard to the upcoming 1990 census
4. A session of a new early childhood intervention project for Latino families, which emphasized mother-child participation in the program.

I also interviewed the director of the latter project to find out her impressions of the involvement of Latino mothers.

INTERPRETATION OF DATA

In interpreting the data I used the constant comparative method described by Glaser and Strauss (1967). In this approach, incidents are analyzed for similarities that reflect general categories; these are constantly compared with one another in order to discover a general theoretical framework that adequately interprets and explains the data. The emerging theory is gradually delimited and reduced to lead to the formulation of a small set of higher-level concepts.

My early analysis began with the identification of about fifty codes, which I gradually refined and delimited to five basic themes, each of which is represented by Chapters 6 through 10. For example, the theme of Chapter 7, parents' theories of the problem, represents my ultimate interpretation of a cluster of explanations about the meanings of disability, which I initially identified with codes such as "retarded or crazy," "language confusion," "language difference versus deficit," "family identity," "kindergarten curriculum," and "placement changes." As I listened to parents I realized that their comments constituted a body of theories about the role of cultural conflict in their children's schooling.

Thus I see the findings of this study as contributing to a growing body of information that seeks to clarify the dynamics of cross-cultural interaction between low-income minority populations and schools. The foregoing chapters have emphasized that the disability framework under which special education services operate has come under increasing attack by scholars who focus on the dissonance between schooling and culturally diverse communities. This study adds to that debate the voices of parents.

Lofland (1971) has made a distinction between "static" and "phase analysis" of social settings, the latter being more appropriate to the interactional and dynamic nature of human perspectives. In keeping with this formulation, the design of this study allowed for a process-oriented interpretation of the perspectives of the parents. The ability of this methodology to capture a process is evident in the data of the study. The research shows not a static picture of parents in conflict with a school system but an outline of the dynamics of cross-cultural confrontation, in which processes of challenge, response, retreat, and resolution reflect the uneven flow of change. If nothing else, I would hope that professionals will recognize the cultural assumptions on which their practice is based and the impact that cultural blindness can have on those they seek to serve.

6

Twelve Families
on the West Side

The twelve families who participated in this study lived in an area of the city known as the West Side. With only one exception, they lived on welfare benefits. With the same one exception, they were all first-generation, Spanish-speaking Puerto Ricans who had been living in the United States no longer than 12 years. At the time of the study they all had at least one child in special education, and five families had two or more children in special education. All told, these twelve families accounted for seventeen of the forty-eight Puerto Rican children placed in special education programs at the time of the study. In addition, one family had an older child who had exited the special education class and returned to regular education.

In this chapter I will offer a brief description of these participants and an outline of the main issues that dominate their lives as part of this inner-city Latino community. As described in the previous chapter, twelve professionals who work with this community or with the school district were also informants for the study. While the bulk of the data come from interviews and observations with families, I will also be referring to information and opinions offered by these professionals.

Before turning to an exploration of the data of the study, I will offer a brief profile of each family. For the most part, I will describe the mothers, referring specifically only to those fathers whom I interviewed. I will then give a more in-depth illustration through a close-up profile of one mother. All names have been changed, and the ages of children refer to their ages at the time of the study. The first mother, Ana, is the one who was introduced in Chapter 1.

PROFILES OF TWELVE FAMILIES

ANA, 28 years old, had been in the United States for 12 years. She is light-skinned with gray eyes and just a trace of Africa in her features, while her husband is much darker. Ana usually speaks Spanish but can also use a fluent mixture of English and Spanish, marked by a heavy Spanish accent. Her 12-year-old son, José, had been placed in special education in the first grade when the family was living in Connecticut. When he entered school in this district, he was placed in a regular first grade since Ana deliberately did not bring any records with her. José has remained in regular education ever since. Her second child, Gina, age 9, has been in a self-contained special education class since the first grade and was classified "mildly mentally retarded."

Francisca, age 57, had been in the United States for 12 years. She is light-skinned and speaks only Spanish. Her daughter, age 16, had been placed in special education between the ages of 10 and 14, with the classification "mildly mentally retarded," but had returned to regular education at the time of the study. Francisca was also the guardian of her 6-year-old granddaughter, Rosita, who was in a self-contained special education class, classified as "mildly mentally retarded."

Rita, age 32, speaks clear, increasingly fluent English after 6 years in the United States. Rita describes herself as "trigueña" (brown-skinned), with mixed African-European features. She is a single mother of five children whose daily schedule included taking her preschooler to and from school in the mornings, going to English classes for 3 hours in the afternoons, and then attending a cosmetology course from 4:00 p.m. to 9:00 p.m. Her eldest son, Rafael, was placed in a self-contained special education class upon entering the seventh grade 1 year prior to the study. He was classified as "learning disabled/language." Rosemary, Rita's 9-year-old, had been in a self-contained special education class since the first grade, classified as "mildly mentally retarded."

Dora, age 32, who had graduated from high school in Puerto Rico, had lived in the United States for 12 years. She understands English very well but lacks the confidence to speak it. Dora represents the type of racial mixture typically referred to in the English-speaking Caribbean as "Spanish," with light brown skin ("trigueña"), flashing dark eyes, and wavy black hair. She is a single mother of two children. The eldest, Maria, age 9, was in her first year in a special education resource program for reading and math, classified as "learning disabled/reading".

Margarita, age 36, looks 10 years younger than her age, has the same kind of looks as Dora, and is very petite. Like Dora, she understands English very well but is reluctant to speak it. She had been in the United States for 12 years and is the mother of six children, ranging in age from 2 to 17. Her 9-year-old son, Miguel, had recently been placed in a resource program, classified as "learning disabled/language."

Delia, age 38, had been in the United States for 6 years. She is light-skinned, very shy and soft-spoken, and speaks only Spanish. She is the mother of three children, with ages ranging from 5 to 14. The two eldest are in special education, labeled "learning disabled," one in a self-contained class and the other in a resource program.

JOSEFINA, who would be described as "piel oscura" (dark-skinned), is in her late 30s. Soon after the study began, she returned to join her husband in Puerto Rico after some 10 years in the United States. Josefina is the mother of five children, ranging in age from 5 to 21. One of the older boys had been in a special education resource program for some years in middle school and high school. Her youngest was in a self-contained class, classified as "mildly mentally retarded."

INÉS, age 27, had been in the United States for 2 years and speaks only Spanish. She describes herself as "trigueña" (brown-skinned). She is the only mother who says her child showed learning problems before coming here and the only parent who came to the United States specifically to seek education and treatment for her son. She is the mother of 3 children, the eldest of whom, Ricardo, age 11, is in a self-contained class and is classified as "learning disabled/reading."

RAMONA, age 27, was the only mainland-born participant in the study and speaks English with native fluency. Her husband is from Puerto Rico and speaks mostly Spanish. She is the only participant in the study who appears to be Caucasian rather than of mixed race. She has two children and the younger, 10-year-old Marisa, has been in a self-contained special education class since the first grade. She is classified as "mildly mentally retarded."

MARIA and JUAN, in their late 20s, had been in the United States for 5 years but returned to Puerto Rico shortly after the termination of the study. They speak only Spanish. Maria is dark-skinned while Juan is light-skinned. They have four children, the eldest of whom, Juanita, is Juan's child from a previous union. Juanita had been in a self-contained special education class since she came to the United States to join her father 2 years earlier. Her classification had recently been reviewed, at her father's request, and was changed from "emotionally disturbed" to "learning disabled/language."

CARMEN and FIDEL, both in their early 30s, had been in the United States for 6 years. They both speak only Spanish and are dark-skinned. They have four children ranging in age from 5 to 12. The two oldest had been in self-contained classes since the first or second grades, one classified as "mentally retarded" and the other as "learning disabled." The third child, age 7, had recently been referred to special education, with placement yet to be decided.

IRIS and ALFONSO are older than the other couples in the study, probably about 40 and 50 respectively. They had been in the United States for 12 or more years. Alfonso understands English and speaks with a marked

Spanish accent, while his wife speaks only Spanish. They have five children between the ages of 11 and 22. The youngest, Mark, had been in a special education resource program since the first grade and was classified "learning disabled." In the year prior to the study, Mark had expressed great unhappiness over his placement. His parents were in tremendous distress as a result.

INÉS:
A CLOSE-UP VIEW OF ONE MOTHER

By way of further illustration I will offer a more detailed sketch of Inés, a mother who was in many ways typical of and in other ways unique among the participants. Through similarities and contrast, I hope to illustrate the typical family situation of this group.

Inés is a tall, heavily built, and attractive woman of 27, whose light brown skin and facial features tell of African and European ancestry. Vivacious and outgoing, she speaks clear, rapid Spanish and no more than a few words of English. She left school in the ninth grade in Puerto Rico to be married at age 16. She had 3 children, Ricardo, age 11, Francisco, age 9, and Nita, age 7. During the course of the study, Inés got married for the second time, to Jaime.

Inés, Jaime, and the three children lived in a three-bedroom, two-story house paid for by welfare benefits and somewhat larger than those of the other families, who lived in duplexes or government townhouses. Like all the others, Inés's house was sparsely but neatly furnished and meticulously clean.

Despite a more spacious house, Inés's economic circumstances were typical of the other families in the study. Since her husband relied on seasonal work, mostly painting houses in the spring and summer, the family depended on welfare benefits. Inés explained that if her husband earned more than the welfare payments, he must forfeit these benefits, and it was seldom that he would get a job paying sufficiently more to make it worthwhile. In addition, their recent marriage had resulted in a reduction in her welfare benefits. Although this was distressing, she was not sorry, since she felt that, "as a Christian," she could no longer live in an unmarried union. She had just begun part-time work in a local laundry, and she said that as soon as her English was adequate she aimed to become independent through a better job. Meanwhile, she attended English classes at a voluntary agency in the area as a requirement of the welfare department.

Inés emphasized that she came to the United States with nothing:

No ha sido fácil! Yo he tenido problemas pero no puedo aceptar estan-
carme. Hay muchas personas que se conforman con lo que tienen, pero yo
no soy así. Cuando yo vine aquí, conseguí todo de donaciónes y poco a poco, podía sacar lo que no era bueno, y avanzar, poco a poco, hasta que me
siento satisfecha con lo que tengo. . . . Al principio, vivíamos en un aparta-
mento pequeño, con personas encima y abajo de nosotros, y nuestros hijos
no tenían ningún lugar donde jugar. Ahora tienen su propio patio y sus cuar-
tos—y yo no me voy a quedar aquí tampoco!

(It hasn't been easy! I have had problems but I can't accept becoming stag-
nant. There are many people who accept their lot, I do not! When I came
here I got everything from donations, and gradually I was able to get rid of
what was not good and progress, little by little, until I feel satisfied with what
I have. . . . At first we lived in a little apartment with people above and below us and my children had nowhere to play. Now they have their own yard
and rooms—and I am not going to stay here either!)

Inés acted on her words: that summer she was searching for an apartment in the area of Harper School, which all her children attended. This
was one point on which Inés was unique among the participants, most of
whom seldom left the West Side and expressed no interest in moving.
Indeed, hers was the only family in the study that made a point of leaving
the West Side so as to expose the children to different environments—they
had traveled by bus to Niagara Falls and New York City.

Inés presented a contrast to the other mothers in the study on several
other dimensions. She had been in the United States for only 2 years, while
the others had been here between 6 and 12 years. Most pertinent to this
study was the fact that Inés came to the United States specifically because
of Ricardo's difficulties and her dissatisfaction with the schooling and
"treatment" he was receiving. After what she described as several "emotional attacks" as a young child, he had been evaluated in Puerto Rico and
described as having "attention deficit disorder." Inés was unique among the
participants in that she accepted the notion of Ricardo's difficulties as a
"disability" but felt that it was mostly emotional in nature and resulted
from unhappy family circumstances in his early childhood. In Puerto Rico,
she had not been satisfied with his placement in a regular, large class and
the hospital's constant changing of medications, which only resulted in
making him apathetic and sleepy.

When I asked her if Ricardo was the only reason she had come to the
United States, she replied: "El problema era Ricardo en el centro, pero
alrededor del centro estaba mi familia, y a resolverse el problema de Ricar-

do era resolverse el problema de todos nosotros." (The problem was Ricardo at the center, but around the center was my family, and to solve the problem of Ricardo was to solve the problem of us all.)

Ricardo, classified for special education placement as "learning disabled/reading," had completed two years in a nongraded self-contained class at Harper School. His psychological evaluation in 1986 described him as showing "low self-esteem, timidity, hostility, and a low tolerance for frustration" and a great deal of "attention-seeking behavior." The report stated that Ricardo "consistently demonstrated average cognitive skills" but added that his ability in drawing suggested that these scores "may be an underestimate." In a 1986 report, Ricardo was said to know "very little, if any English." Two years later, in the spring of 1988, his teacher reported at the annual review that "Ricardo expresses himself very well in English, better than many of the English-speaking children."

Inés saw Ricardo's problem in terms of "emotional control" and behavior and believed that if he could only settle down, academic progress would follow. Ricardo was a "problem" both at school and at home, and, according to his mother, "even in church." However, my only opportunity to see Ricardo in church was at his mother's wedding, an occasion on which the notion of disability would never have occurred to anyone as being appropriate to the young man who gave away the bride.

Inés and Jaime's wedding was held in a simple evangelical church on Garfield Street, which marks the southern border of the West Side. Of a congregation of some fifty people, at least half were children. I found the ceremony solemn and awe-inspiring, the cadences familiar despite the foreignness of the formal Spanish in which the traditional vows and dedications were offered.

Inés's tall, full figure dominated as she walked slowly up the aisle in step with the wedding march. In front of her was 7-year-old Nita, carrying flowers for her mother, and, next in line, 9-year-old Francisco, bearing the wedding ring. The small figure at Inés's side was Ricardo, his brown curls standing several inches below his mother's shoulder, his earlier excitement transformed into a shy smile and an expression of immense pride. Clutching his mother's elbow and wearing a light gray suit and pink tie, he was the image of any mother's ideal child.

But most days of the week, Ricardo gave his mother "a huge headache." A week after the wedding, Ricardo was in trouble again at school for fighting on the bus and at home for fighting with his brother and sister all weekend. His mother did not believe in spanking him but said that her admonishments and sending him to his room did not really work. Despite her distress, she could not help laughing as she described how sending

Ricardo to his room for fighting over a basketball game with his brother only resulted in his leaning out the window of his room and throwing his little cars into the basketball net!

Inés found it a struggle to keep her patience with Ricardo, whom she described as unable to control his behavior. She said that the worst part of such a problem for a mother is the attitude of other people toward her child:

> A nadie le gusta un niño hiperactivo. Es muy doloroso para una madre ver que nadie quiere estar cerca de su niño—que los demás en la sociedad lo rechazan y dicen que es un niño malcriado y que no se le ha enseñado disciplina. Yo enseño y disciplino a mis hijos, pero Ricardo ha tenido este problema desde que él tenía 3 ó 4 años cuando había gran tristeza en mi matrimonio, y lo afectó. Quiero a todos mis hijos, pero mi corazón está con Ricardo porque él tiene tantos problemas en su vida.

> (No one likes a hyperactive child. It is very painful for a mother to see that no one wants to be near your child—that others in the society reject him and say that he is badly brought up and has not been taught discipline. I do train and discipline my children, but Ricardo has had this problem since he was 3 or 4 years old, when there was great unhappiness in my marriage and it affected him. I love all my children, but my heart goes out to Ricardo because he has so much trouble in his life.)

ACCULTURATION, AUTHORITY, AND THE FAMILY

Inés's intense involvement with her children was typical of all the mothers in the study. Only one mother, Ramona, worked outside the home, and she would have preferred to stay home so that her children would not have to stay with neighbors after school. All saw their chief role as responsibility for the home and the care and training of children. They took great pride in their work.

This pride was expressed in different forms. One was housekeeping; whether the families lived in one floor of a multidwelling house, a four-bedroom government-built townhouse, or a single-family dwelling, and regardless of the outer condition of the buildings, the interiors of these homes were immaculate. Despite shabby or sparse furnishing, the walls and shelves were decorated with statuettes, pictures, and trinkets, many of which were souvenirs of Puerto Rico.

The strongest statement of these mothers' pride in their families could be seen in the children themselves. I commented to Teresa, the social worker who introduced me to several families, that the children were particularly neat and tidy. She replied that one could identify the Latino kids on the street "by the way their hair is combed and the way they are dressed and scrubbed, even if they are wearing old clothes."

Nevertheless, my interviews with the mothers revealed the pervasive conflict between their attempts to fulfill traditional expectations of parenting and the undermining influence of the acculturation process being experienced by their children. The fact that the children spoke English was one contributor to the widening gap in some families. Ana, for example, told of a "trick" her son played on her, by getting her to sign permission for him to be a "walker" to school. She signed the paper and then was horrified to find that her son was now walking to school instead of traveling on the school bus.

Inés explained the problem in this way:

Cuando los niños llegan a la edad de adolescente, es natural que cambien—sus humores, sus pensamientos, sus actos todos cambian. Pero aquí en los Estados Unidos, los niños tienen tanta libertad—hay niños de 6 y 7 años en la calle. Entonces, los niños Latinos ven esta libertad en los Americanos y ellos creen que también ellos tienen derecho a esta libertad.

Pero algunas costumbres de aquí pueden ser muy distintas a las de Puerto Rico, porque en Puerto Rico aunque un niño tenga 12, 13, 14 años y aún 16 ó 18 años, si el papá dice, "Tú no vas para la calle," el niño no va para la calle. Entonces, cuando mi papá a mí me decía, a la edad de 14 años, "Tú no puedes salir de la casa," yo no le decía, "Papá, déjame ir." Dos veces no se lo decía. Pero aquí los muchachos insisten y insisten y hasta aun a veces se van sin permiso. Para nosotros, por lo menos para mí, se me hace difícil. Los niños le responden y argumentan.

(When children get to adolescence, it is natural that they will change—their moods, their thoughts, their actions all change. But here in the United States the children have so much freedom—there are children 6 and 7 years old in the street. So the Latino children see this freedom in the Americans and they feel that they also should have the right to this freedom.

But some customs here may be very different from those in Puerto Rico, because in Puerto Rico even if a child is 12, 13, 14 years old, or even 16 or 18, if the father says "you cannot go in the street," the child does not go in the street. So when my father would say to me at the age of 14 years, "You cannot leave this house," I would not say, "Papa, let me go!" You didn't ask twice! But here the children insist and insist and sometimes they even go without permission. For us, at least for me, this is very difficult. The children answer you back and they argue.)

Beyond having to negotiate new meanings of authority within the family itself, these parents were also faced with the challenge of redefining the relationship of the family unit to the society at large. The pressures of culturally different definitions of the role and authority of parents in the host society were evident in the following comment by Ana:

> The doctor says I am too young to have the operation [tubal ligation] but I don't want any more children because they are too much headache when they start growing up! They don't have so much respect like they used to, especially here, the kids don't respect you because you have too many problems in the family court or in the school or whatever and I don't like that.

Ana's reference to the family court reflects a deep resentment among these families toward the powerful authority exercised by the state over roles traditionally reserved for the family. Ana, for example, objected to the school's referring to her child's absence from school as "illegal." Francisca also said that once she had to go to the family court because the school has to report a certain number of absences, even if the parent sends an excuse. The magistrate, she said, dismissed the complaint because he realized that the doctor had said her granddaughter was sick.

This clash between family and state presented a fearful challenge to the parents' sense of authority. Teresa, a South American social worker who had lived in the United States for 18 years and who had worked with families on the West Side for 3 years, focused on corporal punishment as one example of this conflict:

> In our countries, when children get spanked, they do not think their parents don't love them. I knew my parents did it because they loved me. They taught me manners and to be obedient. That's the way they see it. But here it's a whole different ballgame and the parents feel like they're in a system that is very fearful because if you behave like a parent should behave, you might lose your children. And the kids use the system. I know kids who have turned their parents in. The kid learns the system right away. So the parents feel helpless. . . . It's not that they hit all the time—it's a last alternative, but you use it and there is a case worker at your door. So the parents are frightened, they feel they're losing control of their children. Child Protective—Children's Division! That's the most feared word on the whole West Side!

These comments point to three main concerns: conflicting sociocultural norms regarding acceptable parenting styles; conflicting sociocultural norms regarding the power of the state versus the family; and the influence of social welfare authorities in the lives of low-income families in particular.

Teresa's comments indicate that the first two of these concerns were intertwined as parents experienced the conflict and confusion of those who stand between two cultures, or what Laosa (1981) has described as a "socioculture-contact situation . . . under conditions of rapid change when patterns of behavior that are adaptive within one sociocultural community are considered maladaptive or deviant in another setting or under new conditions" (p. 162). Laosa's use of the term *socioculture*, which indicates the concept of overlap between social class and cultural features, is important in this discussion because of the frequent finding that both lower social class and cultural minority status tend to be associated with more punitive patterns of child rearing (Laosa, 1981). However, there is a third factor in this pattern of overlap—that of changing values within American culture over time, since it is also true that what may be described as culturally normative parenting today in the United States really reflects recent developments in the notion of children's rights, in contrast to traditional assumptions of parental authority in the socialization of children (Hess, 1981). Thus the greater use of physical punishment among lower-class Anglo families may reflect a lag in the acceptance of newly developed cultural norms, which are exemplified more often by the middle class. Further, Hess (1981) has emphasized that "the rise in the influence of children that is evident in the United States has not occurred in many other countries" (p. 221).

To observe cultural and/or social-class differences in child-rearing styles is not, however, tantamount to valuing one style over another, and this is the point so eloquently made in the above comments by Teresa. Laosa (1983) has emphasized that judgments about appropriate parenting can only be made in the context of what is culturally normative for a particular group and that formulae for customary parenting that are efficient under stable social conditions may create conflict under conditions of rapid change. Teresa's comments reveal the difficulty parents experience in understanding the authorities' definitions of child abuse, as well as the confusion and self-doubt occasioned by ambiguous interpretations.

A third area of concern, however, is the possibility of bias against low-income families in judgments concerning child abuse. When such parents use disciplinary measures that are culturally normative for them, they may be more vulnerable to inappropriate accusation than are middle-class parents. McLoyd (1990), in a review of literature on poverty and child abuse, indicated that, while there is an established association between these two factors, there are also studies suggesting that estimates may be biased by social-class prejudice and by the greater involvement of social service agencies in the lives of low-income families.

Indeed, I was struck by the frequency with which I met social workers, parent aides, and various representatives of public authorities in the homes. The impact of this on the role of fathers was also explained to me by Teresa:

> The women deal with the agencies—the welfare, child care, whatever. The man stays in the background because he's embarrassed. You know it's very difficult for them to get any kind of employment. So here is an able-bodied man who is dependent on the government to support his family. It's not that they're lazy—they get caught in a system that does not offer any incentives.
>
> For example, if a man works for a certain time, say, on the farm, he pays taxes; then when the tax refund check comes, Welfare takes theirs right off the top. Or say there is an accident and they get any money from insurance, Welfare gets theirs first. The same goes for SSI benefits—for kids with more severe disabilities they can get SSI, but the parent is cut back from welfare and from the food stamps for the amount they got from SSI. So it's not something extra—the only thing is that SSI is a more secure benefit that you can get without all the hassle of having to go to the civic center, where there are only two bilingual people and one of them doesn't like to let anybody know that she is bilingual. And all the papers for the Hispanic families are in English. All of them, unless it is a fair-hearing paper, you know, telling you the date.

Thus the life of this community is filled with the influences of public assistance, which, while it gives support, also represents a structure of authority that can control and influence the private aspects of one's life. These observations point to the combined power of the acculturation process and official authorities to undermine the cohesiveness and strength of traditional families. A sense of powerlessness, brought about by the devaluing of cultural difference, poverty, and little formal education, was evident in many aspects of these families.

Nevertheless, all the mothers said that their families were financially better off in the United States than in Puerto Rico. Rita, a single mother of five, explained that it is not only because of the increased welfare benefits, but because the society is set up to allow poor people to live cheaper if they have to. Her example of this was the availability of second-hand stores, where she could get anything she wants without having to turn to charity. Dora, another single mother of two, used the example of buying second-hand classical music records for her 9-year-old daughter, Maria, to practice her ballet steps. Further, Maria's ballet lessons were given for a token fee by the local school for the arts.

Yet in spite of their improved standard of living, all the mothers replied with a unanimous "No!" when I asked if they liked the United States better than Puerto Rico. They were here for a purpose, or perhaps, in the words of Morales (1986), because they "just had to try elsewhere."

PUERTO RICAN AMERICAN IDENTITY

One of the first things I tried to find out from these families was how they defined their identity in the United States. The response was consistent: all the participants described themselves as "Puerto Rican Americans." Ramona, the only U.S.-born participant, made the point most strongly:

> I am not American—I am Puerto Rican American. I was born in the United States but I am not ashamed of being Puerto Rican, and if I were to not say I am Puerto Rican, it would be like denying my heritage. I don't really use the word *Hispanic* for myself—if it's on a form I have to fill out, I'll check it, but I think of myself as Puerto Rican.
>
> The thing is, sometimes they don't know if you're Puerto Rican or Cuban or what—but still, like at work, they say, "Oh, it's the Puerto Ricans!" I say, "Don't look at me, I didn't do it. It's not my problem!"

Ramona speaks English with no trace of a Spanish accent. While she also speaks Spanish, she reads and writes only in English, since all her schooling was in the United States. Her husband and all his family are Puerto Rican–born and speak Spanish in the home. This was the only home in the study in which both English and Spanish were used regularly.

Ramona's strong emphasis on a Puerto Rican identity was typical of all the participants, as was the notion that Puerto Ricans are negatively stereotyped and "blamed" for any wrongdoing by Spanish-speaking people. In addition, there is one characteristic that sets Puerto Ricans apart from other Hispanic people, and that is American citizenship. Every participant made this point. Inés's words were typical of the group:

> Yo diría que hay mucho prejuicio contra los hispanos aquí en los Estados Unidos. Lo que sucede es que, entre nosotros los hispanos siempre hay grupitos que hacen cosas que no son correctas, quienes no tienen disciplina, que sean cubanos, puertorriqueños, o del otro lado; y por ese grupo, nos catalogan a todos iguales. Han salido muchos problemas con los latinos en el Westside y cuando se leen los periódicos, hablan como si todos somos así. No hablan del grupo que quiere progresar y quiere estar tranquilo, entonces, como resultado, no nos aceptan.

(I would say there is a lot of prejudice against Spanish-speaking people here in the United States. What happens is that, among us there are always little groups who do wrong, who have no discipline, whether it is Cubans, Puerto Ricans, or from somewhere else, and because of that group, they classify us all as the same. There have been many problems with Latinos on the West

Side and when you read the newspapers, they speak as if we are all like that. They don't talk about the group who wish to progress and to be peaceful, so as a result, we are not accepted.)

Y además, la mayoría de los americanos no saben que NOSOTROS somos ciudadanos americanos, que nosotros no somos como, digamos, como los cubanos—estamos incluidos en los mismos derechos que tienen los ameri-canos. Nosotros no somos extranjeros. Nosotros somos ciudadanos ameri-canos, porque la ley así lo dice.

(And furthermore, the majority of Americans don't know that WE are Ameri-can citizens, that we are not like, say, Cubans—we are included in the same rights as Americans. We are not foreigners. Under the law, we are American citizens.)

Ana's husband, the only father in the study to comment on this issue, emphasized the voluntary nature of their status, pointing out that while Puerto Ricans are American citizens, the Cubans are in the United States "por Castro" (because of Castro) and cannot return to their homeland.

This unique characteristic was used by professionals in the study to explain certain features of the Puerto Rican community, in particular, a marked transience, in which families may come to live in the United States, return to Puerto Rico, and then come back to the mainland. Some professionals in the study attributed "low motivation" on the part of Puerto Rican students to the idea that they felt "they could always go back to Puerto Rico." This mobility was also thought by some to be related to a reliance on public assistance and slow progress in the learning of English. Isabel, a Puerto Rican social worker with one of the voluntary agencies, felt that this dual identity placed Puerto Ricans in a difficult position:

See—the problem with Puerto Rican people is that we are Americans by birth-right. . . . Yet we are excluded by the Americans and we get excluded by the Latino Americans. So we're in the middle of nowhere . . . in search of an identity. . . . The barriers here are not only language. To tell you the truth, I think there are people who are just too white to deal with us. There is al-ways racism in different places, but when I came here I began feeling the weight of racism for the first time. . . . It's a new problem for us that we didn't confront before. They don't want us because we are—what?—Puerto Rican? But we are Americans! No—we are Latinos! No—we are Hispanics! So, it's like—even if THEY were not born here, like people from Ireland or Poland, they are white, white, white! You know, they get nationalized, then they are American. But what about us? We are still Americans. What is the problem?

With the primary identity of "Puerto Rican" established, all the parents accepted the term *Hispanic* as a larger group to which they belonged, and while all were equally comfortable with the term *Latino*, a few adopted the local community organization's (LAA) preference for the latter. Indeed, the controversy over terminology was evident only in my discussions with professionals, such as Isabel, an agency social worker, who explained that the term *Hispanic* was perceived by many people as carrying "a racist connotation . . . a sign of disrespect," since it is used mostly by outsiders referring to Spanish-speaking people. Others, however, preferred *Hispanic* to *Latino*. The parents mostly said it did not matter, since their primary identification was "Puerto Rican."

One thing they all agreed on was that neither term included people from Spain, whom they thought of as "Europeans" or "Spaniards." Thus the identity claimed by all the participants, whether parents or professionals, Puerto Ricans or South Americans, held one factor in common, that of being Spanish-speaking people from the Americas. Along with this was a consensus that Americans are intolerant of the Spanish language; Isabel echoed the comments of many participants when she said that she gets "dirty looks" if she and her husband speak in Spanish in a shopping mall. Beyond the bond of a common language, however, nationality, social class, and race seem to cut across the general identity "Hispanic/Latino."

Nationality, Language, and Social Class

All the parents said that while Spanish is the common factor in the identity "Hispanic," the many differences in vocabulary and pronunciation from one country to another often make communication between South Americans and Puerto Ricans difficult. Both South American social workers, Rosana and Teresa, spoke of their need to earn the acceptance of the Puerto Rican community, and while they described these efforts in different ways, the common denominator seemed to be the challenge of crossing social class rather than national boundaries. In Teresa's words:

> I've never had any trouble working in the field in this community, and the people here are all from Puerto Rico. I think it is because, as one woman told me last week, "You have always treated us like you were one of us . . . you'll always sit down and talk to people, never prejudiced because maybe we are poor or have little education."

Another social worker, Rosana, spoke of language and behavioral adaptations she found it necessary to make in order to be accepted by her Puerto Rican clients:

When I started working here, they didn't understand a word I was saying . . . so I learned to speak like a Puerto Rican! Like one day, I spoke to a parent and she said, "You learning to speak Spanish?" and I said, "No, I speak Spanish." She said, "I don't understand what you're saying." I said, "It's because I have an accent from the central part of my country; if you talk to some people from the coast of my country, they talk with an accent close to yours."

Another thing is commands—like I will say "Please come," but if I say that to a kid, he won't understand me. They would say "Vente!"/"Avanza!" (Come!/Hurry up!). If I don't use that, the kids won't respond the same.

But this is not common in all Puerto Ricans. Some of them are very educated, but we don't have a big group of educated people here. . . . Among educated people the language is the same . . . but the people here are mostly from little towns with less education and different dialects. And they may have different facilities so there are many things for them to get used to. I cannot ask them for any more. So I have learned to greet them as they greet everybody—I go driving down the street, and I will roll my window down and say, "Hi! How's it going?"—that type of thing.

These comments reveal an important point that must always be acknowledged — that values related to social class are an integral part of any culture. Thus, the sharing of a common culture does not preclude communication barriers based on class differences.

Race, Language, and Social Class

With the exception of Ramona, all the parents in the study were either racially mixed or, by American standards, Black, while the professionals, both Puerto Rican and South American, were all predominantly Caucasian. No one used the term *Black*, however, when referring to Puerto Ricans, this term being reserved for Black Americans, while the terms *trigueña* (brown-skinned) or *piel oscura* (dark-skinned) were used to describe themselves. Dora, who would be described as "trigueña," said:

Bien, tú sabes, que ellos tienen dos clases de americanos—negro y blanco. Yo no entiendo esto porque en Puerto Rico hay personas de todos los colores, pero nosotros no llamamos a nadie negro o blanco, ellos son todos puertorriqueños. Yo tengo familia que son de piel oscura pero nosotros nunca hablamos así.

(Well, you know, they have two kinds of Americans—Black and White. I don't understand it because in Puerto Rico there are people of all colors, but we don't call anybody "Black" or "White," they are just "Puerto Ricans." I have family who are dark-skinned but we never speak like that.)

Thus these families did not think of themselves as "Black" and did not think that Americans considered them "Black" either. They explained that they were likely to be the object of racism from American Blacks as well as Whites. Inés, who would be described as "trigueña," made this clear when she complained that a Black teacher in Ricardo's school was very rough with the Hispanic children, and the children believed that he was a "racist." In addition, she complained that the Black children, whom she refered to as "los Africanitos" (the little Africans), were always picking on her children and using very bad language.

The difference in terminology reflects the socially determined nature of racial classifications, which was observed in the Chapter 1 discussion of the U.S. Department of Education's classification of students. The fact that race is seen as dichotomous in the United States can present problems for racially mixed peoples from territories that use more continuous classifications. This does not mean that these societies do not attach differential value to different racial mixtures; indeed, there has been a traditional association of lighter skin with higher social class, use of the standard dialect, and higher education; it is also true, however, that these boundaries tend to be flexible and increasingly responsive to education and social class as levers for social mobility. Lewis (1963), nevertheless, has pointed out that the more subtle racism of postcolonial territories such as Puerto Rico and other Caribbean and South American nations is no less real than categorical racial value systems.

An example of the overlapping of social class, race, and language was evident in the frequency with which many participants in the study advised me that I would probably find the speech of dark-skinned Puerto Ricans from Loiza difficult to understand. This community continues to be seen as more "African" in culture than the wider society, a characteristic that has traditionally been devalued by colonial societies.

Rita's comment that Black Americans "are very different from us" was typical of the view of most parents. Nevertheless, Rita explained:

> In Puerto Rico there is prejudice too, there are some white Puerto Ricans who do not even want to speak to dark-skinned people, but here [in the United States] Puerto Ricans stick together more because the Americans are so prejudiced.

This comment suggests that on the U.S. mainland, Puerto Ricans may feel caught between the racial values of their homeland and those of the United States; as a result, racial classifications take on new dimensions, and "Puerto Rican" becomes almost a "race." For example, Isabel, the social worker who said that in the United States she "felt the weight of racism for the first time," is very light-skinned, with mostly Caucasian features, and would almost certainly be considered White in Puerto Rico or other parts of the Caribbean.

SUMMARY

For parents in this study, living in the United States meant having a better standard of living than in Puerto Rico, despite having to rely on welfare benefits. It meant having to forge a sense of self that would redefine the boundaries of one's authority as a parent, one's role as a husband or wife, one's racial identity within a two-dimensional racial structure, and one's value in a community where one's language and culture are not valued.

Being a Puerto Rican American, then, meant a number of things. It meant being from a Puerto Rican family, regardless of place of birth; it meant being an American citizen; it meant belonging to a larger group called "Hispanic" or "Latino," whose common characteristic is being Spanish-speaking and from Latin America; it meant being of a variety of racial combinations, which may have implications for social class, language, and education; and, in the United States, it meant being classified as "Puerto Rican," not "Black," regardless of race.

Francisca, a parent whose opinions will appear frequently in the following chapters, spoke for everyone in the following exchange:

> *Reseacher*:   Your granddaughter was born here?
> *Francisca*:   Mmhm.
> *Researcher*:   So she is an American?
> *Francisca*:   (smiling) Puerto Rican American!

7

Making Sense
of Disability

Parents' Theories of the Problem

The needs and expectations of a society will determine the measure by which its members' behavior will be labeled deviant and the extent to which that deviance will be stigmatized (Becker, 1969). Our discussion of labeling in Chapter 3 showed how the meanings attached to labels of disability, such as "retarded" or "handicapped," vary among societies and among groups within a society, as well as being subject to change over time. An earlier discussion of differing cultural views, in Chapter 2, emphasized that interpretations of the meaning of disability may be affected by the causes attributed to disability, by views of the family, and by beliefs about the relationship between physical and spiritual phenomena.

The language of the Education for All Handicapped Children Act (EHA), however, reflects none of this ambiguity and the process of reification is nowhere so obvious as in the conception of disability inherent in special education theory and practice—the belief that a child's failure to master certain skills is indicative of an objectively identifiable, intrinsic deficit. The limitations of the assessment process are recognized by the law in its call for measures to ensure unbiased assessment, yet the subjective nature of the process is inescapable and becomes most evident with students from culturally diverse backgrounds. Indeed, the ongoing debate over assessment and instruction of minority students, which was outlined in Chapter 3 (e.g., Duran, 1989; Figueroa et al., 1989b; Heller et al., 1982; Ortiz & Polyzoi, 1986), reflects the elusive nature of the search for a definitive dividing line between special and regular education and the arbitrariness of the designation " disability" for many students with mild learning disorders. For many minority students, underachievement is the point at which regular and special education meet, with many students from what has been called "the mental withdrawal—grade retention—

drop-out syndrome" (Stein, 1986) crossing the border from "normalcy" to "disability."

The argument that disability is a socially constructed phenomenon is readily demonstrated in designations such as "mild mental retardation," "learning disability," and "behavior disorder." Indeed, the arbitrary nature of the term *mental retardation* was dramatically demonstrated by the American Association on Mental Deficiency (AAMD), in its radical revision of the definition from an IQ cutoff point of 85 to a mere 70. Overnight, the population of mentally retarded persons was cut by 13 percent (Hardman, Drew, Egan, & Wolf, 1990).

At the other end of the spectrum, the concept of excellence is equally relative to cultural values and goals. In a provocative discussion of the current emphasis in the United States on excellence in education, Spener (1988) argues that the United States is experiencing not a crisis of literacy, but a crisis of an overeducated workforce, which allows employers to arbitrarily raise educational requirements for jobs. This, he says, has the effect of further enforcing what Ogbu (1978) has called a "job ceiling," which keeps minorities from moving up the social ladder. This argument underscores the way that a society can constantly define and redefine its borders for success and failure.

Chapter 6 outlined certain dimensions of culture that Puerto Rican families entering this society may bring with them, and the ways in which they must redefine their identities to find a place within the mainstream culture of the United States. This chapter will examine the impact of yet another redefinition — the school system's classification of their children as having mild disabilities. These Puerto Rican parents, entering the United States at the bottom of the social ladder, demonstrate that differing perspectives on disability can have far-reaching effects.

PERSPECTIVES ON DISABILITY

Interviews with parents showed three ways in which meanings of disability differed along cultural lines for these families. First, the parameters of "normality" in terms of childrens' development were much wider than those used by the educational system; second, different designations for disability led to parents' confusion of terms like *handicap* and *retarded* with more extreme forms of impairment; and third, these designations sometimes carried particular moral meanings, notably the notion that characteristics ascribed to one family member may reflect on the character and health of the family as a whole. In addition, and no less important, was the fact that the parents held their own theories explaining their children's difficulties. The following sections will use quotations from parents to illustrate the findings.

Francisca:
A Story of Meaning

Francisca is 57 years old. Trim and tidy, she carries herself with a quiet dignity, her mostly gray hair drawn back in a bun or combed down in well-shaped waves around her face. Her expression and voice are at first placid and low-keyed, but both become more varied, sometimes querulous and sometimes imperious, as a conversation develops. As far as I could tell, she speaks no English. All our conversations took place in the immaculately kept living room of her modern three-bedroom townhouse, one of the city's more recent housing projects located in the midst of the older houses on the West Side.

Francisca has had years of experience with the special education system. Her daughter, Angelica, had been placed in a program for children labeled educable mentally retarded (EMR) when she was between the ages of 8 and 12. At the time of the study she had returned to the regular program, but Francisca's 6-year-old grandaughter, Rosita, of whom she was guardian, was at the time in special education, classified as mildly mentally retarded.

The following was Francisca's account of her daughter's initial referral to special education. This story is representative of the way in which many families described the initial referral of a child for special education services. For many it was a moment of crisis, marking the onset of a period of confusion and distress.

Cuando los niños eran pequeños, siempre yo iba a buscarlos y llevarlos a la escuela. Un día, cuando la más pequeña esteba en segundo grado, fui a buscarla y cuando yo estaba caminando por la calle Spruce, la niña vino corriendo y gritando. Yo me asusté y creía que pasaba algo. Cuando ella llegó cerca de mí, me apretó y se me tiró encima, y gritó, "¡Mamí!" Yo dije, "¡Dios mío! ¿Qué te pasó?" Y ella me dijo, "¡La maestra me dijo que yo no fuera más a su clase, que ella no va a bregar más conmigo porque yo soy loca!"

Entonces fui a la escuela y les dije que la nena no es loca, pero me mandaban estas cartas y las llevé a la Asociación Latina Americana y pregunté a alguien que quieren decir las cartas y me dijeron que quieren decir que su hija es retardada. La pusieron en las clases especiales aunque les dije en la reunión que ninguna persona que es retardada, que no tiene una mente buena, puede hacer el trabajo difícil de la escuela como la nena lo

hace. Ella hace todo el trabajo de la escuela, pero mandan esta carta solamente porque la muchacha es lenta.

Entonces, fuí a la escuela y les dije que dejaran de mandar estas cartas
porque la nena las ve; ella sabe inglés y las lee y se pone preocupada y dice,
"Yo no voy más a la escuela hasta que dejen de decir que yo soy loca, porque no soy loca." Les dije que ellos mismos van a hacer que algo entre en la
mente de la nena y me han dado el trabajo de quitar esta idea de la mente
de ella.

Ella ya no está en las clases especiales, y a veces ella baja del punto,
porque ella está en grado nueve, y a veces el trabajo es muy fuerte y tiene
que bajar del punto, pero ella siempre trata y hace el trabajo. . . .

Ahora están diciendo lo mismo de mi nieta, pero ella no tiene nada ma-
lo en su mente tampoco. Se porta bien, y habla claramente en ambos el español y el inglés. ¿Por qué dicen ellos que la nena es retardada?

Ellos dicen que la palabra "handicap" quiere decir muchas cosas, no
solo quiere decir que una persona está loca. Pero, para nosostros, los puertorriqueños, ya entendemos esta palabra como loco. Para mí, una persona
"handicapped" que sea una persona que no esté bien de la mente o que
tenga problema de las manos o de las piernas. Pero mis hijas no tienen nada
de eso, gracias a Dios y la Virgen.

(When the children were small I always used to go and collect them from
school. One day, when my youngest daughter was in the second grade, I
went to get her and as I was walking along Spruce Street the child came running toward me screaming. I was very frightened and thought that something
terrible had happened. When she got close to me she grabbed me and
threw herself on me and shrieked, "Mommy!" I said, "My God! What has
happened to you?" And she said to me, "The teacher told me that I must not
come to her class anymore, that she is not going to deal with me anymore
because I am crazy!"

So I went to the school and I told them the child is not crazy, but they
started sending me these letters and I took them to the Latin American Association (LAA) and asked someone what they said and they told me it said the
child is retarded. They put her in the special class although I told them at the
meeting that no person who is retarded, who does not have a good mind,
can do the hard schoolwork she does. She does all the schoolwork, but they
send this letter just because the girl is slow.

When she got a bit older I went to the school and told them to stop
sending these letters because the child sees them, she knows English and
she reads them and she gets very upset and says, "I am not going back to the
school unless they stop saying I am crazy because I am not crazy." I told
them that they themselves are going to make something wrong with the girl's
mind and they have given me a job to get this idea out of her mind.

She is not in the special class anymore, and sometimes she falls below
the level, because she is in ninth grade, and sometimes the work is very

hard, and she has to fall back, but she always tries and does the work. . . .

Now they are saying the same thing about my granddaughter, but she has nothing wrong with her mind either. She behaves well and she speaks clearly in both Spanish and English. Why do they say she is retarded? . . .

They [Americans] say that the word *handicap* means a lot of things, it doesn't just mean that a person is crazy. But for us, Puerto Ricans, we still understand this word as "crazy." For me, a person who is handicapped is a person who is not of sound mind or has problems in speech or some problem of the hands or legs. But my children have nothing like that, thanks to God and the Virgin!)

The Meaning of the Labels

Most parents were initially as incredulous as Francisca at the assignment of the label mentally retarded. Coming from a background where daily affairs can be managed by a healthy body, common sense, and elementary academic skills, parents explained that the label retarded or handicapped would be applied only to someone whose competence is severely impaired or who is considered mentally deranged. Thus the labeling of Francisca's daughter and granddaughter seemed a contradiction in terms. How could a person who is retarded read and become incensed by the very letter that describes her as retarded? How could a 6-year-old who speaks both English and Spanish be retarded?

In addition to different parameters for normal development, the word *retardado* was tied to the general category of mental illness — a tremendously stigmatized form of social deviance. Ana, speaking in terms very similar to Francisca's, made a clear distinction between "retarded" and "handicapped":

Para mí, retardado es loco, en español es *retardado*. Para mí la palabra *handicapped* es una persona que esté incapacitada, como mentalmente, o que le falte una pierna, o que sea ciego o sordo, que no pueda trabajar y no pueda hacer nada . . . pero, para los americanos *handicapped* es todo el mundo.

(For me retarded is crazy, in Spanish that's *retardado*. For me the word *handicapped* means a person who is incapacitated, like mentally, or missing a leg, or who is blind or deaf, who cannot work and cannot do anything . . . but for Americans *handicapped* is everybody.)

For parents to accept the use of the word *retarded* they must start by differentiating it from the word *loco*. Most parents who made this transition substituted the word *slow*. Rita, for example, had made an effort to understand the school's use of the label "retarded"; however, she differentiated this from a more extreme form of retardation, explaining that it really meant "que mi niña aprende lentamente, pero no está muy retardada como algunos niños que no saben lo que hacen" (that my child learns slowly, but is not very retarded like some children who do not know what they are doing).

Accepting that a child is slow was not always easy, however, since parents would still need to see the child's performance as significantly different from their own expectations. This became confusing for parents whose own level of education was at the third- or fourth-grade level and who had a child already in the fifth or sixth grade or who was bilingual while the parent found English very difficult to learn. The system of nongraded special education classes added to the confusion. One mother, Carmen, exclaimed angrily:

> ¡Ellos me dijeron que la niña necesitaba ir a un salón especial porque estaba loca! Me dijeron un montón de porquería que estaba en los records de la escuela. Yo no estoy muy segura en que grado está mi hija, si en cuarto o en quinto, pero la maestra dice que el año que viene ella va a estar en escuela intermedia, porque ella puede leer y escribir y todo, y ella habla inglés. ¡Así que yo no sé realmente donde está el problema!

> (She told me that the girl needed to go to a special class because she was crazy! Then she told me a pile of nonsense that was in the school records. I'm not even sure what grade my daughter is in, if in the fourth or the fifth, but the teacher says that next year she's going to be in middle school because she can read and write and everything and she speaks English. So I don't really know what the problem is.)

The terms *incapacitado para aprender* or *impedido en el aprendizaje* (literally, "incapacitated or impaired in learning") did not evoke the same confusion for parents, since these terms are usually explained to the parents in term's of the child's being of "normal intelligence" but having trouble learning to read, write, or speak clearly. The parents seemed to understand the term quite readily, but most did not accept it as an appropriate description of their child. While all agreed that their children were having difficulty learning in school, only one parent interpreted the difficulty as a disability. The following section will explain parents' theories of both categories.

PARENTS' THEORIES OF THE PROBLEM

Parents' interpretations of their children's difficulties varied in the specifics, but from all the interviews there emerged three distinct themes: the importance of family identity in the interpretation of a child's development patterns; the detrimental effects of second-language acquisition on school learning; and the detrimental effects of educational practices such as frequent changes in placement, out-of-neighborhood placement, an unchallenging curriculum, and inflexible reading instruction.

Family Identity and Reputation

The strong familism of Hispanic cultures is well documented (Condon et al., 1979; Escobar and Randolph, 1982). With reference to Puerto Rican people in particular, Canino and Canino (1980), have described the typical family as tending to show an "enmeshed" rather than a "disengaged" structure. In this pattern, there is a strong emphasis on the family's identity as a group rather than as a collection of individuals, which, Canino and Canino say, may lead to features such as prolonged mother-child interaction, overlapping of nuclear and extended family roles, and a perception of illness as a problem that resides within the family rather than solely within the individual. This concept of the family may be important in terms of both the identity the family defines for itself and the reputation accorded the family by the community.

While confidentiality is always important for professionals, it becomes crucial in the tightly knit, socially isolated communities in which many non-English-speaking ethnic minority families live (Leung, 1988; Owan, 1985). Several parents told me a story that was illustrative of this.

I first heard the story from Iris and Alfonso, a couple who give an overwhelming impression of combined dignity and deference. Alfonso, a man of about 50, tall, trim, and graying dramatically against dark brown skin, is a model of exemplary adherence to the traditional requirements of "respeto" and "dignidad" in interpersonal behavior. Always seating himself last, he would most often respond to a question with a slight smile, a deferential tilt of the head, and a softly spoken reply of no more than two or three sentences.

This couple told me that some years before, their family had been disgraced by their child's special education placement, because the social histories written about their child as well as children in other families gave the false impression that their difficulties resulted from family immorality, such as child abuse, drug dealing, or prostitution. The contents of these records had not originally been shown to parents but were later divulged to some parents by a social worker from an agency in the area. Three families in the study had been among the group.

Iris and Alfonso had been so distressed by this event that, in desperation, they moved to the north side of the city, in the hope that their son would be sent to school in that area. They were greatly disappointed to be told by the district that the only appropriate program for Mark would still be at Spruce Street School and that he would be bused there. They subsequently moved back to the southwest side, where all their friends and grown-up children lived.

Iris would not specify the origin of the derogatory social histories. By waving her hand in a direction upward and away from her house as she spoke of "ellos" (them), she hinted only that "they" were somehow part of the school system. Although the damaging stories had been written several years earlier, Iris's distress was intensified by her son's growing unhappiness with being placed in special education.

Iris and Alfonso's story was subsequently corroborated by Ana and Carmen. It was also corroborated by the professional who had written the social histories, who explained that the information she wrote in the histories had come from neighbors and family members; she felt information about family environment and practices was important for the psychologist to know but was not intended for public consumption. She told me that after the parents were shown the histories they denied much of the information and complained to the school district. As a result, the histories had to be rewritten in a more positive vein.

This incident raises complex questions about confidentiality and the recording of sensitive information. Beyond the fact that the law provides for parents' access to their children's records, the questions of whether the histories should have been more euphemistically written and whether the truth of the stories was properly verified before being recorded are ones that all responsible professionals must face.

In any case, it is evident that the interpretations arising from this episode had a negative impact on one of the most sensitive areas of Puerto Rican people's identity—family reputation. In addition to these families' traditional association of "retardation" with mental illness, disability thus took on an extra stigma, that of being tied to bad family character—an extra burden to bear in redefining identity.

While family identity can be influenced by community opinion, families' essential self-definitions arise from their own history. Parents' interpretations of children's strengths and weaknesses were intimately tied to family self-definitions. An intriguing feature of this is the fact that, while a strong concept of group identity makes the whole group vulnerable, there is also a resilience created by the assumption of a group identity; that is, inasmuch as the individual may bring shame to the group, so may aspects of the group's identity serve to protect the individual. Thus all parents spoke of their childrens' strengths and weaknesses in terms of a range of family characteristics.

There is a certain acceptability in a child's difficulties "coming from the father," or being "just like his aunt." While some mothers modified the term *retarded* and others rejected it outright, in either case they described the children in terms of marked family traits not considered to be outside the range of normal behavior. Thus they felt that the school's labeling process did not recognize the child's individuality and family identity. Francisca, for example, explained both her daughter's and her granddaughter's difficulties at school in terms of the school's preference for more expressive types of personality. Her children, she said, were very quiet, both by heredity and because of the family's lifestyle:

> Como les dije en la escuela, el único problema que tiene la muchacha es que ella es callada; no habla mucho. Pero eso de no hablar mucho viene de la familia porque el papá de estos muchachos es muy callado. ¡Él, si le hablan, habla; si le saludan, saluda, si no, nada! Entonces eso es por la herencia, la muchacha no tiene problema de hablar ni es retardada ni nada.
>
> Y la nena mía—ella es muy tímida, tú sabes, la he criado aquí y ella no juega con otros niños afuera, solamente en la escuela. En la casa, solamente la dejo ir afuera si va con alguien de la familia, pero sola, no.

> (As I told them at the school, the only problem my child has is that she is very quiet. She does not talk much. But this quietness comes from the family, because the father of these children is very silent. He—if you speak to him he speaks, if you greet him he greets you, if not, nothing! . . . So this is by heredity, the child has no problem in speech nor is she retarded or anything.
>
> And my granddaughter—she is very timid, you know, I brought her up here and she does not play with other children outside, only at school. At home I only let her go outside if she goes with the family, but alone, no.)

In a similar vein, another mother, Ramona, acknowledged that her 10-year-old daughter was progressing more slowly than most children in academic work, but she did not agree that this meant her daughter was mentally retarded. Rather, she described her daughter as very unsure of herself because of extreme shyness, similar to that of her "father's family" and of herself. Ana, whose 9-year-old, Gina, was also classified as mentally retarded, agreed that her daughter needed a special class because she was slow in learning and her behavior was very erratic. Ana understood what "Americans" mean by "retarded" but considered it irrelevant: Gina, she said, is simply "like her father." He never did learn to read and write and has a quick temper. He has always been like that, and she feared that Gina would be too:

> I think she won't change because she is the same thing as my husband. He is always "con coraje" (mad). You tell him something, he talks to you back. He can't stay quiet. He spoils Gina—he says, "I love her because she is just like me!"

Two mothers, Inés and Dora, emphasized the role of unhappy family circumstances that they felt affected their children in early childhood. Dora thought that her daughter Maria's progress in school was affected by this, but she put much greater emphasis on the role of "confusion" between English and Spanish, as well as on inappropriate teaching methods. Inés was the only parent in the study who accepted the term *disability* as a description of her child's difficulties in behavior and attention, and her views were much more in line with the medical model that underlies special education placement and programming.

"A Causa del Idioma"
(Because of the Language)

The notion of language "confusion" expressed by Dora reflected a common theme among parents of children labeled learning disabled. Since Spanish was the primary language in all of the homes in the study, even those children born in the United States learned Spanish as their first language. Thus English became a requirement only upon entrance into school in the United States, which, for most, was between kindergarten and the third grade. These children were placed directly into regular education, English-speaking classes with varying amounts of "pullout" for the English as a second language (ESL) program. Those labeled mentally retarded were identified within a year or two and those labeled learning disabled were referred to special education between the second and sixth grades. All of the latter group had repeated one grade, and in several cases two grades, before being referred.

Parents of children classified as learning disabled said that the children had been "doing fine" in prekindergarten and kindergarten and that their problems began when they entered the elementary grades. Of those children who had started school in Puerto Rico, parents said that they had had no problem in school there. Inés's son, Ricardo, who had been classified as having attention deficit disorder in Puerto Rico, was the only exception to this.

Some parents interpreted the second-language difficulties in school as a reflection of American intolerance and unreasonable expectations on the part of teachers. Josefina, for example, whose 14-year-old son had been in a special education class since the fourth grade, said:

> Es por el lenguaje—nada más! Al principio, mi hijo no sabía inglés, pero tenía que aprender a leerlo y escribirlo. Entonces, cuando ya lo sabía, su pronunciación no era perfecta como un americano porque tiene que tener un acento de Puerto Rico, pero ellos querían que él lo supiera correcto.

Cuando yo fui a la reunión, decían que el niño tiene un nivel alto en la matemática, pero el leer . . . Entonces, les dije que yo supongo que un niño de Puerto Rico no pueda aprender el inglés tan rapido. Puede aprender leerlo pero no tan perfecto como el Americano.

(It is all because of the language—nothing more! At first my son did not know English, but he had to learn to read it and write it. Then when he learned it his pronunciation was not perfect like an American because he must have a Puerto Rican accent, but they wanted him to know it correctly. When I went to the meeting they said that the child is at a high level in math but the reading . . . So I told them that I suppose that a child from Puerto Rico could not learn English so quickly. He can learn to read it but not so perfectly as an American.

Another mother, Delia, illustrated the impact of this process by drawing a comparison between her older children, who began school in Puerto Rico and were doing "alright" until they entered the first and second grades in the United States, and her youngest child, who was born in the United States and went to prekindergarten here. She said that at the end of the semester there was a great family joke when the little girl came home from her kindergarten class with a certificate for good reading:

Los nenes se echaron a reír, pero, sabes, se sintieron abochornados porque están atrasados en la lectura. Pero es porque ella empezó aquí en los Estados Unidos desde "prekinder," no como ellos que empezaron en Puerto Rico y después, al venir a este país, se encontraron con otro idioma.

(The children all had to laugh, but, you know, they felt embarrassed because they are behind in reading. But it is because she started here in New York in the pre-k, not like them starting in Puerto Rico and then coming to this country to meet with a new language.)

While parents were adamant regarding the role of language confusion, it was evident that they did not have a clear idea of exactly how this worked in school. Parents used the terms ESL and *bilingual* interchangeably and expressed the belief that this program was the source of the children's confusion. However, none of the children in the study were old enough to have been in the district's bilingual program, which had been discontinued about 8 years earlier. Thus one important implication of parents' comments on language programs in the school is the extent of their unawareness of the educational programs their children were in. This recalls similar observations made by Figler (1981) and Delgado-Gaitan (1987).

The belief that bilingual or ESL classes confuse children presented a dilemma for most of the parents: they felt that a choice had to be made between English and Spanish, and all were adamant that they would choose English for their children. Yet they said that one disadvantage of being educated in English only was that the children never learn to read and write in Spanish and might even forget the language after a while. For families who thought they might like to return to Puerto Rico, this was particularly worrying. Others simply felt that the ability to speak two languages would be an advantage for the children when they grow up.

Detrimental Educational Practices

Parents of children classified as mentally retarded conceded that their children's overall development was slow, and most did not object to placement in a smaller class for extra attention. As shown earlier, the interpretation of this as a disability and the stigma of that label were the main things they objected to. However, they expressed great disappointment in the way these programs were implemented, saying that they tended to hinder rather than help the children. Parents laid two particular charges in this respect: first, that frequent changes of school placement had hindered the children's progress, and second, that the curriculum in the "special class" was infantile and repetitive. One parent of a child labeled learning disabled had an additional concern — methods used in the teaching of reading. I will discuss each of these in turn.

Placement and Curriculum. Between kindergarten and age 9, Rita's daughter, Rosemary, had been moved to five different schools in the district's attempt to locate the most appropriate program. To her mother's relief, Rosemary had finally been placed in a school where the district said she would remain until age 12. Rita liked this school, since Rosemary was finally beginning to show progress and had recently passed the kindergarten levels and begun first-grade work.

Similarly, by the age of 7, Francisca's granddaughter had been placed in three different schools. Francisca was angry about the moves and about the child's being placed in a school outside the neighborhood. She was also angry about the nature of the curriculum, which she said emphasized kindergarten activities such as painting and coloring:

> Le dan un papelito de animales y entonces ella tiene que marcar si es una vaca, o si es un perro, y cosas así! Yo la veo mucho mas despierta que eso, y ella puede aprender a contar y escribir. . . . Todo el día ella está perdiendo el tiempo, porque no están enseñándole nada. Si ella necesita aprender pintar, la puedo enseñar aquí en la casa.

(They give her a little paper with animals and she has to mark if it is a cow
or a dog, and things like that! I see her as much more alert than that and she
could learn to count and write. . . . All day long she is wasting time, because
they are not teaching her anything. If she needs to learn to paint I could
teach her at home.)

Ana expressed the same sentiments. She agreed with special class
placement for her daughter because of the small groupings where she
could get more attention. However, she said that four school changes in 3
years had done 9-year-old Gina "a lot of harm" and had delayed her
progress. In addition, she said that for 3 years her special education program was more like kindergarten than first grade. Ana had encountered
the same problem when her son had been placed in special education some
years before in another city. Upon relocating, she found her own way of
solving the problem:

When I moved down here I was tired of José staying down in the special
class. He was always in kindergarten, they never let him pass to the first
grade because they say he doesn't know the work. But how can José know
something if you don't tell him how to do it? All they did was painting and
some little stuff—every day the same thing. So when I came here I told them
I lost the school papers and I put him in regular first grade. He failed one
year but the next year he passed, and he never failed since then, and he gets
A's and B's in the regular class because he is very intelligent.

Teaching of Reading.   The teaching of reading became the focus of one
mother's concern. Dora, whose daughter, Maria, was labeled learning
disabled, was the only mother who had completed high school. At the time
of the study, Dora was pursuing an understanding of the methodology used
to teach reading and had concluded that inflexible use of a direct-instruction, phonic method, along with repeated grade retention, had compounded her daughter's language-induced difficulties. Dora did not consider her daughter learning disabled:

Cuando yo empecé a enseñarle a leer en kindergarten, yo le enseñe a leer
la palabra completa y ella estaba aprendiendo. Pero la manera que ellos le
estan enseñando ahora, la está confundiendo. Todos los niños no son ig-
uales, y ella no está aprendiendo por este método. Esto es solo fonética y
ella se sintió confundida cuando empezó la escuela y tuvo que aprender a
hacer todas las cosas en inglés. Entonces, ella no entiende la diferencia entre las letras del alfabeto y los sonidos que tiene que decir en inglés.

(When I started teaching her to read in kindergarten, I taught her to read the whole word and she was learning, but the way they are teaching her now is confusing her. All children are not the same, and she is not learning by this method. For one thing, it is only phonetics and she became confused when she started school and had to learn to do everything in English; so she does not understand the difference between the letters A B C, and the sounds you have to say in English.)

Both Dora's account and her daughter's school records showed that although Maria had passed the first reading level at the end of the second grade, in repeating the grade she had, somehow, been put back to the same level. Toward the end of her repeating year, Maria's report indicated that she still had not mastered this reading level. Her mother was incredulous:

¡Es algo muy fuerte para entender! ¡Es imposible que María se quede un año completo en el mismo nivel de lectura, especialmente cuando ella lo pasó el año anterior!

(It is a very hard thing to understand! It is impossible that Maria could stay a whole year on the same reading level, especially when she had passed it the year before!)

Beneficial Effects of Special Education Placement

Despite disagreement with the school's interpretations of children's difficulties, there were some parents who expressed satisfaction with the effectiveness of special education placement, notably parents of children labeled learning disabled who felt that the resource program was helping their children. Margarita and Delia, for example, who both explained their children's problems in terms of second language "confusion," agreed that the children were progressing better as a result of the special attention. Inés, who had come to the United States because of Ricardo's learning difficulties, felt that the school was doing its best and she was getting the services she came for. Others, however, such as Dora and Josefina, were skeptical, believing that a combination of intolerance and inappropriate methods continued to hold the children back.

It is important to note that the parents did not object to special assistance as such. On the contrary, all said that small-group instruction should be the main benefit of special education. Even parents who considered the curriculum or the teaching methods inappropriate also felt that the child "would not make it" in a large class. In sum, parents did not object to special class or resource placement per se; they mostly agreed that the children were having difficulty and were willing to accept appropriate and effective help from special education, but they varied in their assessment of the actual success of these programs.

PARENTS' THEORIES AND PROFESSIONAL ARGUMENTS

The views reported in this chapter constitute a cluster of folk theories that are very much in line with certain current arguments in the field of special education. First, they illustrate the argument that conceptions of disability are reflections of social constructions based on cultural values and expectations, a point that has been made by numerous scholars, including Becker (1969), Bogdan and Knoll (1988), Dexter (1964), Goffman (1963), and Lofland (1969). Second, these views also echo ongoing debates within the field regarding appropriate instruction for bilingual students and the efficacy of special class placement.

Cultural Perspectives on Disability

The perspectives outlined here should sharpen educators' awareness of the potential for cross-cultural misunderstanding inherent in the culturally specific classification system used by special education. While parents placed great value on education and saw it as their children's route to success, they did not interpret academic success as an indicator of normalcy or good mental health. In their view, a child may be slower than others and may need extra help in learning to read and write, but that does not make the child disabled. Rather, it may indicate that a number of extrinsic factors in either the home or school environment have interfered with his or her progress, in particular, the learning of the second language.

The notion of limitations stemming from within the child was accepted tentatively by only a few parents. Such parents spoke of their children's development or behavior in terms of a normal range of diversity that was part of the family's identity: it may be a child's nature to be slow in learning or to be extremely shy or quick tempered, but it is not necessarily a disability.

The interpretation of parents' disagreement as a reflection of cultural difference may be challenged in a number of ways. First, it is appropriate to ask whether these parents' views differ significantly from those of mainstream American parents; second, whether parents are simply engaging in a process of denial in order to protect their children's and their families' identities; and third, whether parents' disagreement simply represents a difference in nomenclature — in this case a mistaken translation of the term *retarded* to mean "crazy."

The first two of these arguments reflect the commonsense expectation that parents are likely to engage in behavior designed to protect their children and themselves from social stigma. Wolfensberger and Thomas (1983) have described the stigmatizing of an individual as a process in which a particular characteristic that is negatively valued is attributed as the defining feature of the individual, resulting in the ultimate devaluing of the whole person. It is reasonable to expect, then, that parents may be more likely to accept labels that emphasize a discrete characteristic, precisely because they thereby render the child less vulnerable to the process of stigmatizing. Indeed, this is evident in the findings of a small but consistent body of literature on parents' reactions to disability labels showing that parents tend to reject retardation-related labels (Barsch, 1961; Smith, Osborne, Crim, & Rhu, 1986; Wolfensberger & Kurtz, 1974). Further, it is well known that parent opinion has been a powerful force in the recognition of the classification learning disability. It has also been suggested that parents may actively seek a milder label in an effort to deflect responsibility for negative familial dynamics underlying the child's difficulties (Pollack, 1985).

The notion of denial as a self-defensive mechanism is in keeping with Goffman's (1963) well-known consideration of stigma, in which he observes that labeled persons themselves may engage in actions designed to camouflage their difference so as to "pass" for normal. This theory was applied by Edgerton (1967) to his findings that persons labeled mentally retarded rejected the label and expended considerably energy in disguising their deviance. Edgerton referred to this self-defensive mechanism as a "cloak of competence." More recently, Zetlin and Turner (1984) identified different types of self-perceptions among persons labeled mentally retarded, which included both "acceptors" and "deniers" of the label; they concluded that one significant source of such reactions was the way parents had explained their children's limitations to them.

It is crucial to understand the meaning of the concept of "passing." A standard that has been established by society for the identification of deviance does not represent objective reality or "truth," but simply a social agreement as to the definition of deviance. Bogdan and Taylor's (1982) life histories of persons labeled mentally retarded demonstrate that such persons' self-identifications may differ sharply from the way society has identified them. Bogdan and Taylor point out that these individuals' rejection of society's label simply reveals the existence of differing perspectives, thus underscoring the socially negotiated nature of the labeling process. In other words, one cannot assume that the labeler is "right" and the denier "wrong," since the application of a label is but a social decision reflecting a societal value. To attempt to "pass" is simply to try to assert one's self-definition over the definition imposed by society. Indeed, Goffman (1963) concluded his famous discussion of stigmatized identity by saying: "The normal and the stigmatized are not persons but rather perspectives" (p. 138).

Beyond the need to renegotiate society's labels, however, parents' ability to make realistic assessments of their children's capabilities has also been documented by some studies. Wolfensberger and Kurtz (1974) found that parents who rejected the label mental retardation were, nevertheless, in agreement with professionals' evaluations of their children's mental age and performance level, while Edgerton and Ottina (1986), in a follow-up study after 25 years, found that mothers' assessments of their children's potentials were verified over time and proved more accurate than those of professionals.

Parent-professional disagreement, then, is most typically seen at the level of naming the problem, not at the level of describing children's performance or behavior. In this regard, the parents in this study show a pattern similar to what is known about mainstream parents, in that they reject the labels while acknowledging that their children have difficulties. The reasons for their rejection of these labels, however, are complex.

First, like the mainstream parents in the literature, they find the label mental retardation too stigmatizing. This is exacerbated by the fact that traditional Spanish does not have a word for *retarded*, but rather identifies mental disability with mental retardation under the vernacular term "loco" (crazy). It is not simply a matter of mistranslation, but a reflection of an absence of distinction between mental illness and intellectual impairment, the latter being considered an impairment only at the more extreme end of the spectrum. Prior to the influence of Western conceptions of special education, mild learning difficulties did not earn a separate linguistic classification.

The avoidance of stigma, however, is not the only reason that parents may reject a label. The parents in this study genuinely disagreed that mild deficits in academic skills are tantamount to a handicap, as was made clear by Francisca's incredulity that a child who can read and can speak two languages could be considered retarded. It seems evident that this relates to differing societal norms.

Beyond the issues of stigma and varying societal norms, there is also the question of assumptions about etiology in mild disabilities. The concept of disability by definition suggests some impairment intrinsic to the child. Mainstream parents have argued for more restricted, less global interpretations of children's difficulties but have not rejected the notion of disability as such. In this study, parents of children labeled mentally retarded, when they accepted their children's delay as an intrinsic characteristic, tended to accept it as falling within the normal framework of the family's identity and did not define it as a disability. Parents of children labeled learning disabled, on the other hand, rejected the notion of within-child etiology, identifying the source as extrinsic to the child. These attitudes are similar to the work of Mercer (1972), whose interviews with Black and Chicano parents revealed that they explicitly rejected the mental retardation label on the basis that it was incorrect and was being used as a vehicle to place their children in deadend programs. Thus the views of culturally different parents may differ in some important ways from those of mainstream parents.

Official definitions of mild mental retardation emphasize that the concept does not include the expectation of a biologically based, permanent, and comprehensive incompetence. Nevertheless, the term continues to evoke such an impression, partly because the same term is used for individuals with much more severe intellectual limitations (Reschly, 1988), and partly because the term *disability* inevitably suggests a deficit within the individual. Chapter 3 offered a comprehensive outline of the 20-year-old debate around the disability classification system and some of the current proposals for change, such as recommendations for designations such as "educational handicap" (Reschly, 1988) or "educationally delayed" (Polloway & Smith, 1988), as well as more radical calls for a focus on programmatic needs rather than categorical diagnosis based on the concept of within-child deficits (Reynolds & Lakin, 1987).

This study strongly indicates a need for the latter approach. It is not enough to say that many people misunderstand disability classifications and that it is therefore simply a matter of nomenclature. It is now widely acknowledged that the present assessment system is severely limited in its ability to identify the true nature of students' learning difficulties, especially when these students' cultural experiences predispose them to linguistic, cognitive, and behavioral styles that may differ in important ways from what is considered normative on most assessment instruments (Cummins, 1980a; Figueroa et al., 1989b). Particularly relevant to the views of parents in this study is the observation that the learning disability label is often applied to children whose difficulties are really a reflection of normal second-language development (Ortiz & Polyzoi, 1986). It is time for us to abandon our reliance on a model whose main effect is to locate the source of failure in the child. The concept of disability in the case of underachieving children is simply inadequate and inappropriate in the context of the tremendous diversity of American schools.

Goffman (1963) has spoken of the stigmatizing process as the "spoiling" or "disgracing" of individual identity. For these Puerto Rican families, a broad sense of family identity, with wide parameters of acceptable development and behavior, can protect the individual from such insult, while simultaneously rendering the whole family vulnerable if an individual's difficulties are so extreme as to be considered deviant. Parents' views show how intense can be the stigmatizing effects on families whose cultural base is different, whose knowledge of the school system is minimal, and who already feel powerless and alienated. Correa (1989) has made the point that acculturation must be a two-way process, with professionals in education becoming sensitized to the values and norms of the cultures from which their students come. Prior to this step, professionals need to become aware of their own values and of the fact that most human values are not universal but are generated by the needs of each culture. Such awareness is not too much to ask, since it is through the eyes of the school that a child officially comes to be defined as a success or a failure. The school system must, therefore, accept the tremendous responsibility that accompanies such power.

Instruction and Efficacy

Research on instruction and on the efficacy of special education also parallels the interpretations of parents in this study. Parents' opinion that the curricula of special classes are so watered down as to further retard children replicates a continuing criticism of the field (see Epps & Tindal, 1987, for a comprehensive review of the efficacy of special education programming). Further, out-of-neighborhood placement for these most vulnerable of students clearly undermines the principle of the least restrictive environment, and the call continues for all children to go to school with their brothers and sisters in neighborhood schools (Biklen, 1985).

The most controversial of parents' concerns is the argument that children are handicapped by the transition from Spanish to English in the education process. While parents are unclear as to how this operates, their focus on language is very much in line with current thinking about the education of bilingual children. Cummins (1979) has argued convincingly that children may demonstrate adequate basic interpersonal competence in a second language yet have a level of cognitive-academic language proficiency that is inadequate to the task of literacy or psychological assessment in that language. Indeed, the literature on this topic overwhelmingly agrees that to move children to second-language literacy too soon is to set them up for failure in both languages, thus preparing them for low-status roles in the host society as well as alienation from their native culture (Cordasco, 1976; Cummins, 1986; Lewis, 1980; Ovando & Collier, 1985; Spener, 1988; Stein, 1986).

Grade retention is one evident outcome of prematurely instructing children in the second language, a feature frequently observed among bilingual students, with a common pattern of "overage" students (Walker, 1987). Among the families in this study it was not uncommon to find children as much as 3 years older than the usual age for their grade, and it was the rare child who had not repeated at least one grade level.

Besides language of instruction, research is increasingly focusing on the need for culturally sensitive instructional approaches. In contrast to the direct-instruction, phonic-based approach used with Dora's daughter in this study, more holistic, meaning-based approaches are currently recommended for students from different cultures (Au & Jordan, 1981; Ruiz, 1989). Indeed, Figueroa et al. (1989b), in summarizing the findings to date on assessment and instructional services, call for a paradigm shift from decontextualized, acultural, and asocial interventions toward conditions of high context, both in assessment and instructional approaches. Along with this go recommendations for the targeting of curricula toward the "upper range of bilingual children's academic, linguistic, and social skills" (Ruiz, 1989, p. 130) and for utilizing rather than ignoring the cultural resources of all students (Moll & Diaz, 1987). In this study, Dora's analysis of the inappropriateness of lockstep, decontextualized instruction for her daughter is directly in line with these views.

THE ROLE OF PARENTS IN EMPOWERING STUDENTS

Like the parents in this study, the field is calling for effective, challenging, and culturally appropriate regular and special education programs. The parents' rejection of mild disability labels and their own explanations of their children's difficulties parallel professional arguments so closely as to demonstrate the appropriateness of parental collaboration in children's educational careers. In his proposed framework for the empowerment of minority students, Cummins (1989) uses a sociohistorical perspective to analyze the underachievement of students from what Ogbu (1978) has called caste-like minorities. Cummins argues that only through holistic interventions, which attend to a range of cultural/linguistic, family, community, and pedagogical needs, will minority students be empowered to achieve to their potential.

Most of the parents in this study said that their children were fine until they started school. This should not be relegated to the status of parent/folk lore: it is, increasingly, the comment of careful scholars who have focused their attention on students from low-status minority groups. Trueba (1989) has put the case succinctly:

These disabilities are an attribute of schools. Childrens' seeming "unpreparedness" for mainstream schooling is only a measure of the rigidity and ignorance of our school system, which creates handicap out of social and cultural differences. (p. 70)

Perhaps most important in considering the process of disempowerment is the fact that parents' theories, which this discussion has shown to be consistent with some of the most sophisticated literature in the field, remained unacknowledged by the professionals who worked with these families. Since the assumption of the objectivity of special education procedures and labels precludes the possibility of "truth" in parents' perspectives, parents' interpretations are not legitimated by the system. Indeed, according to the law, parents can challenge the findings of the school's evaluation by having an independent evaluation, a process that utilizes exactly the same evaluation system as that sanctioned by special education. This creates an avenue not for dialogue but rather for an adversarial type of contest between two parties working within the same conceptual framework. For parents' theories to be heard, professionals would have to create genuine dialogue beyond the provisions and constraints of the law.

The data of this chapter underscore the call for a collaborative versus an exclusionary approach to defining the meaning of children's difficulties in school (Correa, 1989; Cummins, 1989, Delgado-Gaitan, 1990). The next chapter will demonstrate that collaboration requires openness to both interpersonal and systemic change.

8

Communication, Information, and Meaning

Chapter 1 of this book introduced a mother whom I have called Ana—a mother who, like many others, centers her life on her children and describes life in the United States as so dangerous that she tries to keep her children "more at home than outside." Ana is the sort of mother whom many professionals in the United States would describe as "overprotective" of her children. Yet for all her efforts, one of the most serious failures of communication reported in the study occurred with Ana's 9-year-old daughter, Gina. Her gray eyes flashing, Ana recounted with renewed indignation a blunder made by the school district about two years before the study. The social worker at her daughter's school had called to say that Gina was sick and needed to be taken home. Ana found a friend from the Latin American Association (LAA) to drive her to the school, only to find that:

> Cuando nosotros llegamos, ellos nos dijeron, "This is the wrong school. Gina does not come here anymore." Me cambiaron la niña mia sin consentimiento mio, y sin decirme nada! Y yo creía que era la misma escuela porque la guagua la recogía aquí, y para mi era la misma guagua!
>
> Entonces, cuando los grandes del distrito escolar hicieron un programa sobre todas las personas puertorriqueñas que tenían complaints sobre los problemas de los niños en la escuela, yo también fuí a quejarme del problema que tuve con la niña mia. Ellos creían que era mentira mia, pero otros padres puertorriqueños también tenían estos problemas, y nosotros firmamos un papel sobre todas estas cosas.
>
> Entonces me hicieron una reunión conmigo. Bueno, que fuimos a la reunión y cuando llegamos, nos cogieron de sorpresa porque ya estaban todos allí esperando, y ellos no me pudieron explicar todo exactamente, ni yo pude hacer algunas preguntas porque no me dieron la oportunidad. Ellos dijeron, "Entiende?" Yo no entendí nada. Yo me vine de allí como si fuera, como según llegué así salimos, porque aunque mi amiga me explicó en español, yo no entendí nada—absolutamente nada!

Pero they asked us to pardon them and now everything that happens with Gina in the school, they notify me right away! Pero si yo no llegué hablar de eso, todo habría seguido pasando así, porqué, por años y años, nadie pudiera entender lo que estaba sucediendo en la escuela con los niños.

(When we arrived, they told us, "This is the wrong school. Gina does not come here anymore." They had moved my child without my consent and without telling me anything! And I thought she was still going to the same school because the school bus collects her right here, and it looked like the same bus to me!

Then, when the big people at the school district called a meeting for all the Puerto Ricans who had complaints about problems with the children in school, I went and complained about the problem I had with my daughter. They thought I was telling a lie, but other Puerto Rican parents were having these problems too, and we all signed a paper complaining about these things.

Then they had a meeting with me. Well, we went to the meeting and they caught us by surprise because when we arrived they were all there waiting, and they could not explain to me exactly what had happened, and I could not really ask questions because they did not give me the opportunity. They said "You understand?", but I did not understand anything! I left there no better off than when I arrived, because although my friend explained in Spanish I understood nothing—absolutely nothing!

But they asked us to pardon them and now everything that happens with Gina at school, they notify me right away! But if I had not gone and complained about this, it would have continued just the same because for years and years no one could understand what was happening to the children at school.)

The only explanation I could get from school district personnel was that Ana had not been present at the meeting where Gina's change of placement was decided but that the decision was recorded on the individual education plan (IEP). I was unable to ascertain whether Ana had actually signed the IEP without observing the change of school, or whether it had never been signed. This story of failure in communication is more dramatic than most, but it exemplifies some of the essential features of the communication system between parents and the school, perhaps the most obvious in this case being the ineffectiveness of a reliance on formal written communication.

Overall, I have characterized the observed patterns of ineffective communication between professionals and parents according to the following themes: trust versus deference, written communication, an absence of information and meaning, and resignation and withdrawal.

TRUST VERSUS DEFERENCE

When parents send their children to school they do so on the basis of trust. If such trust does not exist, every communication between the home and school will be suspect. The review of literature on minority parents' participation offered in Chapter 4 pointed to the common observation that the school is a symbol of authority to which many Hispanic parents defer uncritically (Delgado-Gaitan, 1987; Figler, 1981; Lynch & Stein, 1987; New York City Board of Education, 1958). Figler, for example, found that parents showed "implicit and explicit trust in the school and school staff" (p. 12), who were "generally trusted and held to be infallible" (p. 15).

I cannot say that I found such trust in this study. It is true that much of the distrust expressed by the participants had arisen through miscommunications over a period of several years prior to the study and that, in the year of the study, the school district was engaged in several attempts to improve communication, as will be outlined in the next chapter. What I did observe in this study was a considerable deference for school authorities on the part of parents. Traditional habits and values regarding appropriate interaction with authorities are not easily relinquished. In addition, it is particularly hard for parents who feel that they have no power, and who literally cannot speak for themselves, to confront the very authorities to whom they must, every day, entrust their children.

Rosana, a school social worker for Hispanic families, complained to me that "they [parents] come to the meetings and agree to everything, and then they go away and say they do not like the decisions that were made." Many parents, however, explained that they found it difficult to disagree openly with professionals because of their perceived status. For example, Ana could not bring herself to express to school personnel her strong objection to what she perceived as a repetitive and unchallenging curriculum in Gina's self-contained class. "After all," she said, "that is the teacher!" The identical phrase was used by several mothers in the study.

Trust in the Traditional Setting

Lynch and Stein (1987) have pointed out that parents from traditional Hispanic backgrounds may expect minimal participation in school matters. Parents in this study indicated that within the traditional setting in Puerto Rico they were comfortable with such acquiescence, since it was based on genuine trust. Indeed, they spoke with a fond reverence for the school as they knew it in Puerto Rico, which, while it represented unquestioned authority, also represented safety and love. Once a child was in school he or she was safe and the discipline exercised by the teacher was perceived as a sign of caring for the children. When speaking of the teachers' attitude toward students in Puerto Rico, parents frequently used the words "preocuparse" or "apurarse" (to worry about) — the teachers "worried" more about the children. In Margarita's words:

> Por una parte, me gusta más la escuela en Puerto Rico: hay más comunicación entre el maestro y el niño, más atención. Los maestros se apuran mucho por los niños, y se les dan más cariño—acá, se preocupan por la educación del niño, pero no se preocupan por el niño mismo y sus problemas.

> (In a way I like the school in Puerto Rico better: there is more communication between the teacher and the child, more attention. They worry a lot about children and give more affection—here, they care about the education of the child, but they don't care about the child himself and his problems.)

This emphasis on a personal relationship has been illustrated by Cazden and colleagues (1985) in an ethnographic study of teacher styles in a bilingual-bicultural first-grade classroom in Chicago. They describe the teachers' style as "personalized and characterized by 'cariño' — a close and caring relationship" (p. 160). Some typical features of the teachers' language included addressing the children with explicit terms of endearment as well as habitual use of the diminutive suffix "ito," which may connote smallness but is often used to indicate great fondness for the item or person being referred to. For example, to a child who would not speak up, the teacher said: "Yo quiero que tú me digas con tú boquita, papi — I want you to tell me with your [little] mouth papi [little man]" (p. 162). Further, the authors point out that the intertwining of this style with the fact that the teachers knew and identified with the children's home situations and family values created a very personal form of classroom interaction. For example, the "shared understanding" between teacher and child of the role of grandparents in children's lives brought a tone of intimacy to discussion of family situations. I believe that this is the kind of communication Margarita was referring to and the kind of interaction that leads to genuine trust.

The Undermining of Trust

Against the background of parents' views of the school in Puerto Rico, the school system in the United States seemed impersonal and uncaring to many parents. Occasional blunders and certain ongoing practices regarding placement decisions further undermined the development of trust. The story of Gina's change of placement told at the beginning of this chapter was the worst of these.

Blunders that directly undermined students' self-esteem were also very distressing. Both Dora and Iris told of occasions when their children had been promoted at the beginning of the year "by mistake," only to be returned to the previous year's classroom. Dora was particularly incredulous, since she had "signed all the papers" for Maria to be retained in the second grade and assumed that the decision had been changed when Maria was sent to the third-grade classroom. It was some days before the mistake was discovered and Maria sent back to the second-grade class. What Dora termed "a terrible mistake" dealt a painful blow to 9-year-old Maria.

A recurring problem was the frequent changing of placement, which was mentioned in Chapter 3 as a practice that parents found distressing. Accompanying this was the placement of children in special education programs out of the neighborhood, which applied mostly to children entering self-contained classes. This was a source of great concern to all the parents, whose lifestyle was largely confined to the social networks of the Hispanic neighborhood in which they lived and who saw the city at large as being very dangerous.

Parents who had had satisfactory experiences in this regard stood out in contrast, such as Ramona, who was very happy that Marisa, age 10, had remained in the local school for 3 years, because she would not have wanted her traveling by bus. Ramona walked her child to school and during the 3 years had built trust in the teacher and the school.

Ana, on the other hand, had had little opportunity to build either communication or trust in her daughter's school, since 9-year-old Gina had been moved four times in 3 years. When I expressed confusion over the various moves and asked Ana to explain again, she exclaimed, laughing and gesticulating in an exaggerated fashion: ¡Mira! ¡Ella estaba aquí un año, y después, la cambiaron para allá, y después para acá, y después para otro lado!" (Look! She was here for one year, and then they moved her over there, and then over here, and then someplace else!).

Francisca told a similar story, of having signed permission for her granddaughter to be moved to a special class in another school, and then returning from a brief visit to Puerto Rico to find that Rosita had been moved to yet a different school. The district, she said, had sent a letter in her absence and had gone ahead with the move without her permission. Francisca was assisted by a Puerto Rican social worker in trying to reverse this decision but was refused. Her mistrust of having to send 6-year-old Rosita, whom she described as "sickly," on a bus to a school "so far away" resulted in frequent absences, for which Francisca was ultimately summoned to the family court.

In sum, in Rosita's first 2 years in public school she had been placed in three schools and her grandmother had recently refused the district's recommendation for placement in what would have been a fourth school. In her words:

Entonces, después de todo eso, una señora llegó para hablar conmigo y me dijo que ahora quieren cambiarla a otra escuela porque ella dice, pueden enseñarla mejor ahí. Yo dije que no! Porque la nena va a perder lo poquito que ha aprendido, y esa escuela es aún más lejos.

(Then, after all that, a lady came here to talk to me and said that they want to move her now to some other school because she says they can teach her better there. I said no! I am not going to agree to that because the child is going to lose what little she has learned and that school is even further away!)

Francisca's refusal was unusual for her and for the group as a whole. Indeed, the pattern observed was that parents would only exert control when they were at the end of their tether. Overall, parents felt that they had little control over what seemed to them a capricious and uncaring decision-making process. For the most part, what they felt was mistrust of the system, while what they expressed was an ingrained and habitual deference.

Concerns about control may seem particularly ironic for parents coming from a tradition of not exerting parental control. The difference is that in Puerto Rico they knew what to expect of the school: they had been in that system themselves and had entrusted it with important decisions on behalf of their children. There they were on home ground and knew how, when, and of whom to ask questions. Here everything was foreign — not just the language, but the locations, the formality of school personnel, and the special education rituals. Against this background of mistrust and inadequate information stood the only consistent form of communication — "un montón de papeles" (a pile of papers) from the school, according to Carmen.

WRITTEN COMMUNICATION

Many of my conversations with participants began with the exclamation, "¡Mira! Me mandaron una carta!" (Look! They sent me a letter!). There was always "a letter" parents wanted to talk about. Very early in the project my need to concentrate on the language sharpened my awareness of how often parents used words referring to written communication whenever they spoke of their experiences with special education: "papeles" (papers), "cartas" (letters), "notificarme" (notify me), "firmar" (to sign). Another feature that stood out was the third-person plural, past tense ending, which indicates that "they" did something. A speaker who wants to specify who did the action must use a noun or pronoun, otherwise the subjects are an understood "they." In this context, the parents never specified the subjects: "me mandaron" (they sent me), "la pusieron" (they put her), "lo cambiaron" (they changed him), "lo mudaron" (they moved him), "la examinaron" (they tested her).

What were all these "papers" that must be sent and signed, and why were they so important in the conversation of the parents? And who were "they," the understood "ellos," who did the sending of papers and the putting and moving and testing of children?

The Letters as a Source of Information

The explicit purpose of extensive written communication is to give information and to record decisions and parental permission concerning the various procedures of special education. First comes the initial referral of the child and the requirement that the parent sign permission for an evaluation. Next there are letters about dates for these events and then copies of the evaluation reports. Then come letters informing parents that their child will be placed in special education and inviting them to a meeting at which placement and the "IEP phase 1" will be developed. Records of these meetings must be sent to parents. Then the parent will receive a letter, within a month of placement, to attend an "IEP phase 2" meeting for the purpose of planning with the teacher; the state regulations require this invitation to be sent to the parent no less than 5 days prior to the date set. Then the parent should receive copies of the IEP. From then on, parents receive four classroom reports per school year and invitations to recurring annual review meetings.

For parents of children labeled learning disabled and placed in resource classes there are also letters, usually in the early spring, warning that a child may be retained in the same grade in the coming school year. In addition to all this, of course, are various occasional letters from the school regarding upcoming events and permission for outings and special programs.

Prior to the year of the study, almost all these documents came in English, often without the benefit of discussion. For many parents every letter meant a visit to the LAA to find an interpreter and to seek advice on how to respond. At the time of the study, the school district was engaged in a massive effort to translate all documents into Spanish (and two other "target" languages, Vietnamese and Arabic). This would bring the district into compliance with the requirement that notices to parents regarding identification, evaluation, or educational placement be sent in the native language, "unless it is clearly not feasible to do so" (P.L. 94-142).

With the provision of Spanish documents, however, there still remained the question of the level of readability of special education material, which, according to an analysis by Roit and Prohl (1984), is, on average, at a sixth-grade reading level. Most of the mothers in the study had left school between the fourth and ninth grades, while some of the fathers had completed even less. Equally important was the fact that many documents were virtually incomprehensible because of extensive reliance on educational jargon. Illustrations of this will be given in a later section.

Another school priority at the time of the study was to provide liaison personnel for more personalized information. This was very much needed since many parents did not have telephones and even fewer had cars. These difficulties were compounded by the fact that if there were several children in a family, and if one or two were in special education, parents had two or more schools to deal with. In Ana's case there were two schools plus Head Start for the youngest child, but in bigger families, like Rita's, there were three schools between her four older children plus the prekindergarten program for the youngest.

Just keeping track of the "letters" was a challenge: Inés and Rita were the only parents who could readily locate most of the special education papers and were the two who made the greatest effort to understand and participate in the system. Ana said she had about seven boxes of papers and had to stop her husband from throwing them out. She tried to keep them all but she often became fed up, "especially when all the letters used to come in English." The following quote from Carmen offers an insight into how oppressive the task of deciphering and keeping track of the letters could be:

¡Tantos papeles! Tengo mucho trabajo que hacer—por la mañana yo trabajo en mi casa, y por la tarde cuido a mi mamá, le compro su comida y le lavo su ropa. Yo tengo un montón de cajas llenas de papeles de la escuela y le dije a Fidel que los iba a botar, pero él me dijo "¡no! ¡no!", así que las lleve a la LAA y se los di a ellos. Yo no aguanto tener tantos papeles aquí!

(So many papers! I have a lot of work to do—in the mornings I work in my house, and then in the afternoon I take care of my mother and buy her groceries and wash her clothes. I have a lot of boxes full of papers and I told Fidel I would throw them away and he said, "No, no!" so I took them to the LAA and gave them to them. I can't stand having so many papers!)

The Letters as a Symbol of Power

While written communication functioned as a dubious source of information, for everyone the papers signified the formality and power of the school system. The impact of letters from a relatively unknown power is particularly intimidating and alienating for people whose culture requires the personal touch (Fitzpatrick, 1987). In discussing best practices for communicating with minority families, Marion (1979) has pointed out that the limitation of letters is that the sender is neither seen nor heard. Similarly Figler (1981), in a study of Puerto Rican parents in New York, found written school communication "cold and impersonal."

The concept of high- and low-context cultures (Hall, 1977) adds to our understanding of the cultural dissonance experienced by the parents. In high-context communication there is tremendous reliance on personal delivery, which may include affective as well as factual information, thus making meaning dependent on personal interaction. By contrast, low-context communication relies, according to Hall, on the actual language code, isolated from the interpersonal aspects of communication. The goal of this form of communication is a high level of objectivity — on the assumption that such objectivity reflects greater precision in meaning. The latter will only be true, however, if both parties in the communicative act hold shared meanings of the language being used; indeed, Hall (1977) has observed that "one reason that bureaucrats are so difficult to deal with is that they write for each other and are insensitive to the contexting needs of the public" (p. 93). This was certainly the case with the written communications received by parents in this study.

It is essential to recognize the organizational underpinnings of this form of discourse. Indeed, it is innately bound to the bureaucratic structure of schools and to the legal framework within which they work. This has been discussed at length by Skrtic (1988), who distinguishes between machine bureaucracies and professional bureaucracies, pointing out that while both types share "the principle of standardization to produce standard products or services" (p. 497), the central difference is that machine bureaucracies do simple work "that can be broken down into a series of precise, routine tasks that can be fully determined in advance of their execution" (p. 493), while professional bureaucracies do complex work that "requires the application of general principles to particular cases, and thus involves uncertainty and cannot be prespecified completely" (p. 493). Skrtic maintains that while the work of schools is generally conceptualized as requiring a professional bureaucracy, the society's commitment to a rational-technical paradigm has forced schools to "adopt all the trappings of the machine bureaucracy (centralized power, tight control of personnel, standardized work processes, formalization, regulated reporting, rational planning), even though these do not fit the technical requirements of doing complex work" (p. 494). Skrtic concludes:

> The machine bureaucracy seals off its operations by placing a barrier — formalization — between the worker and the client. . . . Formalization in the machine bureaucracy at least leaves clients with inexpensive products; in the professional bureaucracy formalization leaves clients with impersonal and ineffective services. (p. 496)

This process characterizes the communication between the school system and Puerto Rican parents in this study. Once a letter had been received it meant that the parent must react, but exactly what was required was often a mystery. For parents operating from an inadequate information and experiential base regarding special education, it was practically impossible to interpret the formal documents of the school system. Since parents neither understood nor trusted the system, the school district's "letters" were meaningless, sometimes even threatening, in their formality and foreignness.

Thus the parents spoke of the senders of the letters as "ellos" (they), seldom using personal names or even names of professional roles, such as psychologist. According to Ana, "es un nombre americano" (it is an American name), and she had forgotten it. One or two parents could readily name a child's current teacher, many could not; most could not name a teacher from a previous year. Besides the foreignness of the name, the parent may have met the teacher once or not at all. Even so, it is not the teachers who sign the documents and do the moving; it is mostly administrators or psychologists, and these people were always nameless for the parents. Those parents who did go to placement meetings were not sure who the six or seven people at the meetings were, except that, as Delia said, "they are the ones with responsibility for putting the child in special ed."

One thing was certain, "ellos" were "americanos." The district had recently hired a Spanish-speaking American person to work with families, and at the time of the study the parents who had so far met her described her as "una americana que habla español un poquito" (an American who speaks a little Spanish); none could recall her name. In contrast, parents always referred to the few Hispanic personnel in the district by name.

Thus, for these parents, power was inherent in the written word, which came not only from an unseen and unnamed "they," but in a language that was foreign or without relation to parents' experience. The next letter would be added to an ever-growing pile of incomprehensible papers.

INFORMATION AND MEANING

Parents' lack of awareness and information could be thought of on two levels. First, they had not received information or participated in the required events; for example, they had not been to placement meetings or had not received copies of placement or evaluation documents. This was a common complaint regarding IEP phase 1 meetings. Second, lack of information existed on the more subtle level of functional meaning; for example, parents had received information and even participated in an activity but did not understand its meaning within the special education system.

An Absence of Information: The IEP Phase 1

In this state the document recording decisions taken at an initial placement meeting is called phase 1 of the IEP. This important document records all decisions taken regarding a student's placement for the upcoming academic year. Several of these details are exactly those that parents were most confused about; for example, whether or not the child was in an "ungraded class," which would be the case if the class were described as "option 1,2,3, or 4." This was of concern to the parents because they sometimes did not realize that an ungraded class means that the child would not move up to the next grade. Connected to this are implications for graduation from high school, and this information is also on the document under the heading "diploma-bound." The document also specifies the number of hours per day that the student will spend in special education and the extent of mainstreaming to be included. In addition, there is a record of all important dates regarding the child's referral and placement, including even the date of the next annual review.

Phase 1 of the IEP was a mystery to parents. All the parents who were able to show me documents had a copy of one of these among their papers, but none understood it and certainly none knew its name. The following story illustrates the extent of misunderstanding that can result from inadequate information.

Rita's Story: Uninformed Consent. The most dramatic example of an absence of information was the experience of Rita, who spent a year not realizing that her 14-year-old son, Rafael, had been classified as learning disabled and placed in a self-contained class in middle school.

Rita was one of the best informed and most participatory parents in the study. She kept all her special education papers and tried to go to all the meetings. In the previous year, however, she had missed an important meeting in which Rafael had been referred for the first time to the Committee on Special Education (CSE).

Her information regarding the outcome of the meeting had come from the school social worker, who attended on her behalf and who, she said, told her that Rafael would be getting "extra help in English and math." Rita said she accepted that the decision was up to the school district and was probably in Rafael's best interest. She said no one explained to her that Rafael was going to be in a self-contained special education class. During the year she had talked to the teacher on the phone but had not met him.

There was no copy of Rafael's phase 1 IEP among Rita's many documents, and she did not recall ever receiving it. The only written communication that could have told her that Rafael was full-time in special education was his quarterly report cards, which did state that he was in an "option 1" class. But Rita had not observed this notation, since it meant nothing to her. In the spring Rita received a letter inviting her to an annual review for Rafael. She phoned me and said: "They sent me a letter. I know what it says, but I don't know what it means. I don't know what they are talking about!"

I attended the meeting with Rita, which began with the special education teacher's statement that Rafael's classification was "learning disabled." However, the teacher added that he thought this classification was often related to difficulties in second-language acquisition. He did not expand on this and no one questioned him. He went on to say that Rafael is in an "option 1" class with twelve children. The meeting went very quickly, with the usual reports, and was carried out in a cursory fashion. Toward the end of the meeting, Rita suddenly said to the teacher: "So—has he passed?" The teacher looked startled, hesitated, then began to explain that Rafael was in an "ungraded," or "option 1," class, and would therefore not be going on to another grade. He offered some examples of options that might be available to Rafael at the high school level, such as shop, or art, which was a favorite of Rafael's. He did not address the question of whether Rafael might return to the regular education program or to a graded class.

After this, Rita told the teacher that she had never received a record of the first meeting or the evaluation report, and she asked that these be sent to her. The teacher replied that he would send her a copy of the IEP phase 1, but that it seemed the evaluation had never been sent on from the elementary school. A couple of weeks later, Rita received the IEP in the mail, along with a note from the teacher saying that the evaluation seemed to have been lost and requesting her permission for a reevaluation to be done.

I went through the IEP phase 1 with Rita, and it was evident that she simply did not know how to interpret information such as: "Mainstreaming: as appropriate," or "Placement: option 1," or "Hours per day: 5." When I pointed to the item "Clasificación: Impedido en el aprendizaje (lenguaje)" [Classification: Learning disabled (language)], Rita said this made no sense to her since Rafael's English and Spanish were both fluent — in her word, "normal." She agreed that he was behind in reading and math (at about a fourth-grade level, according to last spring's school report) and thought that this was because Rafael was "lazy" and wanted to spend all his time "por la calle" (in the street) with his teenage friends. Further, Rita said that his math had also been affected by the fact that he had missed math classes for a month in the sixth grade when he was pulled out for English as a second language (ESL) class. (My interviews with senior district personnel confirmed that this was possible.) Rita concluded: "Maybe they decided to call him learning disabled/language because they don't know what else to call him!"

Some months after this discussion, Rita attended the phase 2 IEP meeting to discuss plans for Rafael's upcoming academic year. She told the teacher that she did not like Rafael having the classification learning disabled and that she did not want him to remain in special education. She told me that the teacher explained to her that this classification was not very serious and that he agreed with her that Rafael should return to regular education. He told Rita that as soon as Rafael improved sufficiently in reading and math, he would recommend this. Rita expressed satisfaction with this explanation.

It is useful to summarize the patterns of miscommunication inherent in Rita's experience. First, this mother did not know that her son had been placed in a self-contained, full-time special education class. Second, when she did go to a meeting that should have clarified all this, information was given in such a way as to camouflage rather than explain the meaning of Rafael's classification and placement. Third, when she finally saw the document recording his placement, she did not understand it. Fourth, when this document was fully explained to her, she did not agree with it. Fifth, when she returned, with more understanding, to discuss her questions with the teacher, she received quite a different response; that is, the teacher's opinion that Rafael did not really belong in the class and a commitment from him to recommend Rafael's return to regular education. The moral of the story seems to be that an informed and active parent gets results.

It is clear that within this system of communication between a school system and a group of culturally different parents the burden of acculturation rested entirely with parents. Some district personnel spoke of this in terms of the parents' responsibility; hence they complained that parents would miss meetings and then claim that they had not received documentation. Elizabeth, a district liaison person, admitted, however, that the documentation process was indeed slow and that the district usually had a huge backlog of IEP phase 1 documents; she attributed this to the time-consuming translation process that the district had engaged in. Whether or not letters are received, however, there is literature (Featherstone, 1980; Turnbull & Turnbull, 1986) that points to the need for all parents to be given information regarding disability more than once and in different forms. Reasons for this may include parents' desire to resist unpleasant information, as well as their having an inadequate information base from which to process the new information. Such reasons can only be exacerbated by cultural differences.

In Rita's case, her understanding of Rafael's placement may have been affected by the fact that she did have a prior interpretation of special education, based on her daughter Rosemary's classification as "mildly mentally retarded." Rita had made a great effort to understand and accept Rosemary's classification and special education placement. This understanding seemed to her incompatible with any services Rafael could receive. In other words, it did not occur to her that "they" could be thinking of putting Rafael in special education also, since he clearly had no developmental problems. In her words, "He is not like Rosemary. He is not really in special ed."

This brings us back to our earlier arguments regarding the meaning of disability and the appropriateness of the referral and classification system. Interestingly, the teacher told me in an interview that he did not know what Rafael's ability really was, because he had "never really seen him try." If both the mother and the teacher were correct in thinking that Rafael was "lazy," one cannot help asking if "laziness" is a criterion for placing a 14-year-old in a self-contained special education class at the middle school level. Learning disability, it seems, may have many meanings.

An Absence of Meaning: The IEP Phase 2

The foregoing sections have shown that information may literally be absent or may be given in such a way, either in writing or orally, as to be seriously misunderstood. In addition to this, a more subtle form of miscommunication may occur when a parent actually participates in, but does not understand the importance or meaning of, an event within the special education system. The IEP phase 2, a detailed plan of the child's program, is that point at which the parent is likely to have the most input, since it is concerned with specific goals and activities. Yet this was the most common example of an absence of meaning for the parents involved.

Lynch and Stein (1987), in their study of Mexican American parents' participation, found that fewer than 65 percent of parents remembered signing and receiving the IEP. In the present study, none of the twelve parents were familiar with the term *IEP*, either in Spanish or in English, even when I explained its format and purpose in detail. However, on looking through their documents, I found that both Inés and Rita did have copies of the IEP phase 2 among their papers. When I showed it to them, they both exclaimed, "That is the IEP? I didn't know that was what you were talking about!"

For these two mothers, it could be argued that communication regarding the IEP was observed at least at a minimal level: the information had been given, and the mothers' lack of awareness of it was only at the level of language; that is, they knew about the IEP but simply did not know what to call it. However, the level of language is crucial insofar as it reflects meaning. The language of the special education system is so entrenched in the law itself that there are certain words that repeatedly show up in all the important documents pertaining to placement and progress of a child. Terms such as *IEP, evaluation, annual review, triennial review, initial referral* and *option 1* are among the most common and convey essential concepts on which the law is based.

The problems outlined above were not simply a matter of translation, of parents not knowing the English word for these activities: they did not know the Spanish name for them either. They did not know that they had a name at all. In other words, they did not realize that a particular activity or event was an established procedure, required by law, with a recognized name and a ritualized manner of implementation. Thus these parents had no context in which to evaluate the significance, indeed, the power, of these documents and proceedings in the lives of their children.

Dora's Story: Uninformed Participation.   Dora's first IEP phase 1 meeting illustrates the points that parents may not recognize the significance of events they do participate in and that it is the responsibility of school personnel to rectify this. Dora was very critical of the teaching methods used. She had been very concerned about 9-year-old Maria's retention at the first and second grades and her recent placement in a resource program, with the classification learning disabled. When she received a letter in the spring warning that Maria might be retained yet another year in the second grade, Dora asked for an interview with her daughter's teacher. She asked for the meeting so that she could tell them two things. First, she would not agree to Maria's retention, since this year was already a repeat for her and she had also repeated the first grade. Second, there was "something wrong" with the teaching method because Maria, a child described in her assessment report as being of "average intelligence," had remained on level 1B of the reading program for 2 years. Dora said she had tried to tell the teacher this in a previous meeting at the beginning of the year but concluded, "It seems the teacher didn't understand me and I didn't understand her."

The meeting Dora asked for was led by the special education resource teacher, with the regular class teacher also participating. The focus of the meeting was Maria's difficulties in achieving the reading goals of the program being used (DISTAR—Direct Instruction Strategies for Teaching and Remediation). The teacher's way of speaking revealed that she interpreted the learning disability as distinctly Maria's problem; she emphasized that since reading was "Maria's disability," these difficulties were to be expected. However, on the question of retention, the teacher assured Dora that the school's policy would not allow a child to repeat a grade more than once and that the intent of the letter had been only to inform her of her daughter's slow progress in reading.

The question arises here of why a routine retention letter was sent to Dora if there was really no chance of Maria's being retained. If the purpose of the letter was to let Dora know that Maria was not progressing well in reading, why didn't the teacher send a letter saying just that?

At the end of the meeting, the resource teacher asked both Dora and me to sign a document that listed the goals for Maria's reading, which the teacher had outlined during the discussion. The term *IEP phase 2* was printed on the form, somewhere near the top, along with the date, name of the child, reading program, class placement, and so on. Yet at no point in the discussion had the teacher used the term *IEP* or indicated in any way that this meeting was considered an IEP meeting. Neither was there any documentation of the fact that the parent had initiated the meeting for the purpose of objecting to the possibility of her child's being retained.

This event met none of the criteria for an IEP phase 2 meeting. According to state regulations (New York State Department of Education, 1986, pp. 39–41), an IEP phase 2 meeting is to be initiated by the teacher with 5 days prior advice to the parent and should be held within 30 days of the child's beginning the program. It is required that, for a first IEP phase 2 conference, "a person familiar with [the student's] evaluation must attend" (p. 40). This meeting had been initiated by the parent and was, in fact, the first meeting with her since the CSE meeting at which the IEP phase 1 was done; it was well beyond the 30-day requirement for the phase 2 to be completed, and, most important, there was no one present from the evaluation team.

What did the event mean to Dora? As far as she was concerned, she simply "went to the school to talk to the teacher." Not knowing that an IEP was required or that there were specific procedures for its implementation, Dora thus participated in an important ritual of special education planning quite unaware of its meaning or importance in the system, and certainly unaware that it was out of compliance with state requirements.

To be unaware that such events have names means being unaware of the concepts they represent. The notion of individualized education planning, for example, is a central concept in special education; it represents the intention that each child's learning should be tailored to individual needs, as well as the central tenet of parent input. Similarly, the annual or triennial reviews represent the belief that a child's performance level and needs may change; thus, neither the label nor the program placement are assumed to be permanent.

RESIGNATION AND WITHDRAWAL

Since the problems discussed above reflect not only language but also meaning, participation would seem to be the surest route to clarification and understanding. Many parents, however, did not believe that they had any real power, and they responded to their sense of powerlessness by withdrawing.

Parents who did not go to the meetings simply received news of the outcome by another letter or from someone who went on their behalf and gave the information second-hand. One might ask why parents did not attend meetings more often, why they did not exercise their rights. First of all, a few did, as was illustrated earlier by Francisca's refusal to allow Rosita to be moved to what would have been her fourth school in 2 years. Rita, whose daughter had been to five schools in 3 years, also balked when, at the placement meeting, the Committee on the Handicapped proposed moving Rosemary back to the first school she had been in. Thus it was evident that this kind of participation occurred only in extreme circumstances.

But some parents did not participate at all, and in some cases they were not aware of their most basic rights regarding special education. Parents such as Iris, for example, tended to interpret decision making in terms of personalized interventions as opposed to a process that is intended to be impersonal and routine. Thus they perceived trying to influence a decision in terms of asking a favor.

Others were aware that they could refuse permission for certain things but, instead of doing so, often showed their disagreement by refusing to attend meetings or return forms they were supposed to sign. Ana, for example, said that even if she did not like something she knew that "they will do it anyway," so she might sign a form but fail to show up at a meeting. Thus some parents used a kind of passive resistance in the hope of demonstrating their disapproval. This view of parental participation as a meaningless ritual was typified by the following comment by Francisca:

> Es solo la opinión de ellos la que vale. Si yo no quiero que la nena esté en una clase especial, o si yo quiero que esté en otra escuela, pues todavía ellos van a hacer lo que ellos digan. Porque eso era lo que yo trataba de hacer, y Vera [una trabajadora social de una agencia] me ayudó; y lo intentamos, pero no nos escucharon. La opinión de nosotros no vale.
>
> Muchos padres no quieren que su hijo esté en una clase especial o en una escuela tan lejos, pero se quedan quietos. Es fuerte bregar con éstos americanos. . . . Aquí en América, las escuelas son para los americanos.

> (It is only their opinions that matter. If I do not want the child in a special class, or if I want her in a different school they will still do what they want. Because that is what I tried to do, and Vera [an agency social worker] helped me and we tried, but they did not listen to us. Our opinions are not valued.
>
> Many parents do not want their child in a special class or in a school so far away, but they keep quiet. It is very hard to struggle with these Americans. . . . Here in America, the schools are for Americans.)

PERSONALISM, PROFESSIONALISM, AND ADVOCACY

Interviews with school and agency personnel offered some insights into dilemmas facing the professionals serving these families.

A discussion with Rosana, the school social worker, suggested that it may be difficult for a professional to walk the fine line between personalism and professionalism, and between liaison work and advocacy. Rosana perceived the need to be personal and friendly in working with parents, but she would sometimes have to take a position they disagreed with. At this point, she said, she would lose their trust — "They cannot see a worker within the school as a person — as someone who will advocate for them no matter what." Rosana saw this as a "limitation" on the part of the parents.

This comment shows that Rosana saw her role as liaison in terms of advocacy. Her words illustrate the classic challenge of advocacy — the issue of conflict of interest (Biklen, 1983; Wolfensberger, 1984); that is, that there is a conflict inherent in service providers trying to advocate for their clients. The legalistic framing of special education service undoubtedly exacerbates this challenge, since the notion of parents' rights exists within an adversarial framework, and parents who seriously disagree with a school district's decision must engage in formal hearings in order to register their objections. Despite Rosana's apparent naiveté on this issue, it was clear that parents perceived the inherent potential for conflict.

I asked the other district liaison workers, Gloria and Elizabeth, how they saw this issue. Both said they thought it was a matter of earning parents' trust and felt they could represent parents objectively. However, they both emphasized that parents must be encouraged to bring their own advocates or interpreters to meetings so as not to have to rely on district personnel. Elizabeth felt that one way of meeting parents' needs for support would be to recruit the assistance of more experienced parents, who could act as advocates for their peers.

I asked the same question of two social workers from voluntary agencies, Teresa and Isabel. Isabel agreed that the best solution would be parent advocates. She said that while school district personnel do have a role to play in helping parents act on their rights, their ability to do so is limited because of their alliance with the school district.

Teresa, however, expressed strong opinions on the question of professionalism and advocacy. She emphasized that even the role of interpreter is not simple, since the perceived integrity of the interpreter is central to parents' concerns:

> The thing is, when they need somebody to interpret for them, they want somebody they can trust because that puts them in a very helpless position if it isn't the right person. There is a large amount of distrust because [parents] see a system that they cannot understand, that they cannot deal with on their own. On the other hand, I am a social worker. I don't know so much about the technical aspects of special ed. You know, I may translate the meeting and all that, but that's not my field, really . . . if they tell me, "This is an IEP meeting," I don't know what the requirements are unless they tell me.

While she concluded that it is appropriate for the school district to provide interpreters' services, Teresa was adamant that there is a built-in conflict of interest in district employees trying to advocate for these families:

> A person works, let's say for an agency or the school system, they pay your salary. You have to look out for who you work for, that's how it is. If a person works for the school system, they cannot buck the system to help the parents, because they are employees. So they're caught in the middle. No matter how much they want to help, they've got to answer to a lot of people, so they can't go but so far. You know, that's their meal ticket.

Teresa's view of conflict of interest went further, illustrating that being perceived to be in conflict can be as damaging as being so in actuality. She gave the example of herself, a social worker from a voluntary agency, being asked to interpret for an authority such as the Children's Division in a case where parents' handling of a child is in question. She said that she would only do this if it were a family with whom she already had a strong relationship:

> They don't have one bilingual person working in the Children's Division. When they go, they call on me to translate for them. I will not do it, because if I walk into that interview to translate for Child Protective, I become one of them. If I want to work with that family again, they won't trust me.

The logical conclusion of this argument is that agency personnel may find themselves in an adversarial role with the school district, and this had happened in the past. In Chapter 10, I will examine the role such advocacy activities have played in bringing about current changes in the school district.

SUMMARY

Differences in language, experience, and expectations can set the stage for a tremendous gap in communication between culturally different parents and school personnel. In this study, parents expected and wanted to trust the school and were more comfortable when relationships with professionals had a personal tone. Errors on the part of the school and frequent changes in placement, as well as out-of-neighborhood placement, however, had led to mistrust and confusion. For many years, the district's extensive use of written communication in English compounded these problems. Even when most letters and reports were sent in Spanish, their meaning was still not clear because of the use of educational jargon, the inadequate information and experiential base from which the parents operated, and because of the need for a more personalized style of communication. These failures in communication were made worse when parents who attempted to participate were not aware of the meaning and importance of events in special education. Thus they were not really aware of the implications of their participation and consent. Their consent was truly uninformed.

What constitutes informed consent? The Education for All Handicapped Children Act mandates parents' access to all information regarding their children, their consent to all placement procedures, and their "participation and consultation" in decision making. The data of this study have shown that for culturally different parents to be adequately informed regarding the special education system would require personalized communication not only of a factual nature, but communication sufficiently open-ended and reciprocal as to engage parents in dialogue regarding cultural differences in meanings of disability, lines of authority between the state and the family, parents' preferences and opinions in matters such as placement and teaching methods, and the true extent and meaning of their rights under the law.

Yet, as Skrtic (1988) has observed, the requirements of the law are unrealistic insofar as their successful attainment would require schools to function "like an ad-hocracy (problem-solving organizations in which teams of regular and special education professionals collaborate reciprocally in the interest of individual students)" — a requirement that is difficult to achieve within the machine-bureaucracy of school systems (p. 511). Skrtic concludes that this reliance on bureaucratic controls makes it likely that "P.L. 94-142 monitors will incorrectly interpret procedural compliance as actual implementation of the law. They will be monitoring the myth and not what actually happens to students" (p. 511).

This was the trap into which this school district had fallen with regard to parental participation — a commitment to compliance rather than communication. On the assumption that information could adequately be conveyed within a system of formal written communication, a parent's signature or presence at a meeting would be considered consent, the quality of that consent being the parents' problem rather than the district's. And even within this emphasis on the letter rather than the spirit of the law, there occurred numerous violations of the most minimal requirements for consent.

It is true that most studies of parent participation have shown that a great deal of participation is passive (Gilliam & Coleman, 1981; Lusthaus, Lusthaus, & Gibbs, 1981; Lynch & Stein, 1987; Schuck, 1979). Turnbull and Turnbull (1982, 1986) have made the point that parents have different levels of interest in participation and have the right to participate at their chosen level. Some parents in this study have illustrated this point. However, since a great many findings have been based mainly on White, middle-class parents, it cannot be assumed that this observation should be relevant to a population who, by virtue of cultural and linguistic difference, are patently uninformed. Their consent is required, and the level of information and understanding shown by the majority of the parents points to the impossibility of informed consent, let alone meaningful participation.

While their stories tell of various failures of communication between the school district and the Puerto Rican families, and even major blunders on the part of the district, the pattern that emerges seems circular: parents begin at a disadvantage because the school district has described their children as "handicapped" — a word they consider inappropriate to their healthy children who speak in two languages. They are told that the children will be placed in special classes but feel they have no role in influencing the location of these classes and are disappointed at what they consider a repetitive and watered-down curriculum. Knowing little about the system, they find its impersonal tone alien and intimidating and are fearful of approaching it to find out more. All their information comes through formal letters in a language they do not know and using terms for which their interpreters often do not provide a Spanish equivalent. Finally, their attempts at participation seldom get them what they want, so they withdraw in skepticism and frustration, each communication event an additional source of confusion.

9

Toward Informed Consent

*Legal Compliance Versus
Culturally Responsive Practice*

The legal mandate for parental participation has been met by the development of specific regulations in each state regarding both written and face-to-face communication with parents. As the previous chapter showed, there are documents to be signed, rules and timelines to be observed, and, not the least intimidating for parents, meetings whose sole topic of conversation is their children's learning difficulties. The data so far have shown some events that were not in compliance with the regulations, but more often they show that even when there is compliance, this does not necessarily ensure parental participation or even informed consent. This chapter will focus on meetings that illustrate the difference between compliance with the letter of the law and professional efforts to infuse into that inert structure the breath of culturally responsive practice.

The individualized education plan (IEP) phase 1 meeting is that annual occasion on which parents come face to face with all the representatives of the system. It is a time for communication and decision making and constitutes one of the central procedures of special education administration. In this state, the meeting must be held no later than 40 school days after the student's initial referral, and its main purpose is to review reports of the student's assessment and current performance so as to make recommendations for the next year's placement and program. Phase 2 of the IEP must be developed within 30 days of a student's entry into a program; with the input of the teacher, a member of the team that evaluated the student, and the parent, this document will specify curriculum goals, related services, and mainstreamed activities.

These meetings constitute parents' official opportunity to be influential in the decision-making process. Yet Mehan and colleagues (1986), in their careful analysis of such meetings, conclude that these events represent the ratification of actions that occurred at previous stages in the process. These researchers do not interpret this as a conspiratorial process, but simply as the way that decisions are arrived at, every step of the referral-to-placement process further entrenching the path to the "decision" that will be stated in the official meeting.

Further, their observations of meetings showed that the underlying assumptions that determined the structure of participation were shared by all parties in the process; for example, assumptions of the superiority of technical knowledge over commonsense knowledge and of the greater authority of those who hold higher rank within the school organization. By virtue of such assumptions, the reports of the psychologist and the nurse took on the character of "professional reports" as compared to the "lay reports" of the parent and classroom teacher; typical features differentiating these were that the "professional reports" were "presented" and received without challenge or question, while the "lay reports" were "elicited" through question and answer and appeared more like an interrogation of the mother and classroom teacher, who were "constantly interrupted by questions from other committee members" (Mehan et al., 1986, p. 128).

These participation structures have important implications for the meanings that emerge from such encounters. Mehan and colleagues (1986) observe that, given these assumptions, the use of technical language by professionals removes the usual grounds by which people negotiate meaning and ensures that the professional version of a student's profile will be credentialed. They explain:

> Because the speaker and hearers do not share membership in a common language-community, hearers do not have the expertise to interrupt or to question. To request a clarification of the psychologist, then, is to challenge the authority of the official position of the district and its representative . . . [thus] committee members (including the parents) remain silent, thereby implicitly contributing to the guise that understanding has been achieved. (pp. 130–131)

These process features are mirrored in the actual content of the decisions made, as is nicely illustrated both by Mehan and colleagues' study and a similar analysis of IEP meetings by Bennett (1988). In the former, the researchers illustrate the way educators' "cultural theory" structured and delimited the reasoning process by which a student's classification was arrived at. The process of elimination used in decision making revealed the belief that "situations and individuals, not structural and institutional arrangements, are possible causes of the student's success and failure" (Mehan et al., 1986, p. 132). Thus institutional effects were not considered as possible sources of the students' learning difficulties.

Similarly, Bennett (1988) focuses on the dialogue between an IEP team and a Hispanic mother who had challenged the IEP's description of her son's behavior. Bennett's analysis demonstrates how professionals defined what was appropriate to be included in the IEP; by defining the IEP as being solely concerned with behavior presumably "belonging" to the child, professionals excluded from the discussion the mother's concern with classroom structure. Thus the mother's interpretation of the role of classroom structure in her child's behavior was delegitimated by the meeting.

In the light of these observations, the central question derived from the data of this study is: What is the potential for genuine parental influence within the limits of the decision-making process, the structure of parent-professional discourse, and the cultural theory that informs the entire process of a meeting? Although parents are invited to be present and participate, there is no escaping the fact that they are respondents in the situation. Indeed, the data of this study show unequivocally that culturally different parents come to these meetings as strangers to a system that is legally required to include them, but whose patterns of discourse are so structured as to exclude meaningful dialogue, and, indeed, to delegitimate parents' views. This chapter will show that, while parents' own personal styles will have an impact on the proceedings, it is essentially the structure and atmosphere provided that will either include or exclude parents.

Chapter 8 showed the tremendous miscommunication that had resulted from parents' lack of information as well as careless or inappropriate professional behavior. Nevertheless, the school district was at the same time engaged in intensive efforts to remedy these problems. The provision of family liaison workers and the appointment of a task force to examine issues related to speech and language assessment of limited-English-proficient (LEP) students were two efforts that were beginning to show a beneficial effect. This impact was becoming evident in certain meetings, in particular those of one school-based team whose annual review meetings achieved a standard of excellence not observed in other meetings. These efforts will be reviewed in the following sections.

IEP MEETINGS: IDEAL AND REALITY

Notwithstanding the plethora of research evidence showing that parents are largely passive recipients of professional decision making, the state-of-the-art in this area continues to envisage a collaborative partnership between parents and school personnel.

Of the many recommendations that have been made regarding improving parental participation, a model developed by Turnbull and Turnbull (1986) may be described as the most generic in nature, in that it offers a detailed analysis of the structure, content, and process of these conferences and should be applicable to any population of parents. Recommendations regarding bilingual families in particular have been made by Baca and Cervantes (1984), who have outlined an approach that focuses on broader issues of information, parent-child interaction, and family support. Casuso (1978) has also presented similar recommendations for working with Spanish-speaking families of preschool handicapped children. The most direct attention to minority families in the IEP process has come from Marion (1979), whose step-by-step outline for including minority parents from the initiation of the referral process through placement of the student emphasizes personal contact and the expression of genuine respect for the culture of parents.

Marion's and Turnbull and Turnbull's models represent ideal practice in the implementation of the IEP process and will be used in this chapter as points of comparison for the meetings observed in the study. In particular, Turnbull and Turnbull's model focuses on the structure of the actual conference, which is conceptualized in terms of six components implemented in an "an atmosphere of open communication" (1986, p. 245). Our discussion will be organized around these 6 structural components of an ideal meeting:

1. Preconference preparation
2. Initial conference proceedings
3. Review of formal evaluation and current levels of performance
4. Development of goals and objectives
5. Specification of placement and related services
6. Conclusion

This chapter will focus on information derived from my observations of the following five IEP phase 1 meetings:

- A triennial meeting for Francisca's granddaughter, which Francisca did not attend
- Two annual reviews for Rita's children, Rafael and Rosemary
- An annual review for Inés's son, Ricardo
- A triennial review for Juan's daughter, Juanita

In addition, I will also refer to phase 1 meetings which I did not observe, but which were reported to me by parents. Of the twelve participants, all but three reported having attended such meetings, which they generally remembered quite well because of the formality of the event and the presence of several professionals. Reports of phase 2 meetings were more difficult to elicit, since they often included only the teacher and parents, and, as was explained in the previous chapter, many parents were not sure if they were IEP meetings or simply occasions on which they "went to the school to talk to the teacher." The only phase 2 meeting I observed has already been discussed in the foregoing chapter as an example of the "uninformed participation" of Dora in a meeting that was inappropriately recorded as an IEP phase 2 meeting.

I will use Turnbull and Turnbull's (1986) six components as a framework for examining the meetings observed, and will also refer to reported meetings for further illustration.

Preconference Planning

Turnbull describes two aspects of preconference planning: first, the preplanning done within the IEP team, such as collecting documents, appointing a "case manager," and so on, and, second, the preplanning done with the parents. Since I could not participate in any preplanning done within a team, I could only infer this from their apparent preparedness at a meeting.

Some preconference planning with parents had been done by various district personnel on an ad hoc, individual basis, but efforts toward systematic preconference planning were just being started as part of the district's efforts toward improving communication with Hispanic parents. In those meetings I attended, Francisca was the only one who had any preparation apart from routine information by letter, while a preconference discussion was reported to me by Iris and Alfonso.

These two instances of preconference planning were quite different in nature and pointed to both the strengths and potential dangers of this approach. The strength lies in the potential for ensuring that parents understand all the issues of concern to their child's program and are given an opportunity to prepare their preferences and objectives. One danger revealed was the potential of preconference preparation to be used as a means of persuading rather than preparing the parent. I will illustrate these two possibilities using data from preconference planning with Francisca and with Iris and Alfonso.

Preparing the Parent.   Elizabeth, the newly employed family liaison for special education, used the phrase "bending over backwards" to describe current efforts of the school district to meet the needs of Hispanic parents. Her attempts to prepare Francisca for her granddaughter's upcoming triennial review offered a striking example of this.

Professionals who worked with Francisca tended to describe her as one of the more recalcitrant parents. While she held very strong opinions, and proved to be one of the most informative participants in this study, her attitude toward the school system was one of combined impatience and resignation. Over a period of some 7 or 8 years, Francisca's interaction with the special education system had amounted to what she described as a "struggle." Shocked by the district's classification of her daughter as mentally retarded, she felt that her attempts at advocacy on this issue had been futile; so, too, had been her efforts to have her granddaughter Rosita's placement changed after she had been moved without her permission. Saying that she was "tired of fighting with these Americans," Francisca would participate actively in any meetings held in her home but explained that she usually was not well enough to attend meetings at the school district offices.

Preconference planning with the parent in this case consisted of a home visit, about a month before, by the teacher and Elizabeth, with Vera, a Hispanic social worker, also present. The teacher reviewed Rosita's progress and recommended that she remain in her current placement, but Francisca told them that she still was not happy with her granddaughter's being in a school so far away from home. The school personnel advised her that she could request a move at the upcoming annual review meeting. Francisca was advised in writing of the date of the meeting and reminded of it by phone the night before, but she said she was not well enough to go, although both Elizabeth and myself arrived separately to take her. Elizabeth reviewed with her what she wanted said on her behalf, and at first this was only the request that Rosita be sent back to the neighborhood school. However, as the discussion went on, Francisca commented that another point on which she disagreed was Rosita's label of mentally retarded.

Elizabeth said Francisca had not told her this before and advised her to go to the meeting and say what she thought. When Francisca insisted that her ill health would not permit this, but that she would willingly go some other time, Elizabeth phoned the chairman of the meeting to see if the meeting could be postponed. She spoke at some length with the chairman, who concluded that since the date had already been changed once, and since most of the participants were already waiting, they would go ahead and if Francisca did not approve of any decisions taken she could make a formal appeal later on.

After these impeccable attempts at preconference planning, there was one ironic outcome: in Francisca's absence from the meeting, her wish for a change of placement was not, in fact, presented to the meeting as a whole. Elizabeth reported it to the chairman immediately before the start of the meeting, but it was not included in the otherwise thorough discus-

sion that constituted the meeting itself. The triennial meetings are so structured as to exclude all but the core of the committee for the actual placement decision, so that after the reports, "temporary members" (a term
used by Mehan et al., 1986) are asked to leave the room while the committee decides on placement. It may be that Francisca's request was discussed
at this point, but, if so, this would still have excluded key people such as
Rosita's teacher and speech pathologist and, of course, the parent, had she
been there.

During this break, I questioned Elizabeth about the omission of Francisca's request and she checked with the chairman, who said that she had
remembered the request but that it would not be possible, since the only
other program available would have been at the Harper School, which the
grandmother had already refused because it was too far away.

It appears that since Francisca's wish was considered unreasonable or,
from the district's point of view, impossible, it was discounted without
being presented at the meeting. In an informal discussion outside the
conference room, Rosita's teacher and speech pathologist both expressed
the opinion that Rosita should not be moved since she was just beginning to
get over her shyness and become comfortable in this class. The point at
issue here is not whose opinion was right, but that the committee's failure
to even discuss the parent's request in her absence made a mockery of the
careful attempts at preconference preparation — indeed, of the claim that
parents' input is valued.

After the meeting, Elizabeth returned to Francisca's home and reported the outcome with great care. She emphasized that if Francisca was still
dissatisfied with the committee's decision on either placement or classification she could make a "formal appeal in writing," asking the committee to
review her classification or her placement. Elizabeth said this three times,
and each time Francisca looked out of the window, replying, with a shrug
and expression of resignation, that she supposed it would be okay since
Rosita seemed happy in the school and loved the teacher. Regarding the
classification, Francisca did not reply at all.

There seemed to me no doubt that Elizabeth's meticulous reminders to
Francisca of her right to appeal simply underscored how unlikely it would
be that Francisca would initiate such formal proceedings. The implication
was that, by her own choice, this parent had not attended the officially
designated event and that to choose another avenue of discourse would be
far more difficult.

The attempt at preconference preparation in this instance was impeccable. The fact that it failed to unearth Francisca's disagreement with the
classification reflected her resignation at her inability to do anything to

change it, since she had been through this before with her daughter, Angelica. This demonstrates how the accumulation of a parent's negative experiences with the system can undermine even the best professional attempts at communication. On the other hand, it is also evident that Francisca's resignation was well founded, since the outcome of the meeting was that both Rosita's classification and current placement were retained. Indeed, the committee's failure to adequately represent the parent's wish seemed to render the whole process farcical. Not so much the outcome, as the process of the meeting validated Francisca's statement that "La opinion de nosotros no vale" (Our wishes are not valued).

Persuading the Parent. One other event in the course of the study, which might be described as an attempt at preconference preparation, suggests the possibility of negative effects if such meetings are not handled properly. This was an informal meeting initiated for Iris and Alfonso by Rosana, the school's bilingual liaison worker. This meeting was an informal discussion, prior to the triennial meeting, regarding these parents' desire to have their son, Mark, moved to another school.

Although only the teacher, liaison worker, and family were present, the family interpreted this discussion as the official decision-making event and said they were unaware that there was another, more formal, meeting to be held. They came away from the meeting believing that they had no choice but to agree to the school personnel's advice that Mark should stay at his present school. This was particularly distressing to the family, since Mark had expressed great unhappiness with his current placement.

In this instance, the notion of preconference planning seems to have been used as an attempt to persuade parents out of their wishes. In a discussion of the imbalance of power between parents and professionals, Gliedman and Roth (1980) have argued that professionals have the right to try to persuade parents to appreciate the professional point of view, but they emphasize that professionals have no right to use their "immense practical and moral power to intimidate or manipulate the parent" (p. 145). Persuasion, however, can be an insidious business, ranging from what Gliedman and Roth refer to as "the power of kindness" to overt manipulation to which parents are particularly susceptible when they are not fully aware of available options or procedures. Indeed, Mehan and colleagues (1986) have referred to the very process of these meetings as "the discourse of persuasion" (p. 109). When the participation structures inherent in such discourse are practiced with parents who have no cultural context for participation, the outcome is, in effect, their effective exclusion from the entire process.

Initial Proceedings

Every event needs an introduction, and, as in all social occasions, the style and content of the introduction set the tone for much of what is to come. Turnbull and Turnbull (1986) describe the initial proceedings of the IEP meeting as functioning to introduce participants, set the atmosphere, and give information regarding the agenda as well as parents' legal rights. They point out the importance of this in the light of observations that many parents feel intimidated by the conferences. Marion (1979) has particularly emphasized the negative impact of a large group of professionals on minority parents and the importance of courteous treatment, such as addressing parents by the titles Mr. and Mrs. He says that such basic courtesies are often not accorded to minority parents.

One of the most successful meetings began with a very traditional greeting initiated by the parent, Juan — a round of spontaneous handshakes with every member of the meeting. This customary formality is particularly valued in traditional Hispanic cultures and symbolizes the importance of respect for each individual present.

For Hispanic people, the requirements of the tradition of "respeto" call not only for the use of titles on formal occasions, but also for appropriate choice of formal or informal second-person pronouns ("usted" vs. "tú"), which indicate the importance of an occasion or differences in age or social role among participants. Thus the American style of using first names even on formal occasions can be confusing. If this informal style is used, however, it is a matter of courtesy and mutual respect that it be applied to all participants. The meetings showed that this was not always the case.

In addition to the style of address being an indicator of mutual respect, foreign names and customs may create difficulties for both groups. As mentioned in an earlier discussion of communication difficulties, the Puerto Rican parents said they had trouble remembering the "American" names. It is even more complicated for Americans, since the challenge is not only in remembering a name that sounds strange but in knowing which surname to use. Hispanic professionals in the study told me that some Americans believe that Hispanics try to confuse them by using different surnames. However, it is traditional that the child receives both the father's and mother's family names, but if the name is to be abbreviated, it is the father's that will be used (Fitzpatrick , 1987).

I will use Inés's and Rita's meetings to illustrate the wide range of practice regarding such courtesies. Inés's surname is Valera, and her son is Ricardo Fuentes Valera. The fact that he is known in school as Ricardo Fuentes led the chairman to introduce Inés as "Mrs. Fuentes." Inés resolved the difficulty herself by saying, when her turn came to introduce herself:

"My name is Inés Valera — not Fuentes — and I am Ricardo Fuentes's mother." Titles and surnames were used consistently throughout Inés's meeting, and the tone was friendly yet respectful.

The meeting with Rita for Rafael, on the contrary, presented a striking contrast and illustrated many of the points made by Marion (1980a) about discourteous treatment. While the classroom teacher met us in the main office and led us in a very courteous manner into the meeting, what seemed like a good beginning was soon overshadowed by a marked lack of courtesy and an unmistakably careless style throughout the meeting itself.

The teacher introduced Rita to the committee in a friendly enough manner, as "Rita Rodriguez, Rafael's mother"; he did not offer his own first name, however. He introduced a student teacher in Rafael's class but he did not introduce two other people sitting at the end of the table, nor did they introduce themselves. Rita told me later that she assumed they were school district representatives. One of these, a man, gave Rita and me a document to sign, indicating our participation. Since he was in charge of the records, I assumed he was the chairman of the meeting, although the teacher took the lead. Since the teacher had not indicated his first name, and Rita already knew him by his surname, she continued to address him as "Mr. Richards," while he called her "Rita."

Review of Formal Evaluation and Current Performance

The formal reviews constitute the information-giving phase of these meetings. This is particularly challenging because of the complex and academic nature of much of the information. The formal evaluation is usually reviewed at initial referrals, triennial meetings, and meetings for change of label, but current levels of performance are reviewed at all meetings. In addition, the student's classification is stated at this time.

Although the responsibility for these procedures necessarily falls to the professionals, parents' input can be useful and they should be fully informed of the outcome of the assessment process in a way that can be constructive for the family (Fulmer, Cohen, & Monaco, 1985). Turnbull and Turnbull (1986) point out that since this information can be highly technical, IEP teams ought to seriously consider separate evaluation conferences prior to the decision-making conference. In meetings with non-English-speaking parents, the need for translation further complicates an already challenging task.

The report of a student's current level of performance, which is usually given by the teacher or other persons working directly with the student, is the less technical of the two reports, since it refers to everyday school activities, achievement levels, and behavior of the child. Thus the best of these meetings were marked by the use of this report as a time for some interchange between parent and teacher regarding observations of the student's progress. In Rita's meeting for Rosemary at Watkins School, for example, she was encouraged to talk at some length about her views of Rosemary's progress.

In all the meetings I observed, the amount of information was appropriate and relevant to decision making, but there was a strong tendency to use educational jargon. Even those teachers who used only minimal jargon used some terms that a parent, and certainly one with limited English, would not understand, such as, "time-on-task," "a hands-on-approach," and "option 1." Other teachers consistently used more extreme jargon, such as "We are emphasizing a lot of manipulatives," or "decoding skills," or "expressive" or "receptive language."

The report on current performance includes information regarding the child's current program placement and, as I pointed out in the previous chapter, this information is often misunderstood by parents. At Rita's meeting, her misunderstanding of her son's placement became evident at the meeting's end, when she asked if Rafael had "passed" the grade. The teacher had begun the meeting by saying that Rafael was in an "option 1" class, which actually indicates that the class is ungraded, but Rita did not know that. This represented unusually careless practice, however, and in all the other meetings such information was given more appropriately.

Regarding the formal evaluation, the main challenge is to present in lay terms information that is considered esoteric even by professionals in education. There are two main decisions to be made by the person reporting: how much detail to give and what kind of language to use. The report must be accurate and comprehensive, but it must be done in lay terms if it is to be meaningful to parents. The use of jargon is most typically observed in these reports, and Marion (1979) and Turnbull and Turnbull (1986) have observed that it has the effect of confusing parents. Mehan and colleagues (1986) have charged that technical language is actually used as a reinforcer of power. Their observation that this language was never questioned or challenged by committee members was also true at meetings observed in this study, with the exception only of the interpreter, whose intervention will subsequently be discussed at length.

In most of the meetings the reports of the formal evaluation relied heavily on technical language, but one meeting stood out as an illustration that the ideal of effective communication is indeed attainable—the meeting at Harper for Juanita. Juanita's father, Juan, was a quiet participant who seemed, by his answers and by his own occasional questions, to understand the main import of the report. This was particularly important because Juan had requested the reevaluation since he did not agree with the label emotionally disturbed, and one of the purposes of this meeting was to report on the decision about Juanita's classification. I will focus on the main features that made this report so successful.

Second-Language Acquisition and the Assessment Process.

It was evident that the Committee on Special Education was aware of the complexity of the evaluation process with children who are in transition between two languages. In all phase 1 meetings I observed, the question of the importance of native language in the assessment process was raised. The committee at Juan's meeting, however, was exemplary in its attention to this issue. Reports from the psychologist and speech pathologist paid detailed attention to the differing levels of performance evidenced by Juanita in Spanish and English.

The psychologist concluded that Juanita showed a large discrepancy between language and performance skills but that within language there was not a great overall difference between her English and Spanish. She said she would classify Juanita as learning disabled but was not sure whether the source of her difficulty was her overall language development or her reading skills. Saying that "maybe Dad can help us here," she asked Juan what he thought of this. He replied: "Yo creo que el problema el el idioma, porque cuando ella está hablando con los otros niños en inglés, y yo le pregunto a ella qué es lo que ellos estaban diciendo, ella no puede traducirlo bien al español, aunque ella habla bastante bien en español." (I think the problem is language, because if she is talking with the other children in English and I ask her to tell me what they were saying, she cannot translate it into Spanish, although she speaks quite well in Spanish.)

This discussion led into the report of the speech pathologist, who addressed Juan directly, looking at him instead of at the interpreter. After asking him several questions about language in the home, she asked perhaps the most important question of the meeting—whether Juanita's development in Spanish stopped when she came here and had to start speaking in English. Juan replied: "Si, porque ella aprendió el Inglés rapidamente y está olvidando el español ahora." (Yes, because she picked up English quickly and is losing her Spanish now.)

The speech pathologist concluded, after some more questioning of Juan, that she thought that Juanita had not developed a primary language fully before beginning to acquire a second. She recommended that the family should encourage Juanita to speak in Spanish at home and continue to develop her vocabulary and become more advanced in Spanish. The school, meanwhile, would work on her English.

This discussion reflected some of the literature on second-language acquisition described in Chapter 3 and was the most probing and sophisticated approach I heard in any meeting. Rather than a "report" from professional to parent, the presentation of the formal evaluation emerged into a shared exploration of the meaning of this student's learning difficulties.

The question of the amount of assessment information to report is difficult to resolve. It would be unethical to report differing amounts according to the information level of the parent, yet it does seem that an undue amount of detail in a formal evaluation may create an information overload; I felt that this may have been the case in some parts of Juán's meeting. This is where parent education programs and preconference planning, or a special evaluation conference, would help by developing parents' information base, thus making it more likely that this component of the IEP meeting will be meaningful.

The Role of the Interpreter.   None of the foregoing reporting could have been accomplished without an efficient interpreter. There are two particularly important features of interpretation to consider. First, and most basic, the interpreter must report accurately and honestly everything that is said. Second, if there is a marked gap in knowledge between the speaker and listener, the interpreter must decide how to modify without omitting or distorting information or meaning.

On the simpler level of accuracy and honesty, some parents in the study expressed dissatisfaction with interpreters they had had. Both Rita and Ana told me that they do not let interpreters know how much English they know, so they cannot be fooled. They said that there are certain interpreters whom they do not trust and will not use. The question of the level at which to offer translated information is more subtle but equally important. With a good interpreter it could be that the parent using a different language may actually have the advantage of receiving a simplified yet equally accurate report.

In the case of Juan's meeting, Elizabeth's careful, lay translation of the report made it a meaningful, though difficult, exercise. The interpreter insisted that every statement in the report be given in lay terms in English, and then she would translate into Spanish in almost identical words. In other words, she did not accept the English jargon and take it upon herself to translate it into lay Spanish; she continually asked the speakers to simplify in English, in this way relying on them to give the exact meaning they intended. This served two purposes: first, it emphasized the fact that she was concerned about being accurate, and, second, it forced the speakers to be more aware of their use of jargon. After the meeting the psychologist said to me that she had not realized how much jargon she used. Some typical exchanges in this meeting were:

Psychologist: Juanita is performing in the borderline range.
Interpreter: Please clarify that for me.
Psychologist: It means she is below the average child of her age but not low enough to be in the retarded range.
Interpreter: Esta significa que ella está bajo del niño promedio por su edad pero no tan bajo para estar en la clasificación retardada.

*   *   *

Psychologist: She shows some decoding difficulties.
Interpreter: Please explain that.
Psychologist: She has trouble breaking the word into parts.
Interpreter: Ella tiene dificultades en dividir las palabras.

*   *   *

Psychologist: She does have trouble with spatial memory tasks.
Interpreter: Could you give some examples?
Psychologist: [Gives concrete examples using sketches and hand demonstrations.]

Besides explaining the meaning of individual bits of jargon, it is also important for the interpreter to explain the importance of events being referred to. In the previous chapter, I pointed to many parents' lack of awareness of the names and importance of some special education events, such as the IEP meeting or annual or triennial review. This meeting with Juan provides a good example of the power of the interpreter on this issue. Toward the end of the meeting, after it had been confirmed that Juanita's classification would be changed from emotionally disturbed to learning disabled, the chairman said that the committee would consider this meeting Juanita's triennial, since it would have been due next year, but all the testing had been done a year early. In translating this, Elizabeth said in Spanish:

Ahora su clasificación ha sido cambiada a *learning disabled*. Esto no significa *mentally retarded*, solamente que ella está un poquito bajo del niño promedio por su edad, y ella está incapacitada para aprender a leer y para el desarrollo del lenguaje. Ella se quedará en la educación especial y tendrá una evaluación cada 3 años, porque, según la ley del estado, esta tiene que ser hecho. En cualquier parte del estado donde viva, ella tiene que tener una nueva evaluación cada 3 años, porque siempre hay la posibilidad que su clasificación pueda cambiar mientras ella cambia. El próximo año sería el tercer año desde que ella entró en la educación especial, pero ya que se acaba de hacer esta evaluación, esta reunión se considera como su "evaluación trienial"—su evaluación de cada tres años—y dentro de tres años ella tendrá otra.

(Her classification has now been changed to learning disabled. This does not mean mentally retarded; she is just below the average child for her age and is learning impaired in reading and in language development. She will remain in special education and will have an evaluation every 3 years, because under state law this must be done. Wherever you may live in the state she must have a new evaluation every 3 years because there is always the possibility that her classification could change as she changes. Next year would have been 3 years since she was in special education, but since this reevaluation has just been done, this meeting will be considered as her "triennial evaluation"—her review of every 3 years— and 3 years from now she will have another.)

In this way the interpreter gave the parent the Spanish term for "triennial" as well as a full explanation of its importance. In emphasizing the legal implications of the event she also made it clear that these meetings are not held at the whim of the school district or parent.

Decisions about Goals, Placement, and Related Services

Information from formal evaluations and teachers' reports leads to decision making about goals and objectives as well as placement and related services. Turnbull and Turnbull (1986) conceive of these as two separate functions, but in the meetings I observed they were usually presented together. These two components are actually the decision-making part of the meetings and, in Turnbull and Turnbull's model, parents are expected to have a great deal of input. In the meetings I observed and was told about by parents, the norm was minimal parental input, with the two meetings at Harper School standing out in contrast.

I will illustrate with examples involving Francisca and Ana, both of whom had told me of their dissatisfaction with their children's repetitive and unchallenging curriculum. Yet neither offered their opinions in this regard when it came to the annual reviews. Francisca was absent and had asked Elizabeth only to address the issue of placement in a closer school. I did not attend Ana's meeting but received a report of it from her and from Vera, the social worker who went with her to interpret.

Ana had planned to tell the committee about two concerns she had: first, she was anxious to know whether or not they were going to keep Gina at her present school; second, she did not think Gina was making any progress, because the goals seemed not to have changed since the previous year. After the meeting, however, she told me that it had been "very quick—only about 10 minutes" and everyone was "very nice," but that when the teacher said that Gina was progressing she felt she could not disagree with her because "she is the teacher." So she said nothing, but felt very happy that they had decided to keep Gina at this school for another 3 years.

Ana's delight with the committee's decision not to move her daughter reflected both her assumption that it was totally their decision and the fact that this 9-year-old had already been moved four times in 3 years. Further, Ana's history with the committee had led her to the conclusion that "they will do what they want anyhow." She had learned this, she said, in the year that Gina had been moved without her knowledge: despite this distressing event, at the annual review that year the committee decided to move Gina back to Phillips School, where she had been the year before. Ana told me about that meeting:

> Había siete personas, todas eran señoras—muy agradables—la maestra, la señora importante, dos otras quienes no las conozco, una secretaria, mi interprete y yo. Me explicaban del progreso de Gina en la matemática y todas sus clases, y opinaban si debían cambiarla de esa clase a un nivel más alto—en nivel 3—no es el grado 3 pero nivel 3. Entonces yo hablé y les dije que quería que Gina se quedara en la misma clase; no quería que cambiara a otra escuela y otra escuela y otra escuela, porque le está haciendo daño a ella. Pero ellos dijeron que no, porque ella iba a un nivel más alto, entonces tenían que pasarla por otra escuela.

> (There were seven people there, all ladies—very nice—the teacher, the lady in charge, two others who I don't know, a secretary, my interpreter and I. They explained to me about Gina's progress in math and all her classes and they discussed whether she should be moved from this class to a higher level—level 3—not grade 3 but level 3. Then I spoke and I said that I wanted Gina to stay in the same class; I didn't want her changing to another school and another school and another school because it is harming her. But they said no, because she has gone up to a higher level, so they have to move her to another school.)

Other reports of placement decisions made at meetings in the past reinforced my impression that parents' opinions were influential only in extreme circumstances and that the norm was for the placement decision to be made either without, or in spite of, the parent's opinion. Perhaps the best example I got of this was Rita's explanation of how the committee came to change their recommendation at one of her annual reviews.

I have previously referred to the practice at triennial meetings of asking parents and other invitees to leave the room while the placement decision is made. Accordingly, Rita left the room, then returned to be told that, although Rosemary had been moved four times in 2 years, the committee was now recommending that she be moved back to Spruce Street School, to the first class in which she had been placed. Rita became very angry and told her interpreter to tell the committee that she would go back to Puerto Rico rather than agree to that, since her daughter had been very unhappy in that class. The chairman then asked Rita and her representative to leave the room once more, and on their return, the chairman said that the committee had changed their decision and would move Rosemary to Watkins School instead.

There is no question that the exclusion of parents at the presumed moment of decision making refutes the espoused notion of collaboration. It must be expected that parents will have preferences regarding choice of school, especially for a young, supposedly handicapped child; if their opinions cannot be influential in such a matter, it would be totally unrealistic to expect them to be influential in technical matters such as instructional approaches or goals. Further, and more ironic, is the fact that a parent's objection could, indeed, be influential, as Rita's ultimately was. Given this, why should the committee go through the charade of excluding the parent from the placement decision? Such a strategy — to be required to leave the room while a decision is made, and to return to be given the "verdict" — is the ultimate declaration of who holds power. Indeed, Rita had to leave the room for a second time in order for the committee to yield to her objection!

It is true that in all meetings the committee asks for parents' opinions at some point, or on some particular issue, and some professionals say that the parents do not comment even when invited to do so. There are many factors that may explain parents' lack of response. Both Francisca and Ana expressed a feeling of resignation, based on past experience, that the committee's preference would stand regardless of the parent's opinion. Many also echoed Ana's sentiment that, on the matter of educational goals and curriculum, it is not appropriate to disagree with the teacher's judgment. One parent, Delia, simply explained she gets so "nervous" she could not say anything at the meetings.

One example of an exemplary attempt to include the parent in the placement decision, however, occurred in Juan's meeting at Harper School. The committee explained to Juan that they were trying to keep Juanita in the same class as her friend, since they felt that this affiliation was crucial to her growing self-confidence. They asked Juan, however, whether it was important to him whether his daughter had a male or female teacher, since this would be part of the decision. Juan indicated that he trusted the committee to make this decision. This discussion demonstrated a respectful concern for both the student and the parent.

Conclusion of Meetings

The manner of concluding a meeting is as important as all other aspects. Both the pace of the entire meeting and the way in which parents are dismissed send a message regarding the importance of their role in the event.

Rita's meeting for Rafael, which began with incomplete introductions of committee members and inadequate information regarding Rafael's placement, was concluded in a perfunctory and unusually careless manner. The first attempt to conclude the meeting came unexpectedly, when, at the end of reports from two teachers and the speech pathologist, there was a pause, broken after a few seconds by an interjection from the man seated at the head of the table, who had never been introduced either by name or status, but who seemed to be chairing the meeting. He said suddenly: "So, are we finished?"

Before anyone could answer, he rose and left the room. The others remained seated, and Rita, who had spoken only twice so far, quickly asked the classroom teacher if Rafael had "passed" the grade, revealing, as was discussed at length in Chapter 8, her total lack of information. As the teacher was concluding his response to Rita, the man who had left the room returned, took his seat, and said again: "So, are we finished?"

The teacher stood up and thanked Rita and me for coming and said that she should feel free to call him if she had any questions. He was very courteous and walked us to the door of the school and stood outside in a relaxed manner, obviously willing to chat for a while. And there began what I would call the "meeting after the meeting," in which Rita asked him to tell her more about what kind of job he would try to get for Rafael and I asked him to clarify his comment that the classification "probably had a lot to do with second language issues." He agreed to give me an appointment to discuss his impressions of this with me. (In that interview, Mr. Richards explained that he believed the current testing procedures were culturally inappropriate for many limited-English-proficient students, and that many of these students were functioning too well to be really cognitively impaired.)

Rita's meeting lasted 15 minutes and reflected many of the issues raised by participants in the study: inadequate information regarding the non-graded class and its implications for high school graduation, inadequate respect for and courtesy to the parent, a presentation of the label that hinted at the role of second-language acquisition without explaining it, and even a lost evaluation.

By contrast, Inés's meeting at Harper School went on for an hour and a half, and then for another half an hour to discuss problems raised by Inés about the upcoming placement of her nephews, who were soon to arrive from Puerto Rico. At this meeting it felt as if the participants were prepared to go on all day; indeed, the meeting stood out as proof that the essential features of Turnbull and Turnbull's (1986) and Marion's (1979) models are attainable. This model meeting demonstrated the best of this school district's progress toward informed consent for culturally different parents.

TOWARD THE IDEAL: A MODEL MEETING

The first striking feature of Inés's meeting was the fact that it was the second annual review held that spring for Ricardo. She told the school that she had not been aware of the first meeting and requested another. (As it turned out in discussion at the end of the meeting, Inés had received notice of the first and had signed it, indicating she could not come at that time; she had not realized that the meeting would go ahead without her.) The second meeting was held with the full complement of committee members as well as Inés, myself, and Elizabeth and Gloria, both bilingual district liaison personnel. Gloria is Puerto Rican and Inés had requested her presence to assist Elizabeth in interpretation if necessary.

In addition to the appropriate and thorough attention paid to all components of the meeting, there were three features that stood out: a tone of absolute support for the student, Ricardo, whose behavior had proven a continuing challenge to the school administration; an atmosphere of absolute respect for the parent; and a model of effective parent participation presented by Inés. I will illustrate these with a few examples.

Inés came prepared with notes. Quite early in the meeting, the teacher reported that Ricardo behaves and works well in class because it is very structured but that he has difficulty in less structured parts of the school day. He added that he believed that Ricardo thinks that everything he does is okay and does not distinguish between when he is right or wrong. After he concluded, there was a pause, and then Inés said:

> ¿Me permiten hablar? Ricardo se porta bien en el salón de clase porque no se siente rechazado por el maestro, así que él lo respeta. Pero fuera del salón de clase él se siente rechazado por los demás, así que él hace estas cosas para llamar la atención. Él sabe bien cuando hace algo bien o cuando hace algo mal. Yo he tratado de corregir a Ricardo y lo castigo a menudo, pero yo no puedo castigarlo todo el tiempo porque no quiero perder su confianza. Yo quiero que él confíe en mi, así que debo tener cuidado con él. . . . Yo agradezco la ayuda que la escuela me da, y estoy dispuesta en ayudar a la escuela en cualquier forma posible.

> (May I speak? Ricardo behaves well in the class because he does not feel rejected by the teacher, so he respects him. But outside of the class he feels rejected by others, so he does these things to get attention. He is conscious of his behavior and of when he is right or wrong. . . . I try to correct Ricardo and punish him often, but I cannot always do so since I do not want to lose his confidence. I want him to trust me, so I must be careful with him. . . . I appreciate the school's help and am willing to cooperate with the school in every possible way.)

There was brief and positive response to this, and before the committee could go on, Inés looked at her notes and said that she had a few requests. The first was whether it would be possible for Ricardo to receive some counseling in school from the psychologist. A brief discussion of this led to the decision that, while the psychologist is not available for individual counseling, Ricardo could be assigned to the school's behavior specialist, who works with small groups.

Inés thanked the committee and went on to her next request — that some solution be found regarding Ricardo's frequent suspensions from the school bus, since this form of punishment is not helpful in that it often means he misses school. The chairman promptly replied that they agreed with Inés and had come to a decision that since most of Ricardo's suspensions were a result of his fighting on the bus, they had requested a small bus to pick him up at the door, and they hoped this would come through in September. Part of the reasoning here was that Ricardo most often fights with his sister, so this would separate them.

Inés thanked them and looked at her notes again. This time she spoke about an incident in which Ricardo had forged a letter from her to the teacher saying that he was sorry for his misbehavior and was requesting permission to be allowed to resume play in the gym. Before Inés could finish what she wanted to say on this, the teacher, chairman (who is one of the school's vice-principals), and speech pathologist were all nodding and chuckling.

The teacher laughed out loud, saying that it was particularly funny because the handwriting was so obviously not Inés's. He told Inés that he had reprimanded Ricardo on the one hand but had also congratulated him on writing such a good letter; he told Ricardo that the only thing wrong with the letter was that he forged his mother's name—he should have taken responsibility for his own statements. Inés, who had appeared very serious when she raised the topic, laughed in relief along with the others. It was an example of the supportiveness of this group that they sought the positive aspects of the student's misdemeanor, and their good humor in doing so was heart-warming.

After this, the chairman began her report of plans for Ricardo next year and when she spoke of Ricardo's being mainstreamed in at least one "special," such as art, music, or gym, Inés immediately interjected that she would like the school to give him some extra attention in art, since he is good at it and this could help him develop a direction for the future. This suggestion elicited a chorus of agreement from the committee regarding Ricardo's talent in art—one voice exclaimed "gifted!" Elizabeth then initiated discussion of a summer program at a local school for the arts, and the chairman suggested that the Latin American Association (LAA) be approached for a scholarship.

The interpretation approach previously described was also very influential in this meeting. For one thing, the fact of interpretation slowed down all the reports and forced the speakers to simplify their language. Second, it could even be that the fact of the foreign language afforded Inés an extra air of sophistication and respect. However, this is hard to separate from the effect of this mother herself: she had a lot to say and her tone and words were reasonable and supportive of the school, yet it was clear that she expected a lot of the school and was prepared to ask for it. Undoubtedly, great credit must go to the interpreter, whose careful concern for accuracy and understanding modeled respect for the parent. It would have been hard for other members of the committee to do otherwise.

One more lesson to be learned from this meeting is that every member of the committee can make a useful contribution. Turnbull and Turnbull (1986) recommend that, since a very large committee can increase the parents' discomfort, it might be a good idea to hold some members "on call" just for the portion relevant to them. This was a striking feature of this meeting: both the English as a second language (ESL) teacher and the nurse were called in only for their particular concerns. They both were very informative and offered examples of "problem solving" in the group, an ideal recommended by Turnbull and Turnbull but which I did not see in any other meeting.

The nurse's input was invaluable. She had requested clarification on Ricardo's medication, and there were about 10 minutes of discussion about what medications Ricardo had been on and which had been terminated and why. It was evident that Inés herself was not completely clear on the answers. With patient questioning and explanation of the differences between three medications, the nurse was eventually successful in discovering exactly what Ricardo's past and current medication was. Most important, she was able to clarify for Inés the functions and effects of the various medications.

At the end of the meeting, the chairman asked Elizabeth to congratulate Inés on her "excellent contribution" to the meeting and to tell her that the committee's job would be made much easier if all parents were as prepared and expressive as she. The chairman added that Inés's participation in this meeting presented a dramatic contrast to previous meetings, when Ricardo had first been placed in the school. Inés, she said, had "come a long way since then."

SUMMARY

These meetings show how wide can be the range of practice within one school district. Most of the process variables described by Marion (1979) and Turnbull and Turnbull (1986) were violated in Rita's meeting about Rafael, while all were observed in the two meetings at Harper School. In the latter, the difference was made simply at the level of the school-based team, who, operating within the same regulations as all others in the district, and having no extra training in parent facilitation or culturally appropriate practice, combined sensitivity and respect with the skills of a meticulous interpreter to create nearly ideal practice. Indeed, these meetings demonstrated that parents who do not speak English need not be at a disadvantage at all.

Earlier discussions have pointed to the power of the law simultaneously to protect and to confine. With regard to P.L. 94-142, we are concerned in this study with two essential areas: the medical model of disability, by which the practice of special education is bound (Skrtic, 1988), and the requirement for parental participation, which allows for, but does not require, a truly collaborative partnership between professionals and parents. There is an essential tension between these two provisions. By locating learning difficulties within children, and expertise within designated professionals, the law undermines the likelihood of collaboration and reinforces the tendency of professionals to engage in a process of reifying concepts such as disability and remediation. Even a professional such as Rafael's special education teacher, who knew that his student's difficulties were "related to the second-language problem" rather than to any innate disability, was reluctant to address this belief directly at a meeting whose express purpose was to identify the source and nature of the student's disability, thus validating the assumption of within-child deficits.

Professionals who remember that this model is but a societal construct and not a representation of objective reality (Bogdan & Knoll, 1988) can free themselves to look at students as individuals within an ecological framework whose myriad interactions may account for learning difficulties. Similarly, professionals who see students in this way will know that there are many other sources of information and expertise beyond those persons granted official permission to act as experts. Further, if professionals view compliance with the law as an end in itself, its implementation will inevitably be in the mode of confinement, since the law exists only as an abstraction—a set of principles whose actualization can only be documented by measures such as deadlines, statistics, and, in the case of parents, signed consent forms. Professionals who view the law as a vehicle for the assurance of equity, however, will devise strategies for including rather than excluding parents, for sharing rather than appropriating power; rather than placing the burden of assimilation entirely on the shoulders of culturally different parents, they will demonstrate the posture of the professional team at Harper School—a "posture of reciprocity" (Harry & Kalyanpur, 1991).

Regardless of professionals' orientation, however, it is crucial to note that parental initiative is always needed. In Inés's meeting, for example, although committee members knew of Ricardo's talent in art, they had not thought of focusing specifically on this in his program; nor had they planned to include him in the behavior management group, although his behavior was of daily concern to the school. Similarly, it was up to her to inform the committee of her correct name. In Juan's meeting, his spontaneous handshake to all members represented a traditional form of courtesy in Hispanic cultures and helped to place him on an equal footing with school personnel. Here were two very different parents: a father whose shyness and diffidence were evident, yet whose input proved invaluable, and a mother whose self-confidence and determination on her child's behalf brought her into full bloom as an advocate, encouraged by a supportive and caring team with whom she had been building a relationship over a period of only 2 years. Indeed, it is within this kind of setting that the low-context, abstract framework of the law can be given meaning and the reciprocal nature of genuine collaboration can be expressed.

While it is evident that professionals need increased awareness of culturally appropriate behavior, Bennett (1988) has emphasized that the central concern in producing culturally sensitive practice is "with certain processes that produce power arrangements" that disempower families (p. 149). The challenge of changing such structures should not be identified with the creation of further legal frameworks. Bennett (1988) has made this point eloquently:

> It will not do simply to rationalize the bureaucracy further by making our goals more explicit, and developing rational means of implementation and evaluation to carry them out. . . . This has been an increasing tendency in educational policymaking, and is certainly embodied in what most people have seen as the progressive legislation for special education in the U.S. and other First World countries. But as we have seen, some of the very institutional and regulative structures which have in fact gained access to education for large numbers of disabled children who were excluded in an earlier age, can still work to deny access in a different sense: access to a participatory voice in the social and intellectual development of one's children, and more generally, of the children of one's community. (p. 149)

Without a genuine respect for the individual child, as well as his or her family and cultural identity, communication between the special education system and families will fail to represent the true interests of the student. What, after all, is the real purpose of these meetings? As Inés told me:

> Quiero que las personas en las reuniones sepan las fuerzas de mi hijo, en que área está bien, lo que él sabe, que conozcan como es él. Quiero que ellos conozcan de quien estamos hablando, porque no estamos hablando de un objeto, estamos hablando de una persona—una persona que tiene sentimientos.

> (I want the people in the meeting to know what my son's strengths are, what he is good at, what he knows, what he is like. I want them to know who we are talking about, because we are not talking about an object, we are talking about a person—a person who has feelings.)

10

The School District

Challenge and Change

This study reveals two crucial challenges for the school district: establishing effective communication with Hispanic families and meeting the educational and personal needs of students in linguistic and cultural transition. The atmosphere of mistrust, confusion, and dissatisfaction evident in the study reflected parents' perceptions of experiences both past and current. For some parents there was increasing satisfaction and for others, continuing dissatisfaction. This was a study of a school district in the process of change.

Pressure from parents and/or community frequently provides the impetus for school districts to revise their policies. This has been particularly true in the case of Spanish-speaking communities (Cordasco, 1976). It was also true for this district. Three years prior to the study, a challenge from the Latin American Association (LAA) had forced the school district to examine its policies and practice regarding Hispanic students and their families. A district spokesman admitted that it "certainly was" a challenge, which he described in this way:

> It began 3 years ago, when the director of the LAA met with the superintendent. He laid out some concerns, valid concerns, regarding graduation rates, dropout rates, placement of students, regular ed, and special ed. For example, a kid who comes in who is limited English proficient, what grade do you place him in? Is it based on what his grade was in Puerto Rico, or do you put him back a year so he can catch up, or do you hold him back? The other concern was communication—how do parents know what is going on in school?

The district responded by establishing an English as a Second Language (ESL)/Bilingual Committee, which reviewed relevant research as well as current practice in the district and in New York City. One of the results of this was a special board of education meeting with the Hispanic community, which led to the district's investigation of specific individual complaints. Some of the data of this study, such as Ana's complaint that her child was moved without her knowledge, came under scrutiny at that time. But beyond attempts to resolve specific incidents, the initial committee evolved into two study groups, one on communications and one on promotional practices.

Several efforts emerged from these committees, such as translation of materials, the appointment of regular and special education liaison workers, and new policies for placement, screening, promotion, and graduation. The most recent development at the time of the study was the devising of criteria for evaluating the ESL program on an ongoing basis as well as the formation of a speech and language task force that was currently studying the process of speech and language assessment for limited English proficient (LEP) students.

Educational decisions about minority populations reflect the underlying question of whether the prevailing philosophy is one of assimilation of minority cultures into the mainstream of the dominant culture, or of the preservation of minority cultures within an overall national identity. A pluralistic philosophy will be reflected in policies that strive to respect and respond to the needs of culturally diverse children and families (Fitzpatrick, 1987; Lewis, 1980; Poplin & Wright, 1983). In the following sections I will examine the data on the school district's review of its policies in the light of such ideological concerns and in terms of the process of change within school districts.

CULTURAL DIVERSITY AND COMMUNICATION WITH PARENTS

A spokesperson for the LAA emphasized that the district's response to the challenge of home-school communication was appropriate and successful. She said that the forum for Hispanic parents to bring their complaints to the board of education had come about because there were just too many complaints to be handled in individual meetings. She felt that the resulting decisions to translate documents and to employ liaison personnel were "very positive."

The two liaison personnel recently employed were Gloria, who was Puerto Rican, responsible for regular education, and Elizabeth, an American, responsible for families with children in special education. Elizabeth described the district's intention in terms of "making sure the parents really were aware of what was happening when they were asked for permission for a complete evaluation, and what their rights were." She explained that schools had been doing the best they could to explain but that parents were signing and not really understanding.

One aspect of this thrust was to translate documents into Spanish, which became the responsibility of these liaison workers and meant that records of every new event must be rendered in Spanish. For the special education liaison, an ongoing demand was translation of individualized education plan (IEP) phase 1 documents. Since the use of home language in official school documents has long been mandated by P.L. 94-142 this would bring the school district into compliance on this dimension. The data from this study show, however, that making sure parents understand is as important to communication as is the use of Spanish. Elizabeth agreed with this and said that explanation of the IEP phase 1 document was one of her prime targets for the coming year.

Previous attempts at explaining aspects of the system to parents had not proved very successful, and some professionals interviewed in the study pointed to jargon as one of the main reasons for this. Teresa, an agency social worker who described the special education system as "a monstrosity," exclaimed:

> The jargon is the thing that's frightening. . . . The thing is, when you have a workshop, you have to bring it to the level of the people that you are trying to educate so they can understand it. You shouldn't have to have another workshop to explain what you said at the first one.

Elizabeth agreed that the use of jargon adds to parents' already inadequate information about the system and said that after her own orientation for the job, she attended a parent training workshop; coming from a regular education background, she was amazed at how difficult it was for her to get through the jargon. She exclaimed that the level of unawareness among English-speaking parents' underscored how difficult it would be for limited- or non-English-speaking parents.

All professionals interviewed agreed that ad hoc efforts at educating parents in the past had elicited a very limited response. Some interpreted this as reflecting parents' low motivation and concern about special education matters, while others said that other priorities, such as appointments for welfare benefits and lack of transportation and child care, interfered with parents' attendance.

One of Elizabeth's first efforts was a workshop organized in conjunction with a voluntary agency in the area and held at a neighborhood school. Despite the provision of transportation and child care, only six mothers attended out of some thirty who had been invited. The low parent turnout was made more obvious by the presence of twice as many professionals and agency personnel as parents. My interviews with agency personnel beforehand indicated that Elizabeth had been aiming for a very large group and had turned down the offer of using the agency building on the grounds that facilities would not be adequate. One employee of the agency said that she got the impression Elizabeth arranged to use the new conference room at the school because she did not think the modest agency surroundings "nice enough."

This was Elizabeth's first year on the job, and her assessment of the first workshop showed that she was already revising her opinions and expectations:

> At 20 minutes to 10 I thought I was going to have one mother! And then we went out and picked up four of the mothers. And then poor Gloria was running all around to wrong addresses trying to pick up another mother. Actually, I knew that six or seven was a good number, that I should be pleased with that, because when I went to a parent training conference for English-speaking parents, we had four or five. So that's about the number you're going to get, and I've come to realize that.
>
> But I guess I was frustrated after all the work and preparation. My initial reaction was, "Don't they care about their kids!" But now I realize they may have more basic priorities. And one thing I learned is that there were people who didn't come because they don't like to come to that school. So we've got to offer the next ones at flexible times and in neutral locations.

Two of the attending parents were participants in this study, and when I asked the other study participants why they did not come, most said that they had other appointments. Elizabeth's comment about acceptable territory was borne out by two mothers who told me that they did not go because they do not like the school where the workshop was being held and do not trust the people there.

Beyond the giving and explaining of information is the need to establish a mode of communication that Puerto Rican families will be comfortable with. The need for a personal and individualized style of interaction is a consistent theme in the literature on home-school interaction with Hispanic parents (Baca & Cervantes, 1984; Casuso, 1978; Figler, 1981; New York City Board of Education, 1958; Sour & Sorell, 1978); this has also been discussed earlier in this book in terms of the contrast between high- and low-context cultures. The professionals interviewed all confirmed that parents responded best to a respectful but personal approach and were very quiet and acquiescent at formal meetings, even when they had planned beforehand to speak about some particular point. The comment of one social worker, Isabel, offers a poignant example of the concept of a high-context culture:

There is something missing here. I think it's too impersonal, you know? Let me tell you how it happens in Puerto Rico. There, instead of the parent going to the district office, they have the discussion in the child's school, where the parent feels familiar. And also the student comes in for about 5 minutes and they have a little conversation with them. It's more sensitive.

Here you have to go all the way up to the district and they're all dressed up at this big table and everyone is so separated, you know. . . . In Puerto Rico they feel like it's the family—not only my family, but my child's family and they're going to be working with my kid to do everything they can for him. But here it's like you have to be there rigid and listening to everybody and you can hear a pin drop or something!

You don't feel like they know who they're talking about, you know? It's just one more case that comes to the table and it's really sad. When I took the parent training program, they said that parents should show them pictures of the kid. But the formal setting doesn't allow that. And even if they had the picture, they don't feel like taking it out. Okay—I'm going to pass my child's picture around—*No!* Why should I show my picture? *No!*

Mr. Thomas, a bilingual teacher in the district, spoke in a similar vein. He said that the school buildings themselves are "awesome" to parents from Puerto Rico. His solution was to do a lot of home visiting to develop rapport with families:

You need to develop a positive situation, so that when it comes time for a negative situation parents are more receptive. I told the administration, "Every time you guys call on me it's to tell the family, 'Your son is in trouble,' 'your daughter's going to fail.' I don't want those contacts unless you give me time to build some positive ones." And in the last 2 years, I've had the freedom to do that because I have a teacher assistant, and I visit parents regularly. That is the key.

Rosana also spoke of the importance of using a personal and informal style of interaction, which might include engaging in exchanges such as lending records or sharing information about shopping bargains. Elizabeth, who is American, spoke emphatically of the importance of working in a personal way with families:

It was difficult . . . not knowing the people and not knowing if I would be accepted by them. What I found was I tried to treat each person I met with individually—person to person—not as educator to a layperson, but person to person. As I spoke with mothers I found myself speaking woman to woman, mother to mother—in their homes much of the time. And I found that they appreciated it. . . .

I found they were very patient with my Spanish. I don't have a Puerto
Rican accent. I felt, in most cases, they'd realize that I was really there to try
to help them, and I found them more or less willing to work with me. Now
they're starting to call me to go to meetings with them.

The district's efforts at improving communication were beginning to
show results. Parents who had had serious complaints about lack of communication and frequent moving of children, such as Ana and Rita, said
that the current year had been much better. Isabel, an agency social worker, summarized the progress in this way:

Right now the schools are beginning to open up. And still the families are a
little reluctant because they have never been included before. So some of
them are coming in, little by little . . . they're approaching the school now.
. . . But it's something that I think is going to take a little while. Maybe if they
have someone Latino who is a parent too, that person could act as a motiva-
tor for the other parents, and bring in more parents.

CULTURAL DIVERSITY AND EDUCATIONAL CHANGE

The introduction of the new approaches described above reflect an
acknowledgment of the pluralistic nature of the community being served
by this school district. Attempts were being made to make communication
systems more appropriate to families with a different language and communication style. The district's attempts to revise its services to children
themselves, however, appeared much more limited.

The data in the foregoing chapters show that to change assumptions of
power and authority is a slow and uneven process. Skrtic (1988) has offered
a consideration of the nature of change in the bureaucracies of schools. He
maintains that schools are well suited to "incidental" rather than "fundamental" change, because the structure of a professional bureaucracy utilizes a "loosely coupled interdependency among professionals" by which
changes may be made without being "integrated into the ongoing structure; they are simply added on segmentally, making any substantial reor-
ganization of activity unnecessary" (p. 500). Thus demands for change
that can be met by "adding a new program can be accomplished virtually
overnight" (p. 499).

In this study, the school district's response to the communication and
information needs of Latino families was precisely of this nature: the addition of personnel who could translate both written and oral communication and provide information and support to parents on an individual

basis. The impact of such change would depend largely on the skill of the individuals employed to perform this new service. Indeed, the data of this study show the impact of the liaison/interpreter on the process of a meeting, and, in the absence of data on the preconference activities of the Harper School team, one can only assume that specific individuals may have been instrumental in initiating and possibly guiding the changing practice of that team. Thus the role of individuals in change cannot be underestimated, as is evident in the literature on effective schools (Clark, Lotto, & Astuto, 1984). Further, it is precisely the loosely coupled structure referred to by Skrtic that allowed individual school-based teams to develop their own structures for interaction with parents and to utilize the reins of the law to empower rather than to disempower.

Change of a fundamental nature within a school organization, however, is difficult to accomplish. A bilingual program, for example, cannot effectively be "added on" but must be integrated into the existing structure of the school. My discussions with school district personnel pointed to policies related to bilingualism as one of the central features most in need of change, yet most difficult to change in a fundamental way.

In Chapter 3, I offered an overview of the history and current status of research on bilingual education that points to the continuing superiority of educating LEP students in their native language at least until they become literate in that language. Literacy skills, it has been shown, will then be transferred more easily to the second language. This argument is even stronger when applied to young children who speak little or no English and are being introduced to reading for the first time. How can they be expected to begin reading in a language they can hardly speak?

An interview with a spokesperson for the school district revealed that the outcome of the revision process of the previous 3 years was a decision to stay with an English-only instruction model, supported by ESL pullout classes, for both regular and special education students. Against the background of current research, this policy seems inadequate.

Bilingual and ESL Programs

The notion of bilingual education was not new to this school district. Between 1979 and 1983 the school district operated a bilingual program at Spruce Street School, which was the school serving most of the Hispanic children in the district. While I could not get specific documentation from the district office as to the operation of this program, an interview with Mr. Thomas, a teacher who participated in it, suggests that the program evolved from ESL into a bilingual program. He said:

We started off with a program that was initially an ESL pullout program, in which the students were in a regular classroom for a majority of the day and were pulled out for ESL classes. Then it evolved into a half-time bilingual maintenance or transition program in that the students spent half a day with us and half a day in a regular classroom. Then it evolved even further into a full-time bilingual program where the students were taught in a bilingual setting . . . a bilingual, bicultural program.

Mr. Thomas cited two reasons why the program was discontinued: first, the federal seed money for the program ran out, and, second, it was becoming impossible to find qualified bilingual teachers. Another district professional said that the impetus and main support for the program came from one individual, and that when this person left, there was no clear way of integrating required curriculum with what was meant to be a bilingual, bicultural program. She described the situation as follows:

So you wanted to teach the culture and stuff of the Puerto Rican heritage, but you're being stuck in the face with the social studies curriculum for third grade that the city has mandated. So what do you do? Whereas good bilingual programs that have really planned this all out have figured out, like— this is the objective of the third-grade reader, and this is how we'll meet those objectives using Puerto Rican heritage plus anything else that we might have culled out of the regular curriculum. Then you get it approved so that you have just one social studies period and you're learning everything.

So I can't say that we had a really well-thought-out bilingual program, especially after Mrs. Jones left. So then when they decided to bring the ESL program in, it was like, "Oh, we tried bilingual and that didn't work." I don't know. *Did* we try it?

The only official record that I could get from the district regarding the effects of this program was a list of impressions culled from discussion with educational personnel involved at the time. The district administrator who showed me this list said that the following points seemed to constitute the main reasons the program was discontinued:

1. Grouping LEP students together did not take account of the wide range of instructional levels among these children.
2. This heterogeneity created instructional problems for teachers.
3. The students were progressing slowly.
4. Some students were not getting special education, or even Chapter I services, because they were in "bilingual classes."
5. Hispanic students were being segregated.

6. The school was attracting an undue number of Hispanic students because of the bilingual program.
7. It was difficult or impossible to find certified bilingual teachers.
8. Parents were frustrated at their children's lack of progress.

The bilingual program was replaced by ESL programs offered at five elementary schools, one middle school, and one high school. In most cases this model involved a specific number of hours per day during which a student would be "pulled out" for ESL class. At Spruce Street School, however, which had the greatest number of Spanish-speaking children, the kindergarten and first-grade programs were being modified to include bilingual teachers, so that, although instruction would be done in English, the teachers could reinforce the learning of concepts through the native language where necessary. In that school the pullout model began at the second grade.

In the middle school that offered ESL, there was a different approach, initiated by Mr. Thomas, who had formerly taught in the bilingual program. This version resulted in a combined bilingual-ESL model. Mr. Thomas said:

> I felt that the students could learn English and content at the same time. So I proceeded to take the city curriculum—science and social studies—and combine it with the ESL language curriculum so that while a student is learning social studies, they're learning English. The same goes for science and health too. So now the students are getting all their content. They're not being left out because they don't understand English.

Mr. Thomas emphasized that this was simply his classroom — not a program — a good example of "incidental change." This information shows that the school system was essentially in a period of flux, with several, possibly competing, alternatives being sought and offered from school to school and even within schools. The tension between an organization's need for stability and for cultural responsiveness is well illustrated here, with the administration coming to the decision to retain a modified ESL model, which really meant allowing for the possibility of limited bilingual education to occur on an ad hoc basis.

Bilingual Professionals' Views of Bilingual Education.   This tension could also be seen in the political dynamics of the professional body itself. Within this school district, as elsewhere in the country, opinions were divided on the appropriateness of a bilingual versus an ESL approach. Indeed, the district spokesperson said that the opinions in the district essentially came down to an ESL versus bilingual debate. The decision to stay with ESL English-only instruction, he said, was made "to the relief of some and the dismay of others." He explained that the decision was made on the grounds that the ESL program had been evaluated and was thought to be working well.

All the bilingual teachers and liaison personnel I spoke to, however, seemed to be on the side that was dismayed by the decision. They offered the same criticisms found in the literature. First, students lose time in content areas while they are in the process of learning English, both because they are pulled out of other classes for ESL and because, when they do participate in content area classes, it is a while before they understand enough English to know what is going on. One professional told me that there are some teachers who hardly attempt to teach the LEP children in their classes—the children spend most of their time drawing and coloring. Second, the bilingual personnel argued that it is unrealistic to try to teach reading in English to children who are just learning the language and particularly to those who have not yet learned to read in their native language.

In addition to all this, professionals who worked with these children emphasized the difficulties resulting from poverty, transience, and the low level of education of many parents. The district's only bilingual psychologist illustrated the challenge of gaps in instruction as well as the influence of social factors:

> I really think that, for our children at Spruce Street, bilingual education is the best way to go. What Jim Cummins [researcher] says makes a lot of sense to me because the children that we have are developmentally low in their first language due to poverty, parental low education, whatever—so they come in and all of a sudden are hit with this other language.

Parents' Views of Bilingual/ESL Approaches.   In this study it was difficult to ascertain parents' opinions of the bilingual or the ESL programs for two reasons. First, most of the parents had children in special education who, at the time of the study, were between the ages of 7 and 11, which means that they were not in school at the time of the bilingual program. The parents of older children were not able to tell me if the children had been in the bilingual program, although some of them spoke of their children being in ESL.

Second, some parents used the terms *ESL* and *bilingual* interchangeably, like Margarita, who told me that she took her 9-year-old out of "the bilingual class" because she thought it confused him and she wanted him to learn only English at school. Her son was too young to have been in the district's bilingual program, but he, and some of the other younger children, may have been in the modified ESL program in the first grade—a class that had a bilingual teacher, although instruction was, officially, in English. Dora, likewise, said she would not allow her 5-year-old to enter the ESL class in kindergarten in the next year because she believed it had "confused" her older daughter, Maria, by "mixing up" the two languages. Thus I could not be sure which programs parents were referring to, although it was clear that they saw language "confusion" as the source of the children's difficulties.

Those few parents who did understand the way the ESL program worked, however, had a common complaint: that the pullout approach takes away from important content areas. It was mentioned in Chapter 7 that Rita said that her son, Rafael, "did not have math for a month in the sixth grade" while he went to ESL class, and that Rafael's current teacher and a senior district administrator both agreed that this was possible, although they could not verify Rita's report. Josefina and Francisca both blamed ESL pullout for their older children's failure to earn enough credits to graduate from high school.

Parents' misunderstandings and fears about bilingual education echoed those cited in the literature (Lewis, 1980), the primary thrust of this being the fear that the children would not succeed in learning English. All the parents in the study emphasized that learning English was of prime importance for their children. Although they said they would also like them to retain Spanish, they were not sure if this was possible.

Psychological Assessment

The discussion of second-language issues offered earlier in this book pointed out that there are two essential questions underlying the controversy about testing children designated as limited English proficient: the question of how to determine a child's readiness for testing in the second language and the challenge of nonbiased assessment. Embedded in the second question is the challenge of how to interpret test data, not only because it may be culturally biased but because the child's performance may be affected by a great many variables. An interview with the bilingual psychologist in the district underscored the relevance of this very complex concern. I will quote her at some length:

> Let's say I'm called on to test a child who everybody says is having a real hard time; they'd like to know if he has a disability. So I give all the tests, and most usually what I get is problems in reading and math. Well, you have this child who hasn't been taught reading because he doesn't know the lan-

guage. So is he learning-disabled? How would I know if he is or not? He hasn't been taught. The same thing happens with older children that have been here for, say, 3 years. I have to ask, "Okay, how much Spanish did they know? When did they start learning English reading? Did they know Spanish reading when they came?" So they've been here 3 years and they are on second-grade level, but they're 10—is that bad? You can't give them a Spanish reading test, that's not appropriate either—they haven't been taught Spanish reading in 3 years! I'm not even sure, you know—when people go out and they standardize all these tests in Spanish and in English, I'm not sure either one is real appropriate for the kid speaking English for 3 years and caught between the two languages. It's very challenging!

I'm pretty leery of testing kids who have just arrived here unless they walk in with an IEP from Puerto Rico or a psychological report—something that tells me that he's definitely had problems in Puerto Rico before the imposition of all these changes. For example, there was a kid last year who was having some problems—a lot of it seemed to be adjustment—I mean it's an unstable family situation to begin with and just think, here's a kid who was taken away from his school, his culture, his language, his friends, his climate—all those things are changing and maybe he didn't want to come, you know? So what's his only out? He's here. He can't say he wants to stay in Puerto Rico—that won't help. So he behaves inappropriately to let some of his frustrations out. So I observed him a little. He didn't strike me as a disturbed kid.

This year he's still having academic problems, but it turns out that he can read at a middle to late second-grade level in Spanish. He's 11. But the way I figured it out, he left Puerto Rico probably in about the middle of third grade, so to read second-grade Spanish isn't bad, especially if he's remembering it now, a year and a half after leaving. Last year he was probably adjusting to the problems, so he didn't learn anything in either language. And the other thing is that he didn't show any really distinct processing deficits. So here we are. I recommended that he stay in the regular class.

This psychologist's awareness of the subtleties of designating "proficiency" in English point to the challenge of professional decision making and the impossibility of using low-context tools, such as standardized tests, for understanding a process so complex and ambiguous as human learning. Indeed, her frank observations underscore the travesty that is perpetrated in the name of education when an educational system insists that students must be designated "handicapped" in order to gain appropriate services. The psychologist acknowledged that the outcome of the decision to retain this student in the regular class could very well be continued inappropriate service. Thus informed and caring professionals such as she are caught in a classic "Catch 22" position: either to inappropriately label a child in order to access special services or to inappropriately retain the student in the regular class.

A further concern of the psychologist was the difficulty of identifying a child's true level of proficiency, with the result that many children who should be tested in Spanish may never be referred to her:

> I'm basically called to [evaluate] the children who have just come. . . . How about if a kid has been here 3 years and sounds good to the teacher? For example, I was called in to consult in testing a girl who was reported to know enough English to be tested in English. We got to the second question of one of the subtests on the intelligence test, "How are a candle and a lamp the same?" And the girl didn't know what a candle was. That's enough English? I mean . . . she knew what a "vela" (candle) was!

Speech and Language Assessment

Along with the debates over psychological evaluation and language of instruction for LEP students is the challenge of speech and language assessment. This arises where the psychologist recommends such assessment because she suspects that a child's difficulties may be based on deficits in the processing of language. A recent task force on speech and language assessment resulted in district guidelines for a specific series of steps to be observed in the referral process. The emphasis in this document was on the importance of making a differential diagnosis between language-impaired children and children in the normal process of second-language acquisition. Although the district was acquiring some assessment tools in Spanish, the chairman of the task force explained that these instruments are still unreliable since most of them are translations and were not normed on appropriate populations. In an attempt to balance this, the task force was developing informal assessment approaches, including a home-based developmental history and various suggestions for naturalistic assessment. This is in keeping with current recommendations in the literature on speech and language assessment (Baca & Cervantes, 1984).

The task force recommendations would require a trained interpreter to be present at all speech and language assessments "if there is not a qualified bilingual speech/language pathologist available" (task-force chairperson). While there were no such personnel currently in the district, this requirement reflected the awareness of such a need. Indeed, the chairperson of the task force said that the group considered a bilingual speech and language pathologist to be "the ideal" but that without active recruitment out of the area such a person would be hard to find.

The concerns of this committee were beginning to be reflected in evaluation practices. This was evident in the meeting at Harper School in which the speech and language pathologist asked Juan a series of probing questions designed to arrive at the best classification and placement decisions for his daughter, Juanita.

Teaching of Reading: Methodology

Beyond the questionable soundness of teaching reading in a language a child has not yet mastered, there is also the issue of what instructional approach to use. One of the central concepts of special education is individualized educational planning. But what does this mean in practice? In an area as crucial as reading, for example, the method used should reflect this concept. The need for flexibility in the teaching of reading to bilingual students, as well as for an emphasis on contextual and culturally appropriate learning styles, has been emphasized by several scholars (Au, 1981; Baca & Cervantes, 1984; Figueroa et al., 1989b; Ruiz, 1989).

The findings of this study, however, were consonant with those of the Texas and California Institutes as summarized by Figueroa et al. (1989b); that is, a "task-analysis driven, worksheet-oriented" special education approach (p. 176). For example, Dora's daughter, Maria, was reported to have made no progress on reading levels over one year, and Dora felt that DISTAR's (Direct Instruction Strategies for Teaching and Remediation) lock-step method and phonic emphasis were not working with Maria. Her concerns were borne out by the bilingual psychologist, who described the attitude of some teachers as: "This method works! If you can't learn it, it's your problem!" Certain programs, she pointed out, are totally inappropriate for certain children, such as the use of DISTAR with a child who was having difficulty discriminating sounds or following directions. The meeting that I observed between Dora and the special and regular education teachers left no question that they considered Maria's learning difficulties to be intrinsic and that they had at no time considered using any other approach.

PLACEMENT OF HISPANIC STUDENTS

This discussion of the school district's attempts at change would not be complete without some consideration of how its practice related to the nationwide controversy surrounding the placement of minority students generally. The introductory chapters outlined this controversy, summarizing several patterns of placement and the situation of Hispanic students within these patterns. The placement figures for this district reflect trends commonly observed in the literature. I will conclude my report of the findings of this study with an analysis of the status of Hispanic students in the school district.

First, it is appropriate to note that while this study focused on Puerto Rican parents only, the figures available from the district did not distinguish the details of disability classifications for Puerto Rican versus Spanish-surname students. In the following analysis, I will therefore refer to the overall figures for Hispanic students. I would note also that out of fifty-eight such students, only one was labeled moderately retarded. This makes attention to the mild disability categories entirely appropriate for this group of students.

In this district, the overall numbers of Hispanic students in special education were not disproportionate to their numbers in the school district as a whole — that is, these students comprised approximately 2.4 percent of the total population and approximately 2.4 percent of the special education population. A wider look at the figures showed that, while White students accounted for approximately 57 percent of the total, they accounted for only 52 percent of special education students. Black students, on the other hand, accounted for 36 percent of the total and about 42 percent of special education students.

This pattern was in line with the trends (Heller et al., 1982) discussed extensively in Chapter 2:

1. White students are placed in special education at a lower rate than Blacks or Hispanics.
2. Black students are disproportionatedly represented in special education programs.
3. Disproportionate placement of Hispanic students is less likely to be evident where the total Hispanic population is small and in districts where there is a relatively large Black population.

As the Hispanic population of this district grows, it will be important that administrators retain a sharp awareness of the risk of disproportionate placement. The district's recent reviews of promotion policy for LEP students showed awareness of these students' needs. For example, students whose native language is not English must be screened within 2 weeks of enrollment in school in order to decide the amount of ESL support they will receive. They will be placed in the grade appropriate to their age or in the grade indicated by their previous school report. A child who is weak in academic subjects may be placed in a Title I class with other children who have low scores in reading and math, thus offering the advantage of a smaller group.

However, for those children who were placed in special education, a noticeable pattern emerges: Hispanic students were placed in self-contained classes more frequently than other students with mild disability labels. Children labeled learning-disabled (LD), educable mentally retarded (EMR), or emotionally disturbed (ED) could be placed either in the regular class with pullout for resource support or in a self-contained, nongraded special education class. Overall district figures for all Hispanic students with mild disability labels showed that 70 percent of these students were placed in self-contained classes, as against 50 percent of Black and 50 percent of White students in the same disability categories.

A closer look at the classifications revealed an even higher rate. Of a total of fifty-eight Hispanic children, nine were labeled speech-impaired (SI) and were in the regular class, receiving only speech and language services. The SI label is considered the mildest of classifications, and these children are not usually placed in either a self-contained class or a resource program. Thus, if we eliminate the nine students labeled SI, this means that there were forty-nine Hispanic students for whom the choice of placement lay between resource and self-contained class: forty-one of these, or approximately 83 percent, were placed in self-contained classes, and only seven, or 14 percent, were in resource programs. The norm for the district was 50 percent in self-contained classes and 50 percent in resource programs.

Thus, although Hispanic students in this district were not overrepresented in special education programs as a whole, those who were in special education were placed in self-contained classes at a much higher rate than other children with similar disability classifications. Professionals to whom I mentioned this pattern expressed surprise at the figures and said they could only surmise that it was related to professionals' assumption that the students' second-language needs might be more readily addressed in the small classes afforded by self-contained placement. If this interpretation is correct, it would offer one more example of "incidental change," an ad hoc attempt to meet students' needs without changing the fundamental pattern of service. Further, since the self-contained class is a more "restricted environment" in terms of peer group interaction than the resource program, this recalls observations in the literature that the legal requirement for the "least restrictive environment" is often inadequately applied in the placement of bilingual children (Baca & Cervantes, 1984).

SUMMARY

This chapter has presented the school district's efforts as seen by professionals. The data reveal an ongoing process of challenge and change, as well as the dynamics of competing interests and viewpoints within professional ranks. The response of the district to a strong challenge from the Hispanic community 3 years prior to the study demonstrates the power of a group in contrast to the efforts of individuals. The district's response to the challenge of communication with families focused on the translation of documents and the appointment of two Spanish-speaking liaison workers. The challenge of educational practices for LEP students led to a review of placement and promotional practices and examinations of psychological and speech and language assessment approaches and of the effectiveness of the district's ESL program. The outcome regarding the latter concern was a decision to continue a modified ESL approach and to continue to evaluate its success.

In the light of information both from the literature and from the participants in this study, the latter decision seems questionable. While parents were poorly informed about the actual instructional practices to which their children were exposed, data from their interviews showed that, with only one exception, parents of children labeled learning disabled interpreted their childrens' difficulties as stemming from "confusion" over the language. All of these children came into an English-only instructional system between the ages of 5 and 10, the younger ones with no formal instruction in reading their native language, and the older ones with some instruction that had been interrupted by immigration and the sudden thrust into a new language and culture. Interviews with bilingual personnel in the district showed a consistent pattern of disagreement with the use of the ESL/English-only instruction model, their main arguments being that children lose both academic content and self-confidence.

The decision to continue with this model was arrived at after 3 years of study by a committee. It seems paradoxical that the native language would be given increased attention in all areas but instruction; that is, instruction of LEP children would continue to be done in English, while native-language use would increase in psychological testing, speech and language assessment, and communication with the family. The promotion policy would be to place new students with their chronological age group or in the grade indicated by the previous school report, while screening them carefully to ascertain the level of ESL service needed. Students would not be retained in a grade before 20 months of instruction. This instruction, however, would be in a language the child does not understand. Thus a child might be considered too limited in English to comprehend and respond to testing in English, yet this same child would be considered capable of understanding and responding to English-only instruction in the classroom.

Skrtic's (1988) distinction between fundamental and incidental change offers one basis for interpreting this paradox. All of the changes instituted by the administration could be effected by the addition of personnel who could work relatively individually or, with respect to assessment or placement practices, could be implemented without disruption to the fundamental functioning of the school system. The comments of the psychologist regarding the systemic nature of a genuine bilingual program reveal the profound changes that would need to be made to meet the most pervasive needs of non- or limited-English-speaking children—changes in curriculum, class structures, timetables, hiring practices, and, last but not least, changes in the essential cultural program inherent in the school system—the belief that children who do not fit into existing services are in themselves inadequate and should be accommodated by being so labeled and placed in the added-on programs of special education.

The data of this study show a school district willing to respond to cultural diversity but attempting to meet fundamentally changing social circumstances with strategies limited to incidental change. Where such strategies succeed in touching the fundamental assumptions of those individuals who act as change agents, systemic or fundamental change may begin to occur. Unless this happens, what is really created is merely "the illusion of change" (Skrtic, 1988, p. 500), while what is needed is change in the organizational paradigm of schools. Skrtic (1988) states this case as follows:

> Because a paradigm is the conceptual glue holding an organization together, a paradigm shift is a traumatic event. . . . Organizations have long periods of stability maintained by the internal consistency and self-reinforcing nature of the current paradigm. Occasional periods of change are punctuated by the build-up of unreconcilable anomalies that eventually destroy the prevailing paradigm. . . . One way in which anomalies are introduced into organization paradigms is through the availability of technical information that the current paradigm is not working. . . .
>
> When ambiguity increases, it sets the stage for ideology and values to be reshuffled (what we would call a paradigm shift); the people best able to resolve it gain power, as does their vision of the world and the organization. (pp. 501, 504)

This conception of the moment of ambiguity is similar to what Bowers (1984) has referred to as the "liminal space"—the betwixt-and-between moment at which change can occur. In an earlier chapter I pointed to reports of culturally different parents succeeding in stepping into such moments and beginning to create fundamental change in the power relationships between themselves and school systems (Delgado-Gaitan, 1990; Warren, 1988).

In this study, the potential for such change was inherent in the challenge offered by the Latino community to the school district. The changes I observed during the period of the study, however, were essentially of an incidental and superficial nature, with the possibility that, by affecting the basic cultural perspectives of individuals and subgroups, they could spill over into a more fundamental level of professional practice. One central fact was not touched by these changes—the essential balance of power between parents and professionals. As long as change is dependent on the "decoupled" efforts of individual professionals, parents remain vulnerable to whimsical rather than philosophical practice—unless, of course, efforts at change prove to be made by persons who, in Skrtic's (1988) words, can resolve the existing ambiguities in the system, or, as Bowers (1984) would have it, individuals or groups who demonstrate the communicative competence to determine new directions.

Two years after the completion of the study, in anticipation of its publication, I engaged in a limited follow-up study, with the purpose of answering the question of whether the changes initiated at the time of the study had borne fruit and, if so, of what nature. The subsequent brief epilogue will highlight these findings and will attempt to pull together the central threads of the argument that has emerged from the data.

Power and Responsibility in Schools

The data of this study reach into the past, to events experienced by twelve families prior to the time of my first interviews with them, then to what was current in their lives during that year, then into the events of 2 years later. The picture of change that emerges from the study is reminiscent of waves that rise to a crest, break, and spill over in dramatic foam, suddenly white where there was blue, for a moment transformed in shape, color, and texture. Once past its peak, the spray regroups and, rolling forward, gathers back into itself, uneven lines of blue replacing the spew of white. Building and rebuilding upon itself, the process ebbs and flows, ever incomplete.

The dissatisfaction of Latino parents with the blunders and impersonality of the school system had been rising, in Ana's words, "por años y años" (for years and years) and found its crest in a confrontation between the school board and the Latino community. The result was a spate of efforts to transform communication with this community and to reshape the district's approach to instruction for students with limited English proficiency (LEP).

In the spring of 1990, a round of interviews with eight of the original twelve families and with Elizabeth, the family liaison, as well as observations of selected school district and community events, demonstrated the continuing but uneven flow of change. I will briefly outline both instructional and communication issues and attempt to integrate my observations into a concluding discussion of the central findings of the study.

INSTRUCTIONAL ISSUES

The follow-up study revealed that instructional issues were still being hotly debated by professionals, while parents' views tended to reflect the current progress of their own children.

Professionals' Views

The central concerns among professionals were the nature of ESL instruction and the need for native language instruction, particularly for younger students not yet literate in their first language. A small group of bilingual personnel, most of whom had participated in the original study, appeared to have the potential to effect fundamental change in the school district's services to LEP students. Armed with what Skrtic (1988) has called "the technical information that the current paradigm is not working" (p. 502), and with a strong ideological bent that questioned assumptions about the relative roles of special and regular education as well as the assumptions of disability on which the system is based, this group was actively promoting a number of changes in the direction of current thinking in bilingual special education.

Their ideas were being well received by the administration. One new development was that the district did engage in active out-of-state recruitment of a bilingual speech pathologist, an ideal that had seemed out of reach 2 years before. Further, and most surprising, was that what had seemed like a firm decision for an English as a second language (ESL)/English-only approach only 2 years before was once more under some pressure from this group. In sum, among the approaches either already initiated or being recommended by this group at the time of the follow-up study were the following:

- To hire a bilingual teacher for new special ed classes
- To hire a bilingual speech pathologist
- To hire a Latino parent for liaison and parent training
- To engage in "tandem testing" of students, in which more than one professional would collaborate in the testing so as to gain a more rounded picture of the child's capability
- To train teachers in the use of "sheltered English," in which ESL methods are used to teach content areas
- To train teachers to get away from a lockstep approach by teaching to students' higher capabilities in Spanish rather than to the low-level abilities demonstrated in English
- To train teachers in cooperative learning
- To inform teachers on the process of second-language acquisition
- To develop a professional lending library on related issues
- To establish bilingual programs for kindergarten through third grade in the two schools with the largest Spanish-speaking enrollment

Beyond all this, these professionals were very concerned that, while special education was "bending over backwards" to improve its services, there was little change evident in the regular education system. They felt strongly that more appropriate instruction prior to referral would lessen the prevalence of special education placement for all students. Elizabeth, a member of this group, referred to its efforts as "five people trying to do the work of fifteen."

While this group was effectively addressing fundamental issues, this is not the same as saying that the outcome would be fundamental change. The changes being proposed still existed within the framework of the cultural model expressed in the law — the belief that disability is a truth that can be identified and treated by the correct tools and that the differing cultural interpretations of Latino and other minority families hold no legitimate place within the education system.

Parents' Views

Parents' views of progress in instructional matters reflected whatever was happening with their own children, since it was clear that they did not have an overall view of policy in the schools. Most of the children were still in special education programs, making varying degrees of progress, and it was clear that there was much more stability in terms of placement for this group of students.

Most of the students classified as learning-disabled were still receiving resource services, but in one home a wonderful thing had happened: Dora reported that 12-year-old Maria had learned to read in 1 year, through the efforts of a new resource teacher who had dropped the phonics-only approach and used a whole-word emphasis. Dora hoped that Maria would soon be dismissed from special education.

There was evidence, however, that Spanish-speaking beginners continued to be plagued by inexplicably low achievement in reading. Dora, for example, was very worried about her 6-year-old, Emilia, who, she said, had learned "ni una palabra" (not one word) of some 300 that had been sent home on the reading lists. Meanwhile, Ana's 6-year-old, in a different school, was also being considered for retention in the first grade. Both children spoke English fluently and appeared to be very bright, and their mothers were puzzled and frustrated by the school's reports. Dora held two theories: that the exclusive use of phonics, which she felt had kept her older daughter back, was now hindering Emilia, and that her class teacher, who was bilingual, was using too much of a mixture of English and Spanish, thus confusing the child. Dora was, in fact, very much opposed to what seemed to her to be a bilingual approach in the class. Overall, she expressed her confusion in this way:

> ¡Algo está pasando en la enseñanza—yo no sé—porqué la chiquilla as muy normal, y después de un año, no pudo aprender a leer ni una palabra! ¡Yo lo siento, pero es imposible que yo crea una cosa asi! Y siempre la mayoría de los niños hispanos tienen problemas en la lectura. ¡Eso yo no comprendo!

> (Something is going wrong in the teaching—I don't know—because the little girl is completely normal and after 1 year she couldn't learn to read a single word! I am sorry, but it is impossible to believe such a thing! And the majority of Hispanic children are having problems in reading. I do not understand it!)

SCHOOL-HOME COMMUNICATION ISSUES

The provision of a special education family liaison worker and the translation of documents into Spanish were certainly having an impact. Over the course of her first 2 years in the job of family liaison for special education, the parents' view of Elizabeth had evolved from "an American who speaks a little Spanish" to "a great help," "someone you can trust" (Ana). Ana, Delia, Fidel, and Francisca had all come to rely on Elizabeth to interpret at meetings and to explain the system to them. Francisca further commented that Elizabeth's manner was very appropriate, because she was friendly but not intrusive, a trait of some professionals that she found objectionable.

I was unable to observe any placement meetings, and the reported data from parents were not sufficient to be sure whether the kinds of roles played by parents had in fact changed. Only Ana and Francisca were able to offer me a specific picture of current meetings, and both of these seemed to be continuing in their accustomed role of respondent. In Francisca's case, she considered this satisfactory, since she felt that Rosita was now progressing well with a new teacher and a more advanced curriculum. Ana still held reservations about the curriculum, but her manner of dealing with this had not changed. She described Gina's teacher as "very sweet" and told me that she could not say what she expected for the next year since it would depend on what the teacher would say at the annual review. Smiling, she said: "You know that's how it is!"

It was clear that Elizabeth's role had become broader than that of special education liaison. For example, she had played a central role in helping Ana find jobs for herself and her son. When I commented to Ana that I thought Elizabeth was only helping with special education matters for Gina, she replied, "Yes, but when you have somebody you can trust — who is trying to help . . . "

Elizabeth herself interpreted the parents' view of her with some caution, however, exclaiming: "Yes, but I'm still the gringa — the outsider!" Elizabeth's hope was to employ a young woman named Nadya, who is both Puerto Rican and a parent of a child with a disability, to take over some of the liaison work and parent training. The only problem was to find funds to pay her.

Despite her progress in some areas, Elizabeth was experiencing considerable frustration in the work. One aspect of this was her increasingly unrealistic workload. Besides being willing to respond to non-special-education needs of parents, her caseload had doubled in 3 years. Her additional responsibility for staff development regarding Latino students made her a key player in the group of bilingual personnel referred to earlier.

Another source of her frustration was the continuing low response to her efforts at parent education on issues such as child development or the special education process as a whole. Elizabeth's workshops in the previous year had attracted no more than a handful of parents, and the only event that had been successful was a gala "fiesta educativa" (educational festival) cosponsored by local agencies, which attracted forty-seven parents and more than sixty children. Indeed, the event I observed, a workshop on early childhood language development, which parents had expressed an interest in having and which had been widely publicized, was attended by only nine mothers, some six or seven of whom were a kind of captive audience from the preschool playgroup housed in the same building. Both Elizabeth and Gloria, the regular education liaison, were very disappointed.

Elizabeth's attempts to explain low parental response reflected her frustration, as she vacillated between blaming parents and empathizing with them. At times she would conclude that because of lack of motivation or education parents could not see the importance of their participation, while at others she would emphasize that survival needs compete with educational matters for priority and that logistical difficulties like child care and transportation are serious deterrents. Further, she commented that parents "still do not feel welcome in the schools" because of the language barrier. Nevertheless, she concluded that school districts need to come up with ways to "make parents assume more responsibility."

Parents' explanation of their low response to parent training activities tended to emphasize competing priorities such as household responsibilities, child care, transportation inconveniences, and costs. However, there were hints at the questionable relevance and appropriateness of some of the content and methods of such events. These will be explored in the next section.

Professional Goals and Parents' Needs

The data of this study showed parents who were intensely involved in and concerned about their children's development and the challenge of raising children in a new and threatening urban environment. While their own life experience precluded their feeling comfortable in school-like settings and activities, there was no evidence that they did not value education for their children.

I would like to suggest that perhaps there is indeed low motivation — not with regard to their children's needs but with regard to participation in activities whose form and style fail to address parents' real information needs or to utilize a learning style with which parents can be comfortable. I believe that one important aspect of the problem is the way learning is conceptualized. Parent education or parent workshops, as I observed them in both the original and follow-up studies, were based on a model of learning as an essentially verbal and abstract activity and were usually presented in a student-teacher format derived from the school. They also continued to be based on the assumption that a group format provided the most effective and economical use of time. Thus it almost seemed that Elizabeth had forgotten her comment of 2 years earlier that perhaps getting a few parents at a time might be more efficient than getting large groups.

Indeed, while the notion of parent education through group lectures and discussion may work very well and be attractive to many mainstream parents, the very fact of sitting and absorbing information through verbal means only may be of very little interest or value to others. This seemed to be the case in the workshop I observed on early language development. I observed that while the predominant style of presentation was through lecture/discussion, the mothers were ready to share stories or problems relating to their own children. Indeed, the session could probably have proceeded entirely on spontaneous discussion of concerns raised by the mothers. Perhaps the answer to professionals' desire to share information and guidance on child-rearing issues is to offer regular occasions for informal conversations about problems as they arise, with the full understanding that each occasion may attract only a few people who really need the information at that time.

In addition to a preference for spontaneous and personalized discussion, it may also be that many parents do not feel a need to be given abstract information on general processes such as child development. It is true that the workshop observed in the follow-up study was designed in response to parents' request for this topic in a needs assessment. However, the North American approach to child rearing reflects a view of parenting as incorporating a body of knowledge that can be learned through lectures and reading, or various forms of pedagogy, and that may best be learned from experts in various fields. Parents from traditional cultures may feel that the knowledge passed from one generation to another within the family, coupled with their own experience, is their best source.

Conversations with two parents hinted at this as a possible explanation for why parents do not respond more to "educational" events. Margarita said:

> Bueno, yo creo que la mayoría ya ha pasado por esa experiencia, y ya saben lo que van a hablar.

> (Well, I think that the majority of parents must have had the experience already, and already know what is going to be said.)

Ana also commented that very often meetings and workshops "siempre dicen lo mismo" (always say the same thing) and that parents' role is usually to listen while the professionals talk.

Much of the information on early language development presented in the workshop related to basic developmental patterns that any mother with a young child or who had grown up in a family with many siblings would know from experience. Thus it is possible that, while parents may not be able to state their knowledge of developmental patterns, they do know them through experience and casual observation and do not feel a need to be taught about them in a formal and abstract fashion. They do feel a need, however, to discuss with knowledgeable persons the specific problems presented by their own children. To address this kind of need effectively may require an entirely different format and different goals and expectations on the part of professionals.

Activity-Based, Informal Learning

My observation of a fairly new program — a daily playgroup for Latino mothers with their infants and toddlers — suggested that a more interactive approach may be more successful. I interviewed Jennifer, the preschool specialist who initiated and directs the program, and learned that within the first 3 months of the program, daily attendance had grown from one mother with her two children to eleven mothers and sixteen children.

When I observed the program, which was housed in a school district building, the usual attendance was eighteen to twenty mothers in good weather and about ten to twelve in the colder winter months, since some mothers walked as far as ten blocks to attend. There was such demand for the program that Jennifer was trying to find funding for a second program on the south side to serve parents in that area. Learning in this program was activity-based and informal, and while it is true that a program for parents of preschoolers will differ in important ways from one for parents of school-aged children, this principle could nonetheless be adapted.

Parents who are uncomfortable with a student-teacher model of interaction may be easier to reach through opportunities for activities with other parents or with their children. Literature on some minority groups, notably Native Americans, for example, has observed a traditional preference for parallel activities that promote casual and spontaneous rather than preplanned verbal interaction (Philips, 1983). Indeed, for some groups activities that focus entirely on verbal exchange may be very uncomfortable, especially if the style is formal. Mental health providers who work with Puerto Rican families have suggested that what may work best is to be available to parents on an informal and individualized basis (Ambrosino, 1981; McGowan, 1988) rather than relying on specific events with preprepared agendas. McGowan's recommendations focus on a more flexible approach to time, space, and interpersonal relationships in order to "minimize social distance" (p. 59).

A more informal approach could be implemented through "community-based schools" that could provide a center for various parent activities. Elizabeth, in fact, told me that one of twelve statewide grants for this purpose had been awarded a school in a predominantly Black neighborhood in the city. She expressed the wish that a similar allowance could be made for the Latino community. Even in such a case, however, it would be important that planning be done in a manner truly responsive to the needs and style of the community. This could mean having to be willing to revamp one's notions of what constitutes efficiency and using a style that, in its approach to time, space, and professional-client relationships, may be very "un-American."

An excellent example of professionals' ability to learn from and adapt to the behavior of their clients has been offered by Lieberman (1990) in a discussion of parent intervention with recently arrived Central American families. The author shows how a carefully conceived plan to offer a supportive and culturally appropriate woman-to-woman group was rejected by the mothers—"not explicitly but eloquently enough through the most powerful means of communication at their disposal: lack of attendance at the group meetings" (p. 10). The mothers' pattern showed that what they really wanted were opportunities to develop individual relationships with the group coordinator, not with each other. When the agency responded by totally changing its agenda to meet this need, attendance increased by 75 percent.

Central to such considerations, however, is the observation that, while time, space, and relationships should be approached in ways that are appropriate to the cultural group served, "there is no single, correct way" to do this (McGowan, 1988, p. 61). Rather, as Lieberman's discussion shows, decisions about programs should be made through observing what works and finding ways to implement the underlying principles of interaction, rather than continuing to assume that a particular model ought to work and that if it does not, it means that something is wrong with the people the program was intended to serve. Indeed, this assumption regarding parents is identical to that regarding students—as expressed in an ironic tone by the bilingual psychologist in the study: "This works! If you can't learn there's something wrong with you!"

CONCLUSIONS AND RECOMMENDATIONS

Throughout this study I have emphasized that there exists a tension between the mandate to implement the medical model of disability and the mandate to include parents in the process of identifying and treating children classified under this model. The law recognizes that parents may disagree with the model and has built in a system whereby they must become adversaries in order to be heard. Parents from cultures that hold different versions of the concept of disability, and different versions of the concept of participation with schools, may be uncomfortable both with the model imposed upon their children and with the alternative of challenging this model.

In between these extremes lies the possibility of negotiation of meaning between professionals and parents, of collaboration in identifying what actually might explain students' difficulties and determining the most appropriate methods of remediation. One reason that such intermediate interactions seldom take place is that professionals interpret the model inherent in the law as actually transcending culture. They come to believe that the definitions of disability deriving from the technological culture of the United States in fact represent universal truths. Forgetting what Bowers (1984) has referred to as "the human authorship" of the concept of disability, they see the medical model with its postivist assumptions as the only legitimate interpretation of students' learning difficulties and, in so doing, delegitimate all others.

The documents of the school system ensure this delegitimation of other perspectives by the categorical way in which they are framed and by the reliance on technical language that dissembles truth by excluding any information that may be construed as ambiguous or context-dependent. Thus the documents of the special education system become political tools in the enforcement of the cultural program of the law. Even the individualized education plan (IEP), a document that purports to reflect the individualized needs of a whole person, is expressed in language incomprehensible to most parents and is framed in such a way as to exclude the context that surrounds a student's educational career — as if such a career could exist apart from the total ecology of an individual child. By framing the discourse between itself and parents in such a way as to define what may legitimately be said, the special education system succeeds in alienating and, in most cases, excluding parents. The very consent forms that demonstrate compliance with the law become barriers between schools and families.

While the official perspective is currently being challenged by proponents of the regular education initiative, the fact is that professionals must operate within the constraints of the existing framework. The data of this study have shown that culturally responsive practice is possible; one might reasonably assume that such practice is in existence in many school systems across the country. Further research into effective practice in culturally diverse communities is needed, as well as studies conducted in U.S. territories where traditional cultures are more intact. The only such study so far located reveals the cultural incongruity of the assumptions of the law as well as logistical difficulties of its implementation in the Pacific Basin territories (Brady & Anderson, 1983).

There is no escaping the challenge facing schools. The racial and linguistic homogeneity of this nation, which once aspired to the creation of a neo-European melting pot, is now a thing of the past. The English-only movement, for example, is but an illustration of the growing recognition that change is inevitable and, as usual, frightening. The dramatic changes in school populations since the 1954 decision in *Brown* v. *Board of Education*, which required the racial desegregation of schools, as well as the rapidly growing population of immigrants from Third World nations, have changed forever the face of American schools, indeed, American society, which, in the next century, will no longer be predominantly Caucasian. In the not-too-distant future, the term *minority* will no longer be used as a synonym for people of color.

School systems across the country are trying to come to terms with the implications of these changes, and it is the hope of this book that some of the lessons learned in one small urban school district might be instructive for others with similar concerns. Without trying to suggest that the observations of this study are universally applicable to districts serving culturally diverse communities, the concluding pages will propose a list of recommendations that could be considered by systems where similar populations and similar dynamics obtain.

Restructuring Parent-Professional Discourse

The most important point to be grasped in the face of the changes outlined above is that the voices of vast numbers of people in communities representing widely varying racial and ethnic groups need to be heard if public education is to meet the needs of these populations. While cooperation between regular and special education is a salient feature in this process, this book is concerned with what special education must do to equalize the balance of power between its representatives and the families they serve.

At the center of this process is the way discourse between these two groups is structured. A legalistic approach to equalizing power will not be effective for the majority of people from cultures and communities where adversarial behavior and confrontation with authority are unacceptable; unfamiliarity with the social and educational system makes it impossible for many parents to be assertive. It is up to professionals to provide communication structures that will make dialogue possible and mutual understanding likely.

The study reported in this book has emphasized that the only consistent role offered to parents was that of consent-giver, and that the legalistic framing of this role tended to convert the notion of consent into a meaningless ritual of compliance. In a discussion of African American parents (Harry, in press) I have outlined four roles that need to be developed for parents in the special education process. These roles are equally applicable wherever an alteration of the balance of power is needed. These may be appropriate for mainstream parents also, but are particularly appropriate for parents whose cultural backgrounds place them at a distinct disadvantage in dealing with school systems. The proposed roles are as follows:

1. *Parents as assessors:* Parents would be included in the entire assessment process, with professionals relying on parents' intimate knowledge of their children and of historical and cultural features that may account for children's development, learning, and behavioral patterns. Under the present system, by the time parents are invited to the placement

meeting the power and legitimacy of professional expertise have already been established by the exclusion of parents from the assessment process. Precedent for the role proposed here can be found in exemplary projects funded by the Handicapped Children's Early Education Program (HCEEP), where parents were "an integral part of the interdisciplinary team" (Karnes, Linnemeyer & Myles, 1983, p. 186).

2. *Parents as presenters of reports:* Parents would be expected to be present at conferences in order to give an oral or written parent report which would be an official document, part of the child's educational record. This would signal to parents that their input is not only valued, but needed; currently, parents have virtually no role in placement conferences.

3. *Parents as policymakers:* Parents would elect their own representatives to advisory committees at the building, or, at least, the neighborhood level, with responsibility for participating in decision making about special education programming and cultural or community concerns.

4. *Parents as advocates and peer supports:* Parent groups within schools, perhaps overlapping with the advisory committees, would provide peer advocacy, support at IEP meetings, and perhaps most important, serve as mutual interpreters between the cultures of the community and of the school.

With the provision of official channels for reciprocal rather than one-way discourse, professionals can begin the process of developing collaborative practice.

Professional Attitudes: A Posture of Reciprocity

Wolfensberger and Thomas (1983) have argued that a great deal of unfair treatment of clients in human services reflects professionals' unconscious devaluing of the people they are trying to serve. Whether because of training or personal experience, however, there are some individuals who demonstrate genuine caring and empathy for people whose culture they may actually understand only minimally. This section offers suggestions for developing such a professional "posture of reciprocity" (Harry & Kalyanpur, 1991).

Becoming Informed about Cultural Differences. The following strategies will be useful in gaining information on social interaction, family structures and conceptions of disability:

SOCIAL INTERACTION

1. Invite ethnic community leaders to participate in and observe special education meetings in order to help identify those processes that seem to be working—and why.
2. Poll parents as to which individuals or teams they find most comfortable to work with, and then observe the processes used by those groups.
3. Use those teams or individuals who are achieving better communication with parents to serve as district resources for staff development on communication issues.
4. Request permission from ethnic community groups to allow school personnel to participate in their meetings and other events so as to learn about specific cultural styles through participation.

FAMILY STRUCTURES AND PRACTICES

1. Actively seek information from literature and from parents themselves about family structures and roles, and act on this knowledge by inviting and including the input of influential family members other than parents.
2. Actively seek information on culturally appropriate child-rearing practices, especially on issues such as dependence/independence, reward/ punishment, and group rights/individual rights.
3. Where child-rearing practices differ significantly from mainstream practice or from school expectations, seek the advice of ethnic community leaders regarding the range of normative behavior. For example, if corporal punishment is used more frequently than is expected, try to develop a sense of what is considered abusive within the group's norms; similarly, if dependence/independence of children appears to be an issue. Most often, professionals will have to strike a balance between the norms of the cultural group and the goals of a student's special education program.

VARYING CONCEPTIONS OF DISABILITY

1. Ask parents of children who are about to be assessed to describe their impressions of their children's developmental and achievement levels and their interpretations of the sources of any difficulties observed.
2. Be prepared to engage in dialogue with parents regarding perceptions that may differ from those of the school. Present the findings of evaluations and decisions about classification in terms that emphasize an ecological approach; that is, the many aspects of a child's life that may interact to produce difficulties in learning.
3. Seek the advice of community leaders regarding the beliefs of the group

regarding disability, so as to understand the cultural point of reference expressed by parents.

4. Where evaluation reveals unequivocal biological anomalies underlying a child's difficulties, be sure to refer parents to culturally sensitive medical professionals who can follow up on parents' understanding of the diagnosis.

Developing Specific Communication Strategies. Appropriate communication strategies will be effective when implemented by personnel who are genuinely open to different cultures and who have actively sought to gain information and skills regarding an ethnic group that is new to them. In the words of Jennifer, the preschool director interviewed in the follow-up study, "People know when you are not genuine, and they won't come back!" In an atmosphere of genuine respect and reciprocity, the following school district strategies will be helpful:

1. Employ bilingual liaison workers for families with children in special education, placing the emphasis on the worker's ability to be comfortable with the nuances of both culture and language. This should take precedence over familiarity with the school system, which can be provided by training.
2. Employ interpreters who can learn the special education system, and emphasize the importance of translating exactly what is said and offering explanations where necessary.
3. Make the avoidance of jargon a prime target in professional-parent communication, except where it represents terms required for the parent's information, such as *IEP phase 1, triennial*, and so on, in which case the meanings of these terms must be taught to parents. Terms such as *manipulatives* or *time-on-task* can easily be replaced by lay language.
4. Make professionals aware of the usefulness of models of IEP meetings such as those suggested by Turnbull and Turnbull (1986) and Marion (1979).
5. Place more emphasis on the development of personalized, individual relationships with families than on large-group interaction and information giving.
6. Provide personalized, face-to-face information to clarify all documents regarding referral, assessment, and placement of students.
7. When documents are about to be translated into a new language, invite a small group of parents to participate in determining their level of readability.

Providing Support and Developing Advocacy. Providers of services can support parents by providing them with information on district policies, special education materials and processes, and parents' rights. They can assist parents in understanding the school district's point of view and in expressing their own opinions to professionals. They can encourage parents to become effective advocates by demonstrating that school personnel are open to differing viewpoints and to being influenced by the informed wishes of parents. They can assist parents in presenting preferences or even objections to professional recommendations. Because of the adversarial framework of the law, however, service providers who are employees of school districts cannot presume to be genuine advocates for parents when there is any serious difference of opinion regarding the assessment, placement, or instruction of a student in special education. Even the most caring and cross-culturally sensitive professionals need to be aware of this. (For an opposing point of view see Marion, 1981.)

The job of advocacy is always vulnerable to its own need to cooperate with potential adversaries. In this study it was a community advocacy group that confronted the school district on behalf of Latino parents. At the time of the study, the adversarial tone had softened considerably as the school district tried to respond to the challenges of the community. Ironically, this illustrates the next level at which advocacy may run the risk of conflict of interest; that is, when advocates start to achieve their goals, in order to continue doing so, they must become more cooperative with the group they have been challenging. This pattern has been well described in the literature (Biklen, 1983; Wolfensberger, 1984). Indeed, this notion was suggested by Teresa, a social worker in the community, who expressed the opinion that the relationship between the advocacy agency and the school district had come to the point of "romancing each other!"

This is why consumers of a service, supporting each other in groups, will make the best advocates: regardless of the success of their advocacy, they continue to have something at stake. A sharp awareness of the limits of liaison work will require school personnel to attend to the following:

1. Cultivate an awareness of the potential for conflict between the interests of the school district and those of parents if the boundary between liaison work and advocacy is not properly understood.
2. Seek the cooperation of community agencies to train community members to act as advocates for parents of children in special education programs.
3. Encourage parents to form peer advocacy groups, conveying the message that it is genuinely acceptable for parents to bring their own infor-

mal supports to meetings with the school district and that parents will not be considered disloyal in doing so.

Instructional Issues

This book is essentially about parents' views of special education. It is not within its scope to presume to make recommendations regarding specific instructional approaches and curricula for students from culturally diverse backgrounds. The thrust of these final comments is to reiterate that parents' explanations of their children's difficulties are grounded in intimate knowledge and daily observation and, as in the case of this study, may run directly parallel to the most sophisticated theories of the experts in the field.

The central instructional issues identified by parents were language of instruction, frequent changes in and out-of-neighborhood placement, an unchallenging curriculum in self-contained classes, and methods in the teaching of reading. All of these matters are of current concern to the field.

Parents of children classified as learning-disabled mostly identified either linguistic bias on the part of the school system or language "confusion" as a major source of students' academic difficulties. While it is important to note that parents were not adequately informed about the approaches used with LEP students in the district, their almost unanimous conviction that bilingualism played a central role in their children's difficulties must be taken seriously. Some parents felt that the answer would be to teach the children in English only. In fact, most of the children had been taught in English only. Some parents felt that the answer would be to teach them in Spanish only until they learned English. All agreed that their prime goal for their children should be literacy in English, and they were prepared to have them lose Spanish rather than fail in English.

Research on second-language learning shows clearly that students should not have to choose between one or the other language. It also shows that to move children to second-language literacy too soon is to set them up for failure in both languages (e.g., Baca & Cervantes, 1984; Cummins, 1986). Thus the notion that the best way to learn English is to be submerged in it at school has been shown to be a fallacy for young children whose first language is not yet fully developed in either speech or literacy.

Regarding curricula and placement in self-contained classes, the observations of parents in this study were also in line with common criticisms of the field. Parents were accepting of special education services to the extent that they succeeded in enhancing children's progress in school without stigmatizing them. Their criticisms of a watered-down curriculum echo longstanding complaints, while the practice of moving children frequently to wherever there is a program ignores the need of both parents and children for a sense of safety and belonging within their community and for continuity in relationships with professionals.

With regard to reading, the notion of relying totally on one approach for students who are supposed to be having an individualized program must be challenged. While this is true for all programs, it is particularly so for students caught between two languages, whose greater need for meaningful content and context may render phonics-only methods inappropriate.

Labeling in Special Education

Like the parents in the study, this conclusion can only echo the continuing call within the field for a revision of the classification system. While the distress caused by stigmatizing labels applies to all students, it is exacerbated by different cultural perceptions of the nature of disabilities and different expectations regarding the importance of school-based learning.

For children in the United States, there is one predominantly important social role—that of student. Parents in the United States increasingly give over responsibilities for their children to schools or school-like facilities. They increasingly expect and accept the authority of the state in child-rearing matters traditionally relegated to the family. For many minority cultures this pattern is quite alien.

The most important agent of the state is the school. It is through the power of those whom Mercer (1973) has referred to as the "professional diagnosticians" and "legitimate labelers" that deviants are labeled and officially defined as failures (p. 15). The enormous importance of the school's classification process may color a child's whole identity, so that, for many children, to fail at the task of being a student is to be described as being "disabled." This is very different from the way parents in the study talked about school failure. There is a real difference in perspectives between calling someone "disabled" and saying, as did one mother (Ana), that her husband "went to school but never learned to read and write, so after a couple of years he left the school and went to work to help his family."

It is not that such parents do not value school learning; on the contrary, they value it highly because they see it as the only way for their children to achieve a quality of life that they themselves cannot attain. But they reject a global definition of the child that is based on what they consider only a part of the child's identity. In the perspective of these families, the parameters of "normalcy" and acceptability are much wider than are those of the school, and the toleration for human difference much greater. Yet they know that the power of the school is such that to be stigmatized as a student is to be stigmatized as a whole person.

This study can only recommend that the field move toward services based on descriptions of students' needs rather than on the ascribing of disability classifications that stigmatize children. Ethnic minority students already have the burden of battling stigmatizing labels as they struggle to move out of their position at the bottom of the social and economic ladder of the United States. The literature increasingly shows that cultural differences are devalued by an educational system bent on identifying deficits rather than strengths and that the insistence on identifying a rigid border between normality and disability is at best erroneous, at worst malicious.

Culturally different parents cannot afford to become complacent in their struggle for equality, but their empowerment as advocates can scarcely begin without the cooperation of schools. This most powerful of authorities must look inward toward the creation of communication structures that genuinely empower parents. The hope of every generation lies in its children. Indeed, for culturally diverse ethnic minorities of low social and economic status, their children may be all they have to lose.

References

Ada, A. F. (1988). The Pajaro Valley experience. In T. Skutnabb-Kangas & J. Cummins (Eds.), *Minority education: From shame to struggle* (pp. 223–238). Clevedon, England: Multilingual Matters.

Adams, B. N. (1978). Black families in the United States: An overview of current ideologies and research. In D. B. Shimkin, E. M. Shimkin, & D. A. Frate (Eds.), *The extended family in Black societies* (pp. 173–180). Paris: Mouton Publishers.

Adams, D. W. (1988). Fundamental considerations: The deep meaning of Native American schooling, 1880–1900. Facing racism in education. *Harvard Educational Review, 58*(1), 1–28.

Adkins, P. G., & Young, R. G. (1976). Cultural perceptions in the treatment of handicapped school children of Mexican-American parentage. *Journal of Research and Development in Education, 9*(4), 83–90.

Aloia, G. F. (1981). Influence of a child's race and the EMR label on initial impressions of regular-classroom teachers. *American Journal on Mental Deficiency, 85*(6), 619–623.

Ambrosino, S. (1981). Integration of methods. In E. Mizio and A. J. Delaney (Eds.), *Training for service delivery to minority clients* (pp. 131–143). New York: Family Service Association of America.

Anderson, W., Chitwood, S., & Hayden, D. (1982). *Negotiating the special education maze.* Englewood Cliffs, NJ: Prentice-Hall.

Appleton, N. (1983). *Cultural pluralism in education: Theoretical foundations.* New York: Longman.

Argulewicz, E. N. (1983). Effects of ethnic membership, socio-economic status and home language on LD, EMR and EH placements. *Learning Disability Quarterly, 6*(2), 195–200.

Aschenbrenner, J. (1978). Continuities and variations in Black family structure. In D. B. Shimkin, E. M. Shimkin, & D. A. Frate (Eds.), *The extended family in Black societies* (pp. 181–200). Paris: Mouton Publishers.

Attneave, C. (1982). American Indians and Alaska Native families: Emigrants in their own homeland. In M. McGoldrick, J. K. Pearce, & J. Giordano (Eds.), *Ethnicity and family therapy* (pp. 55–83). New York: Guilford.

Au, K., & Jordan, C. (1981). Teaching reading to Hawaiian children: Finding a culturally appropriate solution. In H. T. Trueba, G. P. Guthrie, & K. Au

(Eds.), *Culture and the bilingual classroom* (pp. 139–152). Rowley, MA: Newbury House.

Baca, L. M., & Cervantes, H. T. (1984). Parent and community involvement in bilingual special education. In L. M. Baca & H. T. Cervantes (Eds.), *The bilingual-special education interface* (pp. 213–232). St. Louis: Times Mirror/Mosby.

Baglopal, P. R. (1988). Social networks and Asian Indian families. In C. Jacobs & D. D. Bowles (Eds.), *Ethnicity and race* (pp. 18–33). Silver Spring, MD: National Association of Social Workers.

Barsch, R. H. (1961). Explanations offered by parents and siblings of brain-damaged children. *Exceptional Children, 27,* 286–291.

Basso, K. H. (1979). *Portraits of "the Whiteman."* New York: Cambridge University Press.

Baughman, E. E. (1971). *Black Americans: A psychological analysis.* New York: Academic Press.

Becker, H. S. (1969). *Studies in the sociology of deviance.* New York: Free Press.

Becker, H. S. (1970). *Sociological work.* Chicago: Aldine.

Bennett, A. T. (1988). Gateways to powerlessness: Incorporating Hispanic deaf children and families into formal schooling. *Disability, Handicap & Society, 3*(2), 119–151.

Bernal, E. (1977). Perspective on non-discriminatory assessment. In T. Oakland (Ed.), *Psychological and educational assessment of minority children* (pp. xi-xiv). New York: Brunner/Mazel.

Bickel, W. E., & Bickel, D. D. (1986). Effective schools, classrooms, and instruction: Implications for special education. *Exceptional Children, 52*(6), 489–500.

Biklen, D. (1983). *Community organizing: Theory and practice.* Englewood Cliffs, NJ: Prentice-Hall.

Biklen, D. (1985). *Achieving the complete school: Strategies for effective mainstreaming.* New York: Teachers College Press.

Billingsley, A. (1968). *Black families in White America.* Englewood Cliffs, NJ: Prentice-Hall.

Blakely, M. (1982, October). *Southeast Asian refugee parent survey.* Paper presented at the conference of the Oregon Educational Research Association, Newport, OR.

Bogdan, B., & Biklen, S. (1982). *Qualitative research for education.* Boston, MA: Allyn & Bacon.

Bogdan, R., & Knoll, J. (1988). The sociology of disability. In E. L. Meyen & T. M. Skrtic (Eds.), *Exceptional children and youth: An introduction* (3rd ed.) (pp. 449–478). Denver, CO: Love.

Bogdan, R., & Taylor, S. J. (1982). *Inside out: Two first-person accounts of what it means to be labeled "mentally retarded."* Toronto: University of Toronto Press.

Boggs, S. T. (1985). *Speaking, relating and learning: A study of Hawaiian children at home and at school.* Norwood, NJ: Ablex.

Bowers, C. A. (1984). *The promise of theory: Education and the politics of cultural change*. New York: Longman.

Bowles, S., & Gintis, H. (1976). *Schooling in capitalist America*. New York: Basic Books.

Boyer, L. B. (1979). *Childhood and folklore: A psychoanalytic study of Apache personality*. New York: Library of Psychological Anthropology.

Brady, M. P., & Anderson, D. D. (1983). Some issues in the implementation of P. L. 94-142 in the Pacific Basin territories. *Education, 103*(3), 259-269.

Bram, J. (1968). The lower status Puerto Rican family. In F. Cordasco (Ed.), *Puerto Rican children in mainland schools* (pp. 116-126). Metuchen, NJ: Scarecrow.

Brice, J. (1982). West Indian families. In M. McGoldrick, J. K. Pearce, & J. Giordano (Eds.), *Ethnicity and family therapy* (pp. 123-133). New York: Guilford Press.

Briggs, C. L. (1986). *Learning how to ask*. Cambridge, England: Cambridge University Press.

Bronfenbrenner, U. (1979). *The ecology of human development: Experiments by nature and design*. Cambridge, MA: Harvard University Press.

Bui, T. H. (1983). Meeting the needs of Indochinese students. *Momentum, 25*, 20.

Buriel, R. (1983). Teacher-student interactions and their relationship to student achievement: A comparison of Mexican-American children. *Journal of Educational Psychology, 75*(6), 889-897.

Campos, S. J., & Keatinge, H. R. (1988). The Carpinteria language minority student experience. In T. Skutnabb-Kangas & J. Cummins (Eds.), *Minority education: From shame to struggle* (pp. 299-307). Clevedon, England: Multilingual Matters.

Canino, G. (1982). The Hispanic woman: Sociocultural influences on diagnosis and treatment. In R. Becerra, M. Karno, & J. Escobar (Eds.), *Mental health and Hispanic Americans: Clinical perspectives*. New York: Grune & Stratton.

Canino, I. (1982). The Hispanic child: Treatment considerations. In R. Becerra, M. Karno, & J. Escobar (Eds.), *Mental health and Hispanic Americans: Clinical perspectives*. New York: Grune & Stratton.

Canino, I. A., & Canino, G. (1980). Impact of stress on the Puerto Rican family: Treatment considerations. *American Journal of Orthopsychiatry, 50*(3), 535-541.

Cassidy, E. (1988). *Reaching and involving Black parents of handicapped children in their child's education program*. Lansing, MI: CAUSE Inc. (ERIC Document Reproduction Service No. ED 302 982)

Casuso, V. (1978). Working with families of the preschool handicapped child in Spanish-speaking communities. In P. L. Trohanis (Ed.), *Early education in Spanish-speaking communities* (pp. 17-26). New York: Walker.

Cazden, C. B., Carrasco, R., Maldonado-Guzman, A. A., & Erickson, F. (1985). The contribution of ethnographic research to bicultural bilingual education. In J. E. Alatis & J. J. Staczek (Eds.), *Perspectives on bilingualism and bilin-*

gual education (pp. 153–169). Washington, DC: Georgetown University Press.

Cazden, C. B., & Leggett, E. L. (1981). Culturally responsive education: Recommendations for achieving Lau Remedies II. In H. T. Trueba, G. P. Guthrie, & K. H. Au (Eds.), *Culture and the bilingual classroom: Studies in classroom ethnography* (pp. 69–86). Cambridge, MA: Newbury House.

Cazneave, N. A. (1981). Black men in America: The quest for "manhood." In H. P. McAdoo (Ed.), *Black families* (pp. 176–185). Beverly Hills, CA: Sage.

Chan, K. S., & Kitano, M. K. (1986). Demographic characteristics of exceptional Asian students. In M. K. Kitano & P. C. Chinn (Eds.), *Exceptional Asian children and youth* (pp. 1–11). Reston, VA: Council for Exceptional Children and Youth.

Chan K., & Rueda, R. (1979). Poverty and culture in education: Separate but equal. *Exceptional Children, 45,* 422–427.

Chan, S. (1986). Parents of exceptional Asian children. In M. K. Kitano & P. C. Chinn (Eds.), *Exceptional Asian children and youth* (pp. 36–53). Reston, VA: Council for Exceptional Children and Youth.

Chan, S., Lim-Yee, N., & Vandevier, M. (1985, March). *A model of parent education for Asian and Latino families with special needs children*. Paper presented at the annual international conference of the National Association for Bilingual Education, San Francisco.

Cherryholmes, C. H. (1988). *Power and criticism: Poststructural investigations in education*. New York: Teachers College Press.

Chinn, P. C., & Plata, M. (1986). Perspectives and educational implications of Southeast Asian students. In M. K. Kitano & P. C. Chinn (Eds.), *Exceptional Asian children and youth* (pp. 12–28). Reston, VA: Council for Exceptional Children and Youth.

Clark, D. L., Lotto, L. S., & Astuto, T. A. (1984). Effective schools and school improvements: A comparative analysis of two lines of inquiry. *Educational Administration Quarterly, 20*(3), 41–68.

Clark, R. (1983). *Family life and school achievement: Why poor black children succeed or fail*. Chicago: University of Chicago Press.

Cochran, M. (1987). The parental empowerment process: Building on family strengths. *Equity and Choice, 4,* 9–23.

Cochran, M., & Woolever, F. (1983). Beyond the deficit model: The empowerment of parents with information and informal supports. In I. E. Siegel & L. P. Laosa (Eds.), *Changing Families* (pp. 225–245). New York: Plenum.

Coleman, J. S., Campbell, E. Q., Hobson, C. J., McPartland, J., Mood, A., Weinfeld, F. D., & York, R. C. (1966). *Equality of educational opportunity*. Washington, DC: U.S. Government Printing Office.

Collier, V. P. (1987). Age and rate of acquisition of second-language for academic purposes. *TESOL, 21*(4), 617–641.

Collins, J. (1988). Language and class in minority education. *Anthropology & Education Quarterly, 19,* 299–326.

Collins, R., & Camblin, L. D. (1983). The politics and science of learning disability classification: Implications for Black children. *Contemporary Education*, 54(2), 113–118.

Comer, J. (1980). *School power: Implications of an intervention project*. New York: Free Press.

Condon, E. C., Peters, J. Y., & Sueiro-Ross, C. (1979). *Special education and the Hispanic child: Cultural perspectives*. New Brunswick, NJ: Teacher's Corp Mid-Atlantic Network.

Connery, A. R. (1987). *A description and comparison of Native American and Anglo parents' knowledge of their handicapped children's rights*. Unpublished doctoral dissertation. Northern Arizona University, Flagstaff.

Cordasco, F. (Ed). (1968). *Puerto Rican children in mainland schools*. Metuchen, NJ: Scarecrow.

Cordasco, F. (1976). *Bilingual schooling in the United States*. New York: McGraw-Hill.

Correa, V. I. (1989). Involving culturally diverse families in the educational process. In S. H. Fradd & M. J. Weismantel (Eds.), *Meeting the needs of culturally and linguistically different students: A handbook for educators* (pp. 130–144). Boston: College Hill.

Covello, L. (1967). *The social background of the Italo-American school child*. Leyden, England: Brill.

Cuch, F. S. (1987). Cultural perspectives on Indian education: A comparative analysis of the Ute and Anglo cultures. *Equity & Excellence*, 23(1–2), 65–76.

Cummins, J. (1979). Linguistic interdependence and the educational development of bilingual children. *Review of Educational Research*, 49(2), 222–251.

Cummins, J. (1980a). Psychological assessment of immigrant children: Logic or intuition? *Journal of Multilingual and Multicultural Development*, 1(2), 97–111.

Cummins, J. (1980b). The construct of language proficiency in bilingual education. In J. E. Alatis & J. J. Staczec (Eds.), *Perspectives on bilingualism and bilingual education* (pp. 205–227). Washington, DC: Georgetown University Press.

Cummins, J. (1980c). Institutionalized racism and the assessment of minority children: A comparison of policies and programs in the United States and Canada. In R. J. Samuda & S. L. Kong (Eds.), *Assessment and placement of minority students* (pp. 95–108). Toronto: Hogrefe.

Cummins, J. (1984). *Bilingualism and special education: Issues in assessment and pedagogy*. San Diego: College Hill.

Cummins, J. (1986). Empowering minority students: A framework for intervention. *Harvard Educational Review*, 56, 18–36.

Cummins, J. (1989). A theoretical framework for bilingual special education. *Exceptional Children*, 56(2), 111–119.

Cunningham, K., Cunningham, K., & O'Connell, J. C. (1986). Impact of differing cultural perceptions on special education service delivery. *Rural Special Education Quarterly*, 8(1), 2–8.

Curtis, J. (1988). Parents, schools and racism. In T. Skutnabb-Kangas & J. Cummins (Eds.), *Minority education: From shame to struggle* (pp. 278–298). Clevedon, England: Multilingual Matters.

Dao, M., & Grossman, H. (1985). *Identifying and rehabilitating South East Asian students with special needs and counseling their parents.* Sacramento, CA: State Department of Education. (ERIC Document Reproduction Service No. ED 273 068)

Delgado, M. (1980, September). Providing child care for Hispanic families. *Young Children*, pp. 26–32.

Delgado, M. (1988). Groups in Puerto Rican spiritism: Implications for clinicians. In C. Jacobs & D. D. Bowles (Eds.), *Ethnicity and race: Critical concepts in social work* (pp. 34–47). Silver Spring, MD: National Association of Social Workers.

Delgado-Gaitan, C. (1987). Parent perceptions of school: Supportive environments for children. In H. T. Trueba (Ed.), *Success or failure? Learning and the language minority student* (pp. 131–155). Cambridge, MA: Newbury House.

Delgado-Gaitan, C. (1990). *Literacy for empowerment.* New York: Falmer.

Delpit, L. (1988). The silenced dialogue: Power and pedagogy in educating other people's children. *Harvard Educational Review, 58*(3), 280–298.

Dennis, W. (1941). The socialization of the Hopi child. In L. Spier, A. I. Hallowell, & S. S. Newman (Eds.), *Language, culture, and personality: Essays in memory of Edward Sapir* (pp. 259–271). Menasha, WI: Sapir Memorial Publication Fund.

Deutsch, M. (1967). The disadvantaged child and the learning process. In M. Deutsch (Ed.), *The disadvantaged child.* New York: Basic Books.

De Vos, G. A. (1973). Japan's outcastes: The problem of the Burakumin. In B. Whitaker (Ed.), *The fourth world: Victims of group oppression* (pp. 307–327). New York: Schocken.

Dexter, L. A. (1964). On the politics and sociology of stupidity in our society. In H. S. Becker (Ed.), *The other side* (pp. 37–49). Glencoe, IL: Free Press.

Deyhle, D. (1987). Learning failure: Tests as gatekeepers and the culturally different child. In H. Trueba (Ed.), *Success or failure? Learning and the language minority student* (pp. 85–108). New York: Newbury House.

Diaz, J. O. (1981, February). *Home-school discrepancies and the Puerto Rican exceptional child.* Paper presented at the Council for Exceptional Children Conference on the Exceptional Bilingual Child, New Orleans. (ERIC Document Reproduction Service No. ED 207292)

Dunn, L. M. (1968). Special education for the mildly retarded: Is much of it justifiable? *Exceptional Children, 35*, 5–22.

Dunn, L. M. (1988). *Bilingual Hispanic children on the U.S. mainland: A review of research on their cognitive, linguistic, and scholastic development.* Honolulu, HI: Dunn Educational Services.

Duran, R. P. (1989). Assessment and instruction of at-risk Hispanic students. *Exceptional Children, 56*(2), 154–158.

Eagar, G. R. (1986). Cultural differences and parent programs: Hispanic. In C. Moore (Ed.), *Reaching out: Proceedings from a special education symposium on cultural differences and parent programs* (pp. 49–56). Phoenix, AZ: Western Regional Resource Center. (ERIC Document Reproduction Service No. 284 408)

Edgerton, R. B. (1967). *The cloak of competence: Stigma in the lives of the mentally retarded.* Berkeley: University of California Press.

Edgerton, R. B. (1970). Mental retardation in non-Western societies: Toward a cross-cultural perspective on incompetence. In H. C. Haywood (Ed.), *Sociocultural aspects of mental retardation* (pp. 523–559). New York: Appleton-Century-Crofts.

Edgerton, R. B., & Ottina, J. (1986). *A twenty-five year follow-up study of persons labeled mentally retarded.* Washington, DC: U.S. Department of Education, Office of Special Education and Rehabilitative Services. (ERIC Document Reproduction Service No. 271 912)

Edmonds, R. (1986). Characteristics of effective schools. In U. Neisser (Ed.), *The school achievement of minority children* (pp. 93–104). Hillsdale, NJ: Erlbaum.

Engelmann, S., & Bruner, E. C. (1974). *DISTAR Reading I.* Chicago, IL: Science Research Associates.

Epps, S., & Tindal, G. (1987). The effectiveness of differential programming in serving students with mild handicaps: Placement options and instructional programming. In M. C. Wang, M. C. Reynolds, & H. J. Walberg (Eds.), *Handbook of special education: Research and practice* (Vol. 1) (pp. 213–250). Oxford, England: Pergamon Press.

Escobar, J. L., & Randolph, E. L. (1982). The Hispanic and social networks. In R. Becerra, M. Karno, & J. Escobar (Eds.), *Mental health and Hispanic Americans: Clinical perspectives.* New York: Grune & Stratton.

Escobedo, T. H., & Huggins, J. (1983). Field dependence-independence: A theoretical framework for Mexican-American cultural variables? In T. H. Escobedo (Ed.), *Early childhood bilingual education: A Hispanic perspective.* New York: Teachers College Press.

Falealii, T. (1986). The Samoan family. In C. Moore (Ed.), *Reaching out: Proceedings from a special education symposium on cultural differences and parent programs* (pp. 63–72). Phoenix, AZ: Western Regional Resource Center. (ERIC Document Reproduction Service No. ED 284 408)

Falicov, C. J. (1982). Mexican families. In M. McGoldrick, J. K. Pearce, & J. Giordano (Eds.), *Ethnicity and family therapy* (134–163). New York: Guilford.

Featherstone, H. (1980). *A difference in the family.* New York: Penguin.

Figler, C. S. (1981, February). *Puerto Rican families with and without handicapped children.* Paper presented at the Council for Exceptional Children Conference on the Exceptional Bilingual Child, New Orleans. (ERIC Document Reproduction Service No. ED 204 876)

Figueroa, R. A. (1983). Test bias and Hispanic children. *Journal of Special Education, 17*(4), 431–440.

Figueroa, R. A., Fradd, S. H., & Correa, V. I. (Eds.). (1989a). Meeting the multicultural needs of the Hispanic students in special education [Special issue]. *Exceptional Children, 56*(2).

Figueroa, R. A., Fradd, S. H., & Correa, V. I. (1989b). Bilingual special education and this special issue. *Exceptional Children, 56*(2), 174–178.

Finn, J. D. (1982). Patterns in special education placement as revealed by the OCR surveys. In K. A. Heller, W. H. Holtzman, & S. Messick (Eds.), *Placing children in special education: A strategy for equity* (pp. 322–381). Washington, DC: National Academy Press.

Fitzpatrick, J. P. (1987). *Puerto Rican Americans: The meaning of migration to the mainland.* Englewood Cliffs, NJ: Prentice-Hall.

Florida Department of Education. (1988). *Involving minority and isolated parents in the education of their exceptional students.* Tallahassee, FL: Department of Education.

Fordham, S. (1988). Racelessness as a factor in Black students' school success: Pragmatic strategy or Pyrrhic victory. *Harvard Educational Review, 58*(1), 54–84.

Fordham, S., & Ogbu, J. U. (1986). Black students' school success: Coping with the burden of "acting white." *The Urban Review, 18*(3), 176–206.

Frazier, E. F. (1948). *The Negro family in the United States.* New York: Citadel.

Fuchs, D., & Fuchs, L. S. (1989). Effects of examiner familiarity on Black, Caucasian, and Hispanic children: A meta-analysis. *Exceptional Children, 55*(4), 303–308.

Fulmer, R. H., Cohen, S., & Monaco, G. (1985). Using psychological assessment in structural family therapy. *Journal of Learning Disabilities, 18*(3), 145–150.

Gardner, W. I. (1982). Why do we persist? *Education and Treatment of Children, 5*(4), 369–378.

Ghali, S. B. (1982). Understanding Puerto Rican traditions. *Social Work, 27,* 98–103.

Gibson, G., & Vasquez, E. V. (1982, March). *Racism and its impact on Hispanics: Cognitive and affective teaching and learning.* Paper presented at the annual program meeting of the Council on Social Work Education, New York.

Gibson, M. A. (1987). Punjabi immigrants in an American high school. In G. Spindler & L. Spindler (Eds.), *Interpretive ethnography of education: At home and abroad* (pp. 281–310). Hillsdale, NJ: Erlbaum.

Gilliam, J. E., & Coleman, M. C. (1981). Who influences IEP committee decisions? *Exceptional Children, 47*(8), 642–644.

Gillis-Olion, M., Olion, L., & Holmes, R. L. (1986). Strategies for interacting with Black parents of handicapped children. *Negro Educational Review, 37*(1), 8–16.

Ginzberg, E. (1965). The mentally handicapped in a technological society. In S. Osler & R. Cooke (Eds.), *The biosocial bases of mental retardation* (pp. 1–15). Baltimore: Johns Hopkins University Press.

Glaser, B., & Strauss, A. L. (1967). *The discovery of grounded theory: Strategies for qualitative research.* Chicago: Aldine.

Glazer, N., & Moynihan, D. P. (1963). *Beyond the melting pot.* Cambridge, MA: M.I.T. Press/Harvard University Press.

Gliedman, J., & Roth, W. (1980). *The unexpected minority: Handicapped children in America*. New York: Harcourt Brace Jovanovich.

Goffman, E. (1963). *Stigma: Notes on the management of spoiled identity*. New York: Simon & Schuster.

Goldman, I. (1937). The Zuni of New Mexico. In M. Mead (Ed.), *Cooperation and competition among primitive peoples* (pp. 313–353). New York: McGraw-Hill.

Goldstein, S., Strickland, B., Turnbull, A., & Curry, L. (1980). An observational analysis of the IEP conference. *Exceptional Children, 46*(4), 278–286.

Goldstein, S., & Turnbull, A. P. (1982). The use of two strategies to increase parent participation in IEP conferences. *Exceptional Children, 48*(4), 360–361.

Gordon, I. J. (1977). Parent education and parent involvement: Retrospect and prospect. *Childhood Education, 54*, 71–79.

Gordon, I. J. (1979). The effects of parent involvement in schools. In R. S. Brandt (Ed.), *Partners: Parents and schools*. Alexandria, VA: Association for Supervision and Curriculum Development.

Gordon, M. M. (1978). *Human nature, class and ethnicity*. New York: Oxford University Press.

Gorham, K. A. (1975). Effect on parents. In N. Hobbs (Ed.), *Issues in the classification of children* (Vol. 2) (pp. 154–188). San Francisco: Jossey-Bass.

Gould, S. J. (1981). *The mismeasure of man*. New York: Norton.

Grippo-Gardner, L., & McHugh, C. (1988). Networking in New York State: A green thumb experience. *Family Resource Coalition Report, 7*(2), 17–18.

Groce, N. (1985). *Everyone here spoke sign language*. Cambridge, MA: Harvard University Press.

Hale-Benson, J. (1986). *Black children: Their roots, culture and learning styles*. Baltimore: Johns Hopkins University Press.

Hall, E. T. (1977). *Beyond culture*. New York: Anchor.

Hardman, M. L., Drew, C. J., Egan, M. W., & Wolf, B. (1990). *Human exceptionality* (3rd ed.). Boston: Allyn & Bacon.

Harrison, A. O., Wilson, M. N., Pine, C. J., Chan, S. Q., & Buriel, R. (1990). Family ecologies of ethnic minority children. *Child Development, 61*(20), 347–362.

Harry, B. (in press). Toward a restructuring of African American parents' participation in special education: Altering the discourse of power. *Exceptional Children*.

Harry, B., & Kalyanpur, M. (1991). *Empowering culturally diverse families*. Manuscript submitted for publication.

Heath, S. B. (1983). *Ways with words: Language, life and work in communities and classrooms*. Cambridge, England: Cambridge University Press.

Heller, K. A., Holtzman, W. H., & Messick, S. (Eds). (1982). *Placing children in special education: A strategy for equity*. Washington, DC: National Academy Press.

Herman, R. I. (1983, Fall). Poverty, minority and exceptionality. *The Educational Forum*, pp. 47–63.

Hess, R. D. (1981). Approaches to the measurement and interpretation of parent-child interaction. In R. W. Henderson (Ed.), *Parent-child interaction: Theory, research and prospects* (pp. 207–230). New York: Academic Press.

Hill, R. B. (1971). *The strengths of Black families.* New York: Emerson Hall.

Hines, P. M., & Boyd-Franklin, N. (1982). Black families. In M. McGoldrick, J. K. Pearce, & J. Giordano (Eds.), *Ethnicity and family therapy* (pp. 84–107). New York: Guilford.

Hodgkinson, L. (1985). *All one system: Demographics of education.* Washington, DC: Institute for Educational Leadership.

Houston, S. H. (1973, March). Black English. *Psychology Today*, pp. 45–48.

Ishisaka, H. A., Nguyen, Q. T., & Okimoto, J. T. (1985). The role of culture in the mental health treatment of Indochinese refugees. In T. C. Owan (Ed.), *Southeast Asian mental health: Treatment, prevention, services, training and research* (pp. 41–63). Washington, DC: U.S. Department of Health and Human Services, National Institute of Mental Health.

Jackson, G., & Cosca, C. (1974). The inequality of educational opportunities in the Southwest: An observational study of ethnically mixed classrooms. *American Educational Research Journal, 11*(3), 219–229.

Jencks, C. (1972). *Inequality: A reassessment of family and schooling in America.* New York: Basic Books.

Jenkins, A. H. (1982). *The psychology of the Afro-American: A humanistic approach.* New York: Pergamon.

Jensen, A. R. (1969). How much can we boost IQ and scholastic achievement? *Harvard Educational Review, 39*, 1–123.

Jensen, A. R. (1980). *Bias in mental testing.* New York: Free Press.

Johnson, M. J. (1987). American Indian parents of handicapped children. In M. J. Johnson & B. A. Ramirez (Eds.), *American Indian Exceptional Children and Youth.* Reston, VA: Council for Exceptional Children and Youth. (ERIC Document Reproduction Service No. ED 294 338)

Jones, R. L. (Ed.). (1976). *Mainstreaming and the minority child.* Reston, VA: Council for Exceptional Children and Youth.

Karnes, M. B., Linnemeyer, S. A., & Myles, G. (1983). Programs for parents of handicapped children. In R. Haskins & D. Adams (Eds.), *Parent education and public policy* (pp. 181–210). Norwood, NJ: Ablex.

Keesling, J. W., & Melaragno, R. J. (1983). Parent participation in federal education programs: Findings from the federal programs survey phase of the study of parental involvement. In R. Haskins & D. Adams (Eds.), *Parent education and public policy* (pp. 230–256). Norwood, NJ: Ablex.

Kinzie, J. D. (1985). Overview of clinical issues in the treatment of Southeast Asian refugees. In T. C. Owan (Ed.), *Southeast Asian mental health: Treatment, prevention, services, training and research* (pp. 113–135). Washington, DC: U.S. Department of Health and Human Services, National Institute of Mental Health.

Kitano, H. (1969). *The evolution of a subculture.* Englewood Cliffs, NJ: Prentice-Hall.

Kitano, M. K. (1986). Gifted and talented Asian children. In M. K. Kitano & P.C.

Chinn (Eds.), *Exceptional Asian children and youth* (pp. 54–60). Reston, VA: Council for Exceptional Children and Youth.

Kitano, M. K., & Chinn, P. C. (1986). *Exceptional Asian children and youth.* Reston, VA: Council for Exceptional Children and Youth.

Krashen, S. D., Long, M. A., & Scarcella, R. C. (1979). Age, rate and eventual attainment in second language acquisition. *TESOL Quarterly, 13,* 573–582.

Labov, W. (1972). *Language in the inner city.* Philadelphia: University of Pennsylvania Press.

Landry, B. (1987). *The new Black middle class.* Berkeley: University of California Press.

Laosa, L. M. (1979). Inequality in the classroom: Observational research on teacher-student interactions. *Aztlan, 8,* 51–66.

Laosa, L. M. (1980). Maternal teaching strategies in Chicano and Anglo-American families: The influence of culture and education on maternal behavior. *Child Development, 51,* 759–765.

Laosa, L. M. (1981). Maternal behavior: Sociocultural diversity in modes of family interaction. In R. W. Henderson (Ed.), *Parent-child interaction: Theory, research and prospects* (pp. 125–163). New York: Academic Press.

Laosa, L. M. (1983). Parent education, cultural pluralism, and public policy: The uncertain connection. In R. Haskins & D. Adams (Eds.), *Parent education and public policy* (pp. 331–345). Norwood, NJ: Ablex.

Lareau, A. (1989). *Home advantage: Social class and parental intervention in elementary education.* New York: Falmer.

Lauria, A. (1968). Respeto, relajo, and interpersonal relations in Puerto Rico. In F. Cordasco (Ed.), *Puerto Rican children in mainland schools* (pp. 42–54). Metuchen, NJ: Scarecrow.

LeCompte, M. D. (1981). The procrustean bed: Public schools, management systems and minority students. In H. T. Trueba (Ed.), *Culture and the bilingual classroom* (pp. 178–195). Rowley, MA: Newbury House.

Lee, E. (1982). A social systems approach for assessment and treatment practices for Chinese American families. In M. McGoldrick, J. K. Pierce, & J. Giordano (Eds.), *Ethnicity and family therapy* (pp. 527–551). New York: Guilford.

Leler, H. (1983). Parent education and involvement in relation to the schools and to parents of school-aged children. In R. Haskins & D. Adams (Eds.), *Parent education and public policy* (pp. 114–180). Norwood, NJ: Ablex.

Leung, B. (1986). Psychoeducational assessment of Asian students. In M. K. Kitano & P. C. Chinn (Eds.), *Exceptional Asian children and youth* (pp. 29–35). Reston, VA: Council for Exceptional Children and Youth.

Leung, E. K. (1988, October). *Cultural and acculturational commonalities and diversities among Asian Americans: Identification and programming considerations.* Paper presented at the Ethnic and Multicultural Symposia, Dallas, TX. (ERIC Document Reproduction Service No. ED 298 708)

Lewis, E. G. (1980). *Bilingualism and bilingual education.* Albuquerque: University of New Mexico Press.

Lewis, G. (1963). *Puerto Rico: Freedom and power in the Caribbean*. New York: MR Press.

Lieberman, A. F. (1990). Infant-parent interventions with recent immigrants: Reflections on a study with Latino families. *Zero to Three, 10*(4), 8–11.

Liem, N. D. (1985). Indochinese cross-cultural adjustment and communication. In M. Dao & H. Grossman (Eds.), *Identifying, instructing and rehabilitating South East Asian students with special needs and counseling their parents* (pp. 28–58). Sacramento, CA: Department of Education.

Locust, C. (1988). Wounding the spirit: Discrimination and traditional American Indian belief systems. *Harvard Educational Review, 58*(3), 315–330.

Lofland, J. (1969). *Deviance and identity*. Englewood Cliffs, NJ: Prentice-Hall.

Lofland, J. (1971). *Analyzing social settings*. Belmont, CA: Wadsworth.

Lowry, M. S. (1983). *Obstacles to parental involvement: A study of barriers to participation in the educational process faced by Black, low-income, inner-city parents of handicapped children*. Reston, VA: Office for Special Education and Rehabilitation Services. (ERIC Document Reproduction Service No. ED 244 487)

Lusthaus, C. S., Lusthaus, E. W., & Gibbs, H. (1981). Parents' role in the decision process. *Exceptional Children, 48*(30), 256–257.

Lynch, E. W., & Stein, R. (1987). Parent participation by ethnicity: A comparison of Hispanic, Black and Anglo families. *Exceptional Children, 54*, 105–111.

Macias, J. (1987). The hidden curriculum of Papago teachers: American Indian strategies for mitigating cultural discontinuity in early schooling. In G. Spindler & L. Spindler (Eds.), *Interpretive ethnography of education: At home and abroad* (pp. 363–384). Hillsdale, NJ: Erlbaum.

Maheady, L., Towne, R., Algozzine, B., Mercer, J., & Ysseldyke, J. (1983). Minority overrepresentation: A case for alternative practices prior to referral. *Learning Disability Quarterly, 6*, 448–456.

Malmberg, P. A. (1984). *Development of field tested special education placement committee parent education materials*. Unpublished doctoral dissertation, Virginia Polytechnic Institute at State University, Blacksburg.

Marion, R. (1979). Minority parent involvement in the IEP process: A systematic model approach. *Focus on Exceptional Children, 10*(8), 1–16.

Marion, R. (1980a). Communicating with parents of culturally diverse exceptional children. *Exceptional Children, 46*(8), 616–623.

Marion, R. (1980b). A cooperative university/public school approach to sensitizing majority teachers to the needs of parents of Black EMR children. *Journal of Negro Education, 49*(2), 144–153.

Marion, R. (1981). *Educators, parents and exceptional children*. Rockville, MD: Aspen.

Marjoribanks, K. (1979). *Families and their learning environments*. London: Routledge & Kegan Paul.

Mary, N. L. (1990). Reactions of Black, Hispanic, and White mothers to having a child with handicaps. *Mental Retardation, 28*(1), 1–5.

Maryland State Department of Education. (1988). *Teacher supply and demand in Maryland, 1988-91*. Baltimore, MD: Department of Education.

McCall, G. J., & Simmons, J. L. (Eds). (1969). *Issues in participant observation.* Reading, MA: Addison-Wesley.

McDermott, R. P. (1976). *Kids make sense: An ethnographic account of the interactional management of success and failure in one first grade classroom.* Unpublished doctoral dissertation, Stanford University, Palo Alto.

McDermott, R. P., & Gospodinoff, K. (1981). Social contexts for ethnic borders and school failure. In H. T. Trueba (Ed.), *Culture and the bilingual classroom* (pp. 212–230). Rowley, MA: Newbury House.

McGowan, B. G. (1988). Helping Puerto Rican families at risk: Responsive use of time, space, and relationships. In C. Jacobs & D. D. Bowles (Eds.), *Ethnicity and race: Critical concepts in social work* (pp. 48–70). Silver Spring, MD: National Association of Social Workers.

McKinney, J. D., & Hocutt, A. M. (1982). Public school involvement of parents of learning-disabled children and average achievers. *Exceptional Education Quarterly, 3*(2), 64–73.

McLoyd, V. C. (1990). The impact of economic hardship on Black families and children: Psychological distress, parenting, and socioemotional development. *Child Development, 61*(2), 311–346.

Medicine, B. (1981). American Indian family: Cultural change and adaptive strategies. *Journal of Ethnic Studies, 8*(4), 13–23.

Mehan, H., Hartwick, A., & Meihls, J. L. (1986). *Handicapping the handicapped: Decision-making in students' educational careers.* Stanford, CA: Stanford University Press.

Mercer, J. R. (1972, February). *Sociocultural factors in the educational evaluation of Black and Chicano children.* Paper presented at 10th annual conference on Civil and Human Rights of Educators and Students, Washington, DC.

Mercer, J. R. (1973). *Labeling the mentally retarded.* Berkeley: University of California Press.

Michaels, S. (1981). "Sharing time": Children's narrative styles and differential access to literacy. *Language in Society, 10,* 423–442.

Miller, J., Miller, J., & Miller, D. (1987). *American Indian cultural perspectives on disability* (Monograph). Tucson: University of Arizona, College of Medicine, Native American Research and Training Center.

Mintz, S. W. (1960). *Worker in the cane.* New Haven, CT: Yale University Press.

Minuchin, S. (1974). *Families and family therapy.* Cambridge, MA: Harvard University Press.

Mizio, E., & Delaney, A. J. (1981). *Training for service delivery to minority clients.* New York: Family Service Association of America.

Mohatt, G., & Erickson, F. (1981). Cultural differences in teaching styles in an Odawa school: A sociolinguistic approach. In H. T. Trueba, G. P. Guthrie, & K. H. Au (Eds.), *Culture and the bilingual classroom: Studies in classroom ethnography* (pp. 105–119). Cambridge, MA: Newbury House.

Moll, L. C., & Diaz, S. (1987). Change as the goal of educational research. *Anthropology & Education Quarterly, 18,* 300–311.

Moore, C. (1986). *Reaching out: Proceedings from a special education symposium on cultural differences and parent programs.* Washington, DC: Office of Special Education and Rehabilitative Services. (ERIC Document Reproduction Service No. ED 284 408)

Morales, J. (1986). *Puerto Rican poverty and migration*. New York: Praeger.

Morrow, R. D. (1987). Cultural differences—Be aware! *Academic Therapy, 23*(2), 143–149.

Morrow, R. D., & McBride, H. J. (1988, February). *Considerations for educators in working with Southeast Asian children and their families*. Paper presented at the meeting of the National Rural Special Education Conference, Asheville, NC. (ERIC Document Reproduction Service No. ED 299 730)

Murase, K., Egawa, J., & Tashima, N. (1985). Alternative mental health service models in Asian Pacific communities. In T. C. Owan (Ed.), *South East Asian mental health: Treatment, prevention, services, training and research* (pp. 229–259). Washington, DC: U.S. Department of Health and Human Services, National Institute of Mental Health.

Nebgen, M. K. (1979). Parental involvement in Title 1 Programs. *Educational Forum, 43*(2), 165–173.

New York City Board of Education. (1958). Summary of recommendations made by the Puerto Rican Study. In F. Cordasco (Ed.), *Puerto Rican children in mainland schools* (pp. 374–386). Metuchen, NJ: Scarecrow.

New York City Board of Education. (1989). *Annual school census: Pupil ethnic composition report*. Report No. 81. New York: Author.

New York State Department of Education. (1986). *A parents' guide to special education*. Albany: State University of New York Press.

Norton, D. G. (1990). Understanding the early experience of Black children in high risk environments: Culturally and ecologically relevant research as a guide to support for families. *Zero to Three, 10*(4), 1–7.

Oakley, A. (1981). Interviewing women: A contradiction in terms. In H. Roberts (Ed.), *Doing feminist research* (pp. 30–61). London: Routledge & Kegan Paul.

Ogbu, J. U. (1974). *The next generation: An ethnography of education in an urban neighborhood*. New York: Academic Press.

Ogbu, J. U. (1978). *Minority education and caste: The American system in cross-cultural perspective*. San Francisco: Academic Press.

Ogbu, J. U. (1987). Variability in minority school performance: A problem in search of an explanation. *Anthropology & Education Quarterly, 18*, 312–336.

Ortiz, A. A., & Polyzoi, E. (Eds.). (1986). *Characteristics of limited English proficient Hispanic students in programs for the learning disabled: Implications for policy, practice and research. Part 1. Report summary*. Austin, TX: University of Texas. (ERIC Document Reproduction Service No. ED 267 578)

Ovando, C. J., & Collier, V. P. (1985). *Bilingual and ESL classrooms*. New York: McGraw-Hill.

Owan, T. C. (Ed.). (1985). *South East Asian mental health: Treatment, prevention, services, training and research*. Washington, DC: U.S. Department of Health and Human Services, National Institute of Mental Health.

Padilla, F. M. (1985). *Latino ethnic consciousness: The case of Mexican-Americans and Puerto Ricans in Chicago*. Notre Dame, IN: University of Notre Dame Press.

Pattanayak, D. P. (1988). Monolingual myopia and the petals of the Indian lotus: Do many languages divide or unite a nation? In T. Skutnabb-Kangas & J. Cummins (Eds.), *Minority education: From shame to struggle* (pp. 379–389). Clevedon, England: Multilingual Matters.

Patton, M. Q. (1980). *Qualitative evaluation methods.* Beverly Hills, CA: Sage.

Peshkin, A. (1988). In search of subjectivity—One's own. *Educational Researcher, 17,* 17–22.

Pfeiffer, S. I. (1980). The school-based interprofessional team: Recurring problems and some possible solutions. *Journal of School Psychology, 18*(4), 388–394.

Philips, S. (1983). *The invisible culture.* New York: Longman.

Piestrup, A. (1973). *Black dialect interference and the accommodation of reading instruction in first grade* (Monograph No. 4). Berkeley, CA: University of California, Language-Behavior Research Laboratory.

Pinderhughes, E. (1982). Afro-American families and the victim system. In M. McGoldrick, J. K. Pearce, & J. Giordano (Eds.), *Ethnicity and family therapy* (pp. 108–122). New York: Guilford.

Pipes, W. H. (1981). Old-time religion: Benches can't say "Amen." In H. P. McAdoo (Ed.), *Black families* (pp. 54–76). Beverly Hills, CA: Sage.

Pizzo, P. (1983). *Parent to parent.* Boston: Beacon.

Pollack, J. M. (1985). Pitfalls in the psychoeducational assessment of adolescents with learning and school adjustment problems. *Adolescence, 20*(78), 479–493.

Polloway, E. A., & Smith, J. D. (1988). Current status of the mild mental retardation construct: Identification, placement and programs. In M. C. Wang, M. C. Reynolds, & H. J. Walberg (Eds.), *Handbook of special education. Research and Practice: Vol. 2. Mildly handicapping conditions* (pp. 7–22). New York: Pergamon.

Poplin, M. S., & Wright, P. (1983). The concept of cultural pluralism: Issues in special education. *Learning Disability Quarterly, 6,* 367–371.

Prasse, D. P., & Reschly, D. J. (1986). Larry P.: A case of segregation, testing, or program efficacy? *Exceptional Children, 52*(4), 333–346.

Price, M., & Goodman, L. (1980). Individualized education programs: A cost study. *Exceptional Children, 46*(6), 446–458.

Prieto, A. G., & Zucker, S. H. (1981). Teacher perception of race as a factor in the placement of behaviorally disordered children. *Behavioral Disorders, 7*(1), 34–38.

Programs serving special needs families. (1988). *Family Resource Coalition Report, 7*(2), 18–19

Quain, B. (1937). The Iroquois. In M. Mead (Ed.), *Cooperation and competence among primitive peoples.* New York: McGraw-Hill.

Ramirez, B. A. (1987). Federal policy and the education of American Indian exceptional children and youth: Current status and future directions. In M. J. Johnson & B. A. Ramirez (Eds.), *American Indian exceptional children and youth* (pp. 37–54). Reston, VA: Council for Exceptional Children. (ERIC Document Reproduction Service No. ED 294 338)

Ramirez, M., & Castañeda, A., (1974). *Cultural democracy, bicognitive development, and education.* New York: Academic Press.

Ramirez III, M. & Cox, B. G. (1980). Parenting for multiculturalism: A Mexican American model. In M. D. Fantini & R. Cardenas (Eds.), *Parenting in a multicultural society* (pp. 54–62). New York: Longman.

Ramirez III, M., & Price-Williams, D. R. (1971). *The relationship of culture to educational attainment.* Houston, TX: Rice University, Center for Research in Social Change and Economic Development.

Red Horse, J. (1988). Cultural evolution of American Indian families. In C. Jacobs & D. D. Bowles (Eds.), *Ethnicity and race: Critical concepts in social work* (pp. 86–102). Silver Spring, MD: National Association of Social Workers, Inc.

Reissman, F. (1962). *The culturally deprived child.* New York: Harper & Row.

Reschly, D. J. (1979). Non-biased assessment. In D. J. Reschly & G. D. Phye (Eds.), *School psychology perspectives and issues* (pp. 215–254). New York: Academic Press.

Reschly, D. J. (1988). Minority MMR overrepresentation: Legal issues, research findings, and reform trends. In M. C. Wang, M. C. Reynolds, & H. J. Walberg (Eds.), *Handbook of special education, Research and practice: Vol. 2. Mildly handicapping conditions* (pp. 23–42). New York: Pergamon.

Reynolds, M. C., & Lakin, C. K. (1987). Noncategorical special education: Models for research and practice. In M. C. Wang, M. C. Reynolds, & H. J. Walberg (Eds.), *Handbook of special education. Research and practice: Vol. 1. Learner Characteristics and Adaptive Practice* (pp. 331–356). New York: Pergamon.

Riley, M. T. (1978). Project Laton (Parent programming practices). In P. L. Trohanis (Ed.), *Early education in Spanish-speaking communities* (pp. 41–46). New York: Walker.

Rist, R. (1970). Student social class and teacher expectations: The self-fulfilling prophecy in ghetto education. *Harvard Educational Review, 39,* 411–451.

Roberts, R. N. (1990). *Developing culturally competent programs for families of children with special needs* (2nd ed.). Washington, DC: Georgetown University Child Development Center.

Rodriguez, R. (1982). *Hunger of memory.* Boston: Godine.

Roit, M. L., & Prohl, W. (1984). The readability of P. L. 94–142 parent materials: Are parents truly informed? *Exceptional Children, 40*(6), 496–505.

Ruiz, N. (1989). An optimal learning environment for Rosemary. *Exceptional Children, 56*(2), 130–144.

Rumbant, R. G. (1985). Mental health and the refugee experience: A comparative study of South East Asian refugees. In T. C. Owan (Ed.), *South East Asian mental health: Treatment, prevention, services, training and research* (pp. 433–486). Washington, DC: U.S. Department of Health and Human Services, National Institute of Mental Health.

Safer, N. D., Morrissey, P. A., Kaufman, M. J., & Lewis, L. (1978). Implementation of IEPs: New teacher roles and requisite support systems. *Focus on Exceptional Children, 10*(1), 1–20.

Sarason, S. B., & Doris, J. (1979). *Educational handicap, public policy, and social history.* New York: Free Press.

Schlossman, S. L. (1983). The formative era in American parent education: Overview and interpretation. In R. Haskins & D. Adams (Eds.), *Parent education and public policy* (pp. 7–39). Norwood, NJ: Ablex.

Schuck, J. (1979). The parent-professional partnership — Myth or reality? *Education Unlimited, 1*(4), 26–28.

Sharp, E. Y. (1983). *Analysis of determinants impacting on educational services of handicapped Papago students.* Tucson: University of Arizona, College of Education. (ERIC Document Reproduction Service No. ED 239 468)

Shevin, M. (1983). Meaningful parental involvement in long-range educational planning for disabled children. *Education and Training of the Mentally Retarded, 18*, 17–21.

Shimkin, D. B., Louie, G. J., & Frate, D. A. (1978). The Black extended family: A basic rural institution and a mechanism of urban adaptation. In D. B. Shimkin, E. M. Shimkin, & D. A. Frate (Eds.), *The extended family in Black societies* (pp. 25–148). Paris: Mouton Publishers.

Shimkin, D. B., Shimkin, E. M., & Frate, D. A. (Eds.). (1978). *The extended family in Black societies.* Paris: Mouton Publishers.

Shimkin, D. B., & Uchendu, V. (1978). Persistence, borrowing, and adaptive changes in Black kinship systems: Some issues and their significance. In D. B. Shimkin, E. M. Shimkin, & D. A. Frate (Eds.), *The extended family in Black societies* (pp. 391–406). Paris: Mouton Publishers.

Shon, S. P., & Ja, D. Y. (1982). Asian families. In M. McGoldrick, J. K. Pearce, & J. Giordano (Eds.), *Ethnicity and family therapy* (pp. 208–228). New York: Guilford.

Skrtic, T. M. (1988). The crisis in special education knowledge. In E. L. Meyen & T. M. Skrtic, *Exceptional children and youth: An introduction* (3rd ed.) (pp. 479–518). Denver, CO: Love.

Skutnabb-Kangas, T. (1981). *Bilingualism or not? The education of minorities.* Clevedon, England: Multilingual Matters.

Smith, E. J. (1981). Cultural and historical perspectives in counseling Blacks. In D. W. Sue (Ed.), *Counseling the culturally different: Theory and practice* (pp. 141–185). New York: Wiley.

Smith, M. J., & Ryan, A. S. (1987). Chinese-American families of children with developmental disabilities: An exploratory study of reactions to service providers. *Mental Retardation, 25*(6), 345–350.

Smith, R. W., Osborne, L. T., Crim, D., & Rhu, A. H. (1986). Labeling theory as applied to learning disabilities: Findings and policy suggestions. *Journal of Learning Disabilities, 19*(4), 195–202.

Sour, M. S., & Sorell, H. (1978). Parent involvement. In P. L. Trohanis (Ed.), *Early education in Spanish-speaking communities* (pp. 35–40). New York: Walker.

Spencer, M. B. (1984). Black children's race awareness, racial attitudes, and self-concept: A reinterpretation. *Journal of Child Psychology and Psychiatry, 25*, 433–441.

Spener, D. (1988). Transitional bilingual education and the socialization of immigrants. *Harvard Educational Review, 58*(2), 133–153.

Spradley, J. (1979). *The ethnographic interview*. New York: Holt, Rinehart & Winston.

Stein, C. B. (1986). *Sink or swim: The politics of bilingual education*. New York: Praeger.

Strenecky, B., McLoughlin, J. A., & Edge, D. (1979). Parent involvement: A consumer perspective — in the schools. *Education and Training of the Mentally Retarded, 13*, 427–429.

Strickland, B. (1983). Legal issues that affect parents. In M. Seligman (Ed.), *The family with a handicapped child: Understanding and treatment* (pp. 27–39). New York: Grune & Stratton.

Suarez-Orosco, M. M. (1989). *Central American refugees and U.S. high schools*. Stanford, CA: Stanford University Press.

Sudarkasa, N. (1981). Interpreting the African heritage in Afro-American family organization. In H. P. McAdoo (Ed.), *Black families* (pp. 23–36). Beverly Hills, CA: Sage.

Sullivan, O. T. (1980). *Meeting the needs of low-income families with handicapped children*. Washington, DC: U.S. Department of Health and Welfare, National Institute of Education. (ERIC Document Reproduction Service No. ED 201 091)

Tessier, A., & Barton, S. (1978). Parents learn to help themselves. In P. L. Trohanis (Ed.), *Early education in Spanish-speaking communities* (pp. 27–33). New York: Walker.

Tharp, R., & Gallimore, R. (1988). *Rousing minds to life: Teaching, learning, and schooling in social context*. Cambridge, England: Cambridge University Press.

Thomas, P. (1967). *Down these mean streets*. New York: Knopf.

Thompson, T. M. (1982). An investigation and comparison of public school personnel's perception and interpretation of P. L. 94-142. *Dissertation Abstracts International, 43*, 2840A.

Tomlinson, J. R., Acker, N., Canter, A., & Lindborg, S. (1977). Minority status, sex and school psychological services. *Psychology in the Schools, 14*(4), 456–460.

Tran, X. C. (1982). *The factors hindering Indochinese parent participation in school activities*. San Diego, CA: San Diego State University, Institute for Cultural Pluralism. (ERIC Document Reproduction Service No. ED 245 018)

Trueba, H. T. (1983). Adjustment problems of Mexican and Mexican-American students: An anthropological study. *Learning Disability Quarterly, 6*, 395–415.

Trueba, H. T. (1988). Culturally based explanations of minority students' academic achievement. *Anthropology & Education Quarterly, 19*, 270–287.

Trueba, H. T. (1989), *Raising silent voices: Educating linguistic minorities for the 21st century*. Cambridge, MA: Newbury House.

Trueba, H. T., & Delgado-Gaitan, C. (1988). *Minority achievement and parental support: Academic resocialization through mentoring* (Tech. Rep. No. 143). Santa Barbara: University of California, Graduate School of Education.

Trueba, H., Jacobs, L., & Kirton, E. (1990). *Cultural conflict and adaptation: The case of Hmong children in American society.* New York: Falmer.

Tucker, J. A. (1980). Ethnic proportions in classes for the learning disabled: Issues in nonbiased assessment. *The Journal of Special Education, 14*(1), 93–105.

Tung, T. M. (1985). Psychiatric care for South East Asians: How different is different? In T. C. Owan (Ed.), *South East Asian mental health: Treatment, prevention, services, training and research* (pp. 5–40). Washington, DC: U.S. Department of Health and Human Services, National Institute of Mental Health.

Turnbull, A. (1983). Parental participation in the ιερ process. In J. A. Mulick & S. M. Pueschel (Eds.), *Parent-professional participation in developmental disability services: Foundations and prospects* (pp. 107–123). Cambridge, MA: Ware.

Turnbull, A. P., & Turnbull, H. R. (1982). Parent involvement in the education of handicapped children: A critique. *Mental Retardation, 20*(3), 115–122.

Turnbull, A. P., & Turnbull, H. R. (1986). *Families, professionals and exceptionality.* Columbus, OH: Merrill.

Turnbull, A., Winton, P. J., Blacher, J. B., & Salkind, N. (1983). Mainstreaming in the kindergarten classroom: Perspectives of parents of handicapped and non-handicapped children. *Journal of the Division of Early Childhood, 6,* 14–20.

U.S. Bureau of the Census. (1980). *Census of population,* Vol. 1, Chapter C (PC80-1-C) & Vol. 2, Chapter 1E (PC80-2-1E). Washington, DC: U.S. Government Printing Office.

U.S. Bureau of the Census. (1989). *The Black population in the United States: A chartbook* (Current Population Reports, Series P-20, No. 442). Washington, DC: U.S. Government Printing Office.

U.S. Bureau of the Census. (1990a). *The Hispanic population in the US: March 1989* (Current Population Reports, Series P-20, No. 444). Washington, DC: U.S. Government Printing Office.

U.S. Bureau of the Census. (1990b). *United States population estimates, by age, sex, race, and Hispanic origin: 1980–1988* (Current Population Reports, Series P-25, No. 1045). Washington, DC: U.S. Government Printing Office.

U.S. Bureau of the Census. (1990c). *U.S. population estimates, by age, sex, race, and Hispanic origin: 1989.* (Current Population Reports, Series P-25, No. 1057). Washington, DC: U.S. Government Printing Office.

U.S. Congress Subcommittee on Census and Population. (1987). *Hearing on content of the 1990 census questionnaire. Race, ethnicity, and ancestry.* Washington, DC: U.S. Government Printing Office.

U.S. Department of Education, Office for Civil Rights. (1987). *1986 elementary and secondary school civil rights survey: National summaries.* Washington, DC: DBS Corporation.

U.S. Department of Labor. (1965). *The Negro family: The case for national action.* Washington, DC: U.S. Government Printing Office.

Van Ness, H. (1981). Social control and social organization in an Alaskan Athabaskan classroom: A microethnography of "getting ready" for reading. In H.

T. Trueba, G. P. Guthrie, & K. H. Au (Eds.), *Culture and the bilingual classroom* (pp. 120–138). Cambridge, MA: Newbury House.

Walker, A. (1989). Alice Walker. In Lanker, B. (Ed.), *I dream a world* (p. 24). New York: Stewart, Tabori & Chang.

Walker, C. L. (1987). Hispanic achievement: Old views and new perspectives. In H. T. Trueba (Ed.), *Success or failure?* (pp. 15–32). Cambridge, MA: Newbury House.

Wang, M. C., & Birch, J. W. (1984). Comparison of a full-time mainstreaming program and a resource room approach. *Exceptional Children, 51*, 33–40.

Warren, R. L. (1988). Cooperation and conflict between parents and teachers: A comparative study of three elementary schools. In H. Trueba & C. Delgado-Gaitan (Eds.), *School and society: Learning content through culture* (pp. 137–162). New York: Praeger.

Witherspoon, Y. (1961). *Cultural influences on Ute learning.* Unpublished doctoral dissertation, University of Utah, Salt Lake City.

Wolfensberger, W. (1984). *Voluntary associations on behalf of societally devalued people and/or handicapped people.* Toronto, Canada: National Institute on Mental Retardation.

Wolfensberger, W., & Kurtz, R. A. (1974). Use of retardation-related diagnostic and prescriptive labels by parents of retarded children. *Journal of Special Education, 8*(2), 131–142.

Wolfensberger, W., & Thomas, S. (1983). *Program analysis of service system's implementation of normalization goals (PASSING)* (2nd ed.). Toronto, Canada: National Institute on Mental Retardation.

Wolfram, W. (1976). Sociolinguistic levels of test bias. In W. Wolfram (Ed.), *Seminars in Black English* (pp. 75–93). New York: Plenum.

Wright, R., Saleeby, D., Watts, T. D., & Lecca, P. J. (1983). *Transcultural perspectives in the human services.* Springfield, IL: Thomas.

Yano, C. (1986). Asian families. In C. Moore (Ed.), *Reaching out: Proceedings from a special education symposium on cultural differences and parent programs* (pp. 39–48). Phoenix, AZ: Western Regional Resource Center. (ERIC Document Reproduction Service No. ED 284 408)

Yoshida, R. K., Fenton, K. S., Kaufman, M. J., & Maxwell, J. P. (1978). Parental involvement in the special education pupil planning process: The school's perspective. *Exceptional Children, 44*, 531–534.

Yoshida, R. K., & Gottlieb, J. (1977). A model of parental participation in the pupil planning process. *Mental Retardation, 15*(3), 17–20.

Yu, E. S. H. (1985). Studying Vietnamese refugees: Methodological lessons in transcultural research. In T. C. Owan (Ed.), *South East Asian mental health: Treatment, prevention, services, training and research* (pp. 517–541). Washington, DC: U.S. Department of Health and Human Services, National Institute of Mental Health.

Zetlin, A. G., & Turner, J. L. (1984). Self-perspectives on being handicapped: Stigma and adjustment. In R. B. Edgerton (Ed.), *Lives in process: Mildly retarded adults in a large city* (pp. 93–120). Washington, DC: American Association on Mental Deficiency.

Ziegler, M. (1988). Parent to parent support: A federal program. *Family Resource Coalition Report, 7*(2), 8–9.

Zuñiga, Maria. (1988). Chicano self-concepts: A proactive stance. In C. Jacobs & D. Bowles, *Ethnicity and race* (pp. 71–85). Washington, DC: National Association of Social Workers.

Index

About the Author

Beth Harry is Assistant Professor of special education at the University of Maryland at College Park. She received her high school education in her native Jamaica, then completed a bachelor's degree in English language and literature at the University of Toronto in 1967, a master's degree in education at the Ontario Institute for Studies in Education in 1973, and a doctorate in special education at Syracuse University in 1985.

After teaching English in junior high, high school, and community college in Toronto from 1967–1973, Dr. Harry taught for two years in an in-service training program for high school teachers of English at the University of the West Indies in St. Augustine, Trinidad. In 1975, Dr. Harry entered the field of special education in response to the birth of her first child, Melanie, who had cerebral palsy. Dr. Harry established a small private school for children with disabilities in Port of Spain, Trinidad; the Immortelle Center for Special Education is now a nonprofit organization owned by parents. After Melanie's death in 1981, Dr. Harry continued to be immersed in disability issues, and came to the United States to study in 1985.

Dr. Harry currently lives in Columbia, Maryland, with her son, Mark Teelucksingh.